# GETTING THE
# SCOOP

A MANUAL FOR REPORTERS, CORRESPONDENTS,
AND STUDENTS OF NEWSPAPER WRITING

# ALSO AVAILABLE FROM PJM PUBLISHING

## NON FICTION

The 'Real' Wild West
The Technique of the Mystery Story
'I Do Solemnly Swear' Presidential Inaugurations from George Washington to George W. Bush
Complete Hypnotism

## FICTION

Southern Gothic Shorts
The Lodger by Marie Belloc Lowndes
Nightmare Town by Dashiell Hammett
The Evil Guest and Other Tales by J. Sheridan LeFanu
Sax Rohmer's Fu Manchu
Collected Screenplays of Phillip J. Morledge
Deadeye - The True Story of 'Private Lives'

VIEW THE FULL CATALOGUE ONLINE AT
WWW.PJMORLEDGE.COM

# GETTING THE SCOOP

A MANUAL FOR REPORTERS, CORRESPONDENTS, AND STUDENTS OF NEWSPAPER WRITING

EDITED BY

PHILLIP J. MORLEDGE

PJM PUBLISHING
WWW.PJMORLEDGE.COM

# GETTING THE SCOOP

THIS EDITION
© Copyright Phillip J. Morledge 2008

ALL RIGHTS RESERVED

NO PART OF THIS BOOK MAY BE REPRODUCED IN ANY FORM,
BY PHOTOCOPYING OR BY ANY ELECTRONIC OR MECHANICAL MEANS,
INCLUDING INFORMATION STORAGE OR RETRIEVAL SYSTEMS,
WITHOUT PERMISSION IN WRITING FROM BOTH THE COPYRIGHT
OWNER AND THE PUBLISHER OF THIS BOOK.

COVER DESIGN BY PHILLIP J. MORLEDGE
ORIGINAL PHOTOGRAPHS BY THEILR, SCOTT RETTBERG

FIRST EDITION PAPERBACK 2009

This Edition First Published APRIL 2009
PJM Publishing Sheffield, England

ISBN 978-0-9559765-6-8

Printed in Great Britain for PJM Publishing

## NEWSPAPER REPORTING & CORRESPONDENCE

BY

GRANT MILNOR HYDE, M.A.

AND

## REPORTING FOR THE NEWSPAPERS

BY

CHARLES HEMSTREET

# NEWSPAPER REPORTING & CORRESPONDENCE

A MANUAL FOR REPORTERS, CORRESPONDENTS, AND
STUDENTS OF NEWSPAPER WRITING

BY

## GRANT MILNOR HYDE, M.A.

*INSTRUCTOR IN JOURNALISM IN THE UNIVERSITY OF
WISCONSIN.*

**TO MY MOTHER**

# INTRODUCTION

The purpose of this book is to instruct the prospective newspaper reporter in the way to write those stories which his future paper will call upon him to write, and to help the young cub reporter and the struggling correspondent past the perils of the copyreader's pencil by telling them how to write clean copy that requires a minimum of editing. It is not concerned with the *why* of the newspaper business--the editor may attend to that--but with the *how* of the reporter's work. And an ability to write is believed to be the reporter's chief asset. There is no space in this book to dilate upon newspaper organization, the work of the business office, the writing of advertisements, the principles of editorial writing, or the how and why of newspaper policy and practice, as it is. These things do not concern the reporter during the first few months of his work, and he will learn them from experience when he needs them. Until then, his usefulness depends solely upon his ability to get news and to write it.

There are two phases of the work which every reporter must learn: how to get the news and how to write it. The first he can pick up easily by actual newspaper experience--if nature has endowed him with "a nose for news." The writing of the news he can learn only by hard practice--a year's hard practice on some papers--and it is generally conceded that practice in writing news stories can be secured at home or in the classroom as effectively as practice in writing short stories, plays, business letters, or any other special form of composition. Newspaper experience may aid the reporter in learning how to write his stories, but a newspaper apprenticeship is not absolutely necessary. However, whether he is studying the trade of newspaper writing in his home, in a classroom, or in the city room of a daily paper, he needs positive instruction in the English composition of the newspaper office--rather than haphazard criticism and a deluge of "don'ts." Hence this book is concerned primarily with the writing of the news.

Successful newspaper reporting requires both an ability to write good English and an ability to write good English in the conventional newspaper form. And there is a conventional form for every kind of newspaper story. Many editors of the present day are trying to break away from the conventional form and to evolve a looser and more natural method of writing news stories. The results are often bizarre and sometimes very effective. Certainly originality in expression adds much to the interest of newspaper stories, and many a good piece of news is ruined by a bald, dry recital of facts. Just as the good reporter is always one who can give his yarns a distinctive flavor, great newspaper stories are seldom written under the restriction of rules. But no young reporter can hope to attain success through originality and defiance of rules until he has first mastered the fundamental principles of newspaper writing. He can never expect to write "the story of the year" until he has learned to handle everyday news without burying the gist of his stories--any more than an artist can hope to paint a living portrait until he has learned, with the aid of rules, to draw the face of a plaster block-head. Hence the emphasis upon form and system in this book. And, whatever the form may be, the embodiment must be clear, concise, grammatical English; that is the excuse for the many axioms of simple English grammar that are introduced side by side with the study of the newspaper form.

The author offers this book as the result of personal newspaper experience and of his work as instructor in classes in newspaper writing at the University of Wisconsin. Every item that is offered is the result of an attempt to correct the mistakes that have appeared most often in the papers of students who are trying to do newspaper writing in the classroom. The seemingly disproportionate emphasis upon certain branches of the subject and the constant repetition of certain simple principles are to be excused by the purpose of the book--to be a text-book in the course of study worked out in this school of journalism. The use of the fire story as typical of all newspaper stories and as a model for all newspaper writing is characteristic of this method of instruction. Four chapters are devoted to the explanation of a single principle which any reader could grasp in a moment, because experience has shown that an equivalent of four chapters of study and practice is required to teach the student the application of this principle and to fix it in his mind so thoroughly that he will not forget it in his later work of writing more complicated stories. It is felt that the beginner needs and must have the detailed explanation, the constant reiteration and some definite rules to guide him in his practice. Hence the emphasis upon the conventional form. Since, in the application of the newspaper

# CONTENTS

1. GATHERING THE NEWS
2. NEWS VALUES
3. NEWSPAPER TERMS
4. THE NEWS STORY FORM
5. THE SIMPLE FIRE STORY
6. THE FEATURE FIRE STORY
7. FAULTS IN NEWS STORIES
8. OTHER NEWS STORIES
9. FOLLOW-UP AND REWRITE STORIES
10. REPORTS OF SPEECHES
11. INTERVIEWS
12. COURT REPORTING
13. SOCIAL NEWS AND OBITUARIES
14. SPORTING NEWS
15. HUMAN INTEREST STORIES
16. DRAMATIC REPORTING
17. STYLE BOOK

APPENDIX 1. SUGGESTIONS FOR STUDY
APPENDIX 2. NEWS STORIES TO BE CORRECTED

# 1
# GATHERING THE NEWS

Unlike almost any other profession, that of a newspaper reporter combines two very different activities - the gathering of news and the writing of news. Part of the work must be done in the office and part of it outside on the street. At his desk in the office a reporter is engaged in the literary, or pseudo-literary, occupation of writing news stories; outside on the street he is a detective gathering news and hunting for elusive facts to be combined later into stories. Although the two activities are closely related, each requires a different sort of ability and a different training. In a newspaper office the two activities are rarely separated, but a beginner must learn each duty independent of the other. This book will not attempt to deal with both; it will confine itself mainly to one phase, the pseudo-literary activity of writing news stories.

However, introductory to the discussion of the writing of newspaper stories, we may glance at the other side of the newspaper writer's work - the gathering of the news. Where the newspaper gets its news and how it gets its news can be learned only by experience, for it differs in different cities and with different papers. But an outline of the background of news-gathering may assist us in writing the news after it is gathered and ready for us to write.

**1. Reporter vs. Correspondent** - There are two capacities in which one may write news stories for a paper. He may work on the staff as a regular reporter or he may supply news from a distance as a correspondent. In the one case he works under the personal supervision of a city editor and spends his entire time at the regular occupation of gathering and writing news. As a correspondent he works in a distant city, under the indirect supervision of the city, telegraph, or state editor, and sends in only the occasional stories that seem to be of interest to his paper. In either case the same rules apply to his news gathering and to his news writing. And in either case the length of his employment depends upon his ability to turn in clean copy in the form in which his paper wishes to print the news. Both the reporter and the correspondent must write their stories in the same form and must look at news and the sources of news from almost the same point of view. Whatever is said of the reporter applies equally to the correspondent.

**2. Expected and Unexpected News** - The daily news may be divided into two classes from the newspaper's point of view: expected and unexpected news. Expected news includes all stories of which the paper has a previous knowledge. Into this class fall all meetings, speeches, sermons, elections, athletic contests, social events, and daily happenings that do not come unexpectedly. They are the events that are announced beforehand and tipped off to the paper in time for the editor to send out a reporter to cover them personally. These events are of course recorded in the office, and each day the editor has a certain number of them, a certain amount of news that he is sure of. Each day he looks over his book to note the events that are to take place during that day and sends out his reporters to cover them.

The other class includes the stories that break unexpectedly. Accidents, deaths, fires, storms, and other unexpected happenings come without warning and the reporting of them cannot be arranged for in advance. These are the stories that the paper is most anxious to get and the things for which the whole staff always has its eyes and ears open. Seldom are they heard of in time for the paper to have them covered personally, and the reporting of such stories becomes a separate sort of work--the gathering and sorting of the facts that can be obtained only from chance witnesses.

**3. News Sources** - There are certain sources from which the paper gets most of its tips of expected events and its knowledge of unexpected events. These every editor knows about. The courts, the public records, the public offices, the churches, and the schools furnish a great many of the tips of expected news. The police stations, the fire stations, the hospitals, and the morgues furnish most of the tips of unexpected news. Whenever an event is going to happen, or whenever an unexpected occurrence does happen, a notice of it is to be found in some one of these sources. Such a notice or a casual word from any one is called a "tip" and indicates the possibility of securing a story. The securing of the story is another matter. A would-be reporter may get good practice from studying the stories in the daily papers and trying to discover or imagine from what source the original news tip came. He will soon find that certain classes of stories always come from certain sources and that there is a perceptible amount of routine evident in the accounts of the most unexpected occurrences.

**4. Runs and Assignments** - Between the news tip and the finished copy for the compositor there is a vast amount of news gathering, which falls to the lot of the reporter. This is handled by a system of runs and special assignments. A reporter usually has his own run, or beat, on which he gathers news. His run may cover a certain number of police stations or the city hall or any group of regular news sources. Each day he must visit the various sources of news on his beat and gather the tips and whatever facts about the stories behind the tips that he can. The tips that he secures furnish him with clues to the stories, and it is his business to get the facts behind all of the tips on his beat and to write them up, unless a tip opens up a story that is too big for him to handle alone without neglecting his beat.

Assignments are used to cover the stories that do not come in through the regular sources, and to handle the big stories that are unearthed on the regular beats. The editor turns over to the reporter the tip that he has received and instructs him to go out and get the facts. A paper's best reporters are used almost entirely on assignments, and when they go out after a story they practically become detectives. They follow every clue that the tip suggests and every clue that is opened up as they progress; they hunt down the facts until they are reasonably sure that they have secured the whole story. The result may not be worth writing, or it may be worth a place on the front page, but the reporter must get to the bottom of it. Whether on a beat or on an assignment every reporter must have his ears open for a tip of some unexpected story and must secure the facts or inform the editor at once. It is in this way that a paper gets a scoop, or beat, on its rivals by printing a story before the other papers have heard of it.

**5. Interviews for Facts** - To cover an assignment and secure the facts of a story is not at all easy. If the reporter could be a personal witness of the happening which he is to report, the task would be simpler. But, outside the case of expected events, he rarely hears of the occurrence until after it is past and the excitement has subsided. Then he must find the persons who witnessed the occurrence or who know the facts, and get the

# GETTING THE SCOOP

story from them. Perhaps he has to see a dozen people to get the information he wants. Getting facts from people in this way is called interviewing - interviewing for facts, as distinguished from formal interviewing for the purpose of securing a statement or an opinion that is to be printed with the name of the man who utters it. Although a dozen interviews may be necessary for a single story, not one of them is mentioned in the story, for they are of no importance except in the facts that they supply.

For example, suppose a reporter is sent out to get the story of a fire that has started an hour or two before he goes on duty. All that his editor gives him is the tip from the fire department, or from some other source, of a fire at such-and-such an address. When he arrives at the scene there is nothing left but smoldering ruins with perhaps an engine throwing a stream on the smoking debris and a few by-standers still loitering about. He can see with his own eyes what kind of building has burned, and how completely it has been destroyed. A by-stander may be able to tell him who occupied the building or what it was used for, but he must hunt for some one else who can give him the exact facts that his paper wants. Perhaps he can find the tenant and learn from him what his loss has been. The tenant can give him the name of the owner and may be able to tell him something about the origin of the fire. He must find the owner to get the value of the building and the amount of insurance carried. Perhaps he cannot find any of these people and must ask the fire chief or some one else to give him what facts and estimates he can. If the fire is at all serious he must find out who was killed or injured and get their names and addresses and the nature of their injury or the manner of their death. Perhaps he can talk to some of the people who had narrow escapes, or interview the friends or relatives of the dead. Everywhere he turns new clues open up, and he must follow each one of them in turn until he is sure that he has all the facts.

**6. Point of View** - The task would be easy if every one could tell the reporter just the facts that his paper wants. But in the confusion every one is excited and fairly bubbling over with rumors and guesses which may later turn out to be false. Each person who is interested in the incident sees and tells it only from his own point of view. Obviously the reporter's paper does not want the facts from many different points of view, nor even from the point of view of the fire department, of the owner, or of the woman who was rescued from the third floor. The paper wants the story from a single point of view - the point of view of an uninterested spectator. Consequently the reporter must get the facts through interviews with a dozen different people, discount possible exaggeration and falsity due to excitement, make allowances for the different points of view, harmonize conflicting statements, and sift from the mass what seems to him to be the truth. Then he must write the story from the uninterested point of view of the public, which wants to hear the exact facts of the fire told in an unprejudiced way. Never does the story mention any of the interviews behind it except when the reporter is afraid of some statement and wants to put the responsibility upon the person who gave it to him. And so the finished story that we read in the next morning's paper is the composite story of the fire chief, the owner, the tenant, the man who discovered the fire, the widow who was driven from her little flat, the little girl who was carried down a ladder through the smoke, the man who lost everything he had in the world, and the cynic who watched the flames from behind the fireline - all massed together and sifted and retold in an impersonal way from the point of view of a by-stander who has been everywhere through the flames and has kept his brain free from the terror and excitement of it all.

The same is true of every story that is printed in a newspaper. Every story must be secured in the same way - whether it is the account of a business transaction, a bank robbery, a political scandal, a murder, a reception, or a railroad wreck. Seldom is it possible to find any one person who knows all the facts just as the newspaper wants them, and many a story that is worth but a stickful in the first edition is the result of two hours' running about town, half a dozen telephone calls, and a dozen interviews. That is the way the news is gathered, and that is the part of the reporter's work that he must learn by experience. But after all the gathering is finished and he has the facts, the writing of the story remains. If the reporter knows how to write the facts when he has them, his troubles are cut in half, for nowadays a reporter who writes well is considered a more valuable asset than one who cannot write and simply has a nose for news.

**7. News-Gathering Agencies** - This account of news gathering is of course told from the point of view of the reporter. Naturally it assumes a different aspect in the editor's eyes. Much of the day's news does not have to be gathered at all. A steady stream of news flows in ready for use from the great news-gathering agencies, the Associated Press, the United Press, the City Press, etc., and from correspondents. Many stories are merely summaries of speeches, bulletins, announcements, pamphlets and other printed matter that comes to the editorial office, and many stories come already written. Almost everybody is looking for publicity in these days and the editor does not always have to hunt the news with an army of ferrets. Cooperation in news gathering has simplified the whole matter. But it all has to be written and edited. That is why great reporters are no longer praised for their cleverness in worming their way to elusive facts, but for their ability to write a good story. That is why we no longer hear so much about beats and scoops but more about clean copy and "literary masterpieces."

**8. How the Correspondent Works** - The correspondent gathers news very much as the reporter does, but he does it without the help of a city editor. He must be his own director and keep his own book of tips, for he has no one to make out his assignments beforehand. He has to watch for what news he can get by himself and send it to his paper of his own accord, except occasionally when his paper instructs him to cover a particularly large story. But he gets his tips and runs down his facts just as a reporter does. Just as much alertness and just as much ability to write are required of him.

The correspondent's work is made more difficult by what is called news values. Distance affects the importance of the facts that he secures and the length of the stories he writes. He must weigh every event for its interest to readers a hundred or a thousand miles away. What may be of immense importance in his community may have no interest at all for readers outside that community. He must see everything with the eyes of a stranger, and this must influence his whole work of news gathering and news writing. This matter will be taken up at greater length in the next chapter.

**9. Correspondent's Relation to His Paper** - The relations of a correspondent to the paper or news association to which he is sending news can best be learned by experience. Every paper has different rules for its correspondents and different directions in regard to the sort of news it wants. The rules regarding the mailing of copy and the sending of stories or queries by telegraph are usually sent out in printed form by each individual paper to its correspondents. But while gathering news and writing stories for a distant paper, a correspondent must always regard himself as a reporter and write his stories in the form in which they are to appear in print if he wishes to remain correspondent for any length of time. The following rules are taken from the "INSTRUCTIONS TO CORRESPONDENTS" sent out on a printed card to the correspondents of the St. Louis *Star*.

*QUERY BY WIRE ON ALL STORIES you consider are worth telegraphing, unless you are absolutely certain* The Star *wants* you to send the story without query, or in case of a big story breaking suddenly near edition time. If you have not time to query, get a reply and send such matter as might be ordered before the next edition time; send the story in the shortest possible number of words necessary to tell it, asking if additional matter is desired.

Write your queries so they can be understood. Never send a "blind" query. If John Smith, a confirmed bachelor, whose age is 80 years, elopes with and marries the daughter of the woman who jilted him when he was a youth, say so in as few words as possible, but be sure to convey the dramatic news worth of the story in your query. Do not say, "Bachelor elopes with girl, daughter of woman he knew a long time ago." In itself the story which this query tells might be worth printing, but it would not be half so good a story as the elopement of John Smith, 80, bachelor, woman hater, with the daughter of his old sweetheart.

When a good story breaks close to edition time and the circumstances justify it, use the long-distance telephone, but first be reasonably certain The Star *will not get the story from another source.*

Write your stories briefly. The Star *desires to remunerate its correspondents according to the worth of a story and not for so many words. One good story of 200 words with the right "punch" in the introduction is worth a dozen strung over as many dozen pages of copy paper with the real story in the last paragraph of each. Tell your story in simple, every-day conversational words: quit when you have finished. Relegate the details. Unless it is a case of identification in a murder mystery, or some similar big story, no one cares about the color of the man's hair. Get the principal facts in the first paragraph--stop soon after.*

Send as much of your stuff as possible by mail, especially if you have the story in the late afternoon and are near enough to St. Louis to reach The Star *by 9 o'clock the next morning. If necessary, send the letter special delivery.*

Don't stop working on a good story when you have all the facts; if there are photographs to be obtained, get the photographs, especially if the principals in the story are persons of standing, and more especially if they are women.

Correspondents will appreciably increase their worth to The Star *and enhance their earning capacity by observing these rules.*

# 2
# NEWS VALUES

Before any one can hope to write for a newspaper he must know something about news values - something about the essence of interest that makes one story worth a column and cuts down another, of equal importance from other points of view, to a stickful. He must recognize the relative value of facts so that he can distinguish the significant part of his story and feature it accordingly. The question is a delicate one and yet a very reasonable and logical one. The ideal of a newspaper, according to present-day ethics, is to print news. The daily press is no longer a golden treasury of contemporary literature, not even, perhaps, an exponent of political principles. Its primary purpose is to report contemporary history - to keep us informed concerning the events that are taking place each day in the world about us.

To this idea is added another. A newspaper must be interesting. In these days of many newspapers few readers are satisfied with merely being informed; they want to be informed in a way that interests them. To this demand every one connected with a newspaper office tries to cater. It is the defense of the sensational yellow journals and it is the reason for everything in the daily press. There is so much to read that people will not read things that do not interest them, and the paper that succeeds is the paper that interests the greatest number of readers. Circulation cannot be built up by printing uninteresting stuff that the majority of readers are not interested in, and circulation is necessary to success.

This desire to interest readers is behind the whole question of news values. News is primarily the account of the latest events, but, more than that, it is the account of the latest events that interest readers who are not connected with these events. Further than that, it is the account of the latest events that interest the greatest number of readers. Susie Brown may have sprained her ankle. The fact is absorbingly interesting to Susie; it is even rather interesting to her family and friends, even to her enemies. If she is well known in the little town in which she lives her accident may be interesting enough to the townspeople for the local weekly to print a complete account of it. However, the event is interesting only to people who know Susie, and after all they do not comprise a very large number. Hence her accident has no news value outside the local weekly. On the other hand, had Susie sprained her ankle in some very peculiar manner, the accident might be of interest to people who do not know Susie. Suppose that she had tripped on her gown as she was ascending the steps of the altar to be married. Such an accident would be very unusual, almost unheard of. People in general are interested in unusual things, and many, many readers would be interested in reading about Susie's unusual accident although they did not know Susie or even the town in which she lives. Such a story would be the report of a late event that would interest many people; hence it would have a certain amount of news value. Of course, the reader loses sight of Susie in reading of her accident - it might as well have been Mary Jones - but that is because Susie has no news value in herself. That is another matter.

**1. Classes of Readers** - Realizing that his story must be of interest to the greatest number of people, the reporter must remember the sort of people for whom he is writing. That complicates the whole matter. If he were writing for a single class of readers he could easily give them the news that would interest them. But he is not; he is writing for many classes of people, for all classes of people. And he must interest them all. He is writing for the business man in his office, for the wife in the home, for the ignorant, for the highly educated, for the rich and the poor, for the old and the young, for doctors, lawyers, bankers, laborers, ministers, and women. All of them buy his paper to hear the latest news told in a way that interests them, and he has to cater to each and to all of them. If he were simply writing for business men he would give them many columns of financial news, but that would not interest tired laborers. An extended account of the doings of a Presbyterian convention would not attract the great class of men with sporting inclinations, and a story of a very pretty exhibition of scientific boxing would not appeal to the wife at home. They all buy the paper, and they all want to be interested, and the paper must, therefore, print stories that interest at least the majority of them. That is the question of news values. The news must be the account of the latest events that interest the greatest number of readers of all classes.

This search for the universally-interesting news is the reason behind the sensational papers. Although the interests of any individual differ in almost every aspect from the interests of his neighbor, there is one sort of news that interests them both, that interests every human being. That is the news that appeals to the emotions, to the heart. It is the news that deals with human life - human nature - human interest news the papers call it. In it every human being is interested. However trivial may be the event, if it can be described in a way that will make the reader feel the point of view of the human beings who suffered or struggled or died or who were made happy in the event, every other human being will read it with interest. Human sympathy makes one want to feel joy and pain from the standpoint of others. Naturally that sort of news is always read; naturally the paper that devotes itself to such news is always read and is always successful as far as circulation and profits go. The papers that have that ideal of news behind them and forsake every other ideal for it are called sensational papers. Whether they are good or not is another question.

With this idea of what news values means and the idea that news is worth while only when it interests the largest number of people of all classes, we may try to look for the things that make news interesting to the greatest number of people of all classes. The reporter must know not only what news is, but what makes it news. He must be able to see the things in a story that will interest the greatest number of people of all classes. These are many and intricate.

**2. Timeliness** - In the first place, news must be new. A story must have timeliness. Our readers want to know what happened to-day, for yesterday and last week are past and gone. They want to be up to the minute in their information on current events. Therefore a story that is worth printing to-day will not be worth printing to-morrow or, at most, on the day after tomorrow. Events must be chronicled just as soon as they happen. Furthermore, the story itself must show that it is new. It must tell the reader at once that the event which it is chronicling happened today or last night - at least since the last edition of the paper. That is why the reporter must never fail to put the time in the introduction of his story. Editors grow gray-headed trying to keep up with the swift passing of events, and they are always very careful to tell their readers that the events which they are chronicling are the latest events. That is the reason why every editor hates the word "yesterday" and tries to get "today" or "this morning" into the lead of every story. Hence, to the newspaper, everything that happened since midnight last night is labeled "this morning," and everything that happened since six o'clock yesterday afternoon is labeled "last night." Anything before that hour must be labeled "yesterday," but it goes in as "late yesterday afternoon," if it possibly can. Hence the first principle of news values is timeliness - news is news only because it just happened and can be spoken of as one of the events of "today" or of "late yesterday."

**3. Distance** - Distance is another factor in news values. In spite of fast trains and electric telegraphs human beings are clannish and local in their interests. They are interested mainly in things and persons that they know, and news from outside their ken must be of unusual significance to attract them. They like to read about things that they have seen and persons that they know, because they are slow to exert their imaginations enough to appreciate things that they do not know personally. Hence every newspaper is primarily local, even though it is a metropolitan daily, and news from a distance plays a very subordinate part. It has been said that New York papers cannot see beyond the Alleghanies; it is equally true that most papers cannot see more than a hundred miles from the printing office, except in the case of national news. Any newspaper's range of news sources goes out from the editorial room in concentric circles. Purely personal news must come from within the range of the paper's general circulation, because people do not care to read purely personal news about persons whom they do not know. Other news is limited ordinarily to the region with which the paper's readers are personally acquainted - the state, perhaps - because subscribers unconsciously wish to hear about places with which they are personally acquainted. Any news that comes from outside this larger circle must be nation-wide or very unusual in its interest. A story that may be worth a column in El Paso, Texas, would not be worth printing in New York because El Paso is hardly more than a name to most New York newspaper readers. In the same way, the biggest stories in New York are not worth anything in Texas, because Texas readers are not personally interested in New York - they cannot say, "Yes, I know that building; I walked down that street the other day; oh, you can't tell me anything about the subway." News is primarily local, and the first thing a correspondent must learn is how to distinguish the stories that are purely local in their interest from those that would be worth printing a hundred miles away in a paper read by people who do not know the places or persons involved in the story. Colonel Smith may be a very big frog in the little puddle of Smith's Corners, and his doings may be big news to the weeklies all over his county, but he has to do something very unusual before his name is worth a line in a paper two counties away. He is nothing but a name to people who do not know him or know of him, and therefore they are not interested in him. Every correspondent must watch for the stories that have something more than a local interest, some element of news in them that will carry them over the obstacle of distance and make them interesting to any reader.

It would be impossible to analyze news values to the extent of telling every conceivable element of interest that will overcome the obstacle of distance. Yet there are certain elements that always make a newspaper story interesting to any one.

**4. Loss of life** - One of these is the loss of human life. For some strange reason every human being is interested in the thought of death. Just as soon as a story mentions death it is worth printing, and if it has a number of deaths to tell about it is worth printing anywhere. Any fire, any railroad wreck, or any other disaster in which a number of persons are killed or injured makes a story that is worth sending anywhere. There seems to be a joy for the reader in the mere number of fatalities. A story that can begin with "Ten people were killed," or "Seven men met their death," attracts a reader's interest at once. As a very natural result, and justly, too, newspapers have been broadly accused of exaggeration for the sake of a large number. But at present many papers are inclined to underestimate rather than overestimate, perhaps to avoid this accusation. In a number of instances in the past year, among them the Shirtwaist Factory fire in New York, the first figures were smaller than the official count printed later. That does not mean, however, that newspapers do not want stories involving loss of life. Any story which involves a large number of fatalities will carry a long distance, if for no other reason.

**5. Big Names** - Another element of news values is the interest in prominent people. The mere mention of a man or a woman who is known widely attracts attention. Although Colonel Smith of Smith's Corners has to do something very unusual to get his name in any paper outside his county, the slightest thing that President Taft does is printed in every paper in the country. It is simply because of our interest in the man himself. Some names give a story news value because the names are widely known politically or financially, some names because they are simply notorious. But any name that is recognized at once, for any reason, gives a story news value.

**6. Property Loss** - Akin to man's love for any account that involves large loss of human life, is his love of any story that tells about a huge loss of property. The mere figures seem to have a charm; any story that can begin with awesome figures, like "Two million dollars," "One hundred automobiles," "Ten city blocks," has news value. Hence any story that involves a large loss that can be expressed in figures has the power to carry a great distance.

**7. Unusualness** - It is safe to say that newspaper readers are interested in anything unusual. It does not matter whether it is a thing, a person, an action, a misfortune; so long as it is strange and out of the range of ordinary lives, it is interesting. Many, if not most, newspaper stories have nothing but the element of strangeness in them to give them news value, but if they are sufficiently strange and unusual they may be copied all over the country. An unusual origin or an unusual rescue will give an unimportant fire great news value. And so with every other kind of story.

**8. Human Interest** - Along with the element of the strange and unusual, goes the human interest element. Any story that will make us laugh or make us cry has news value. Hundreds of magazines are issued monthly with nothing in them but fictitious stories that are intended to arouse our emotions, and newspapers are beginning to realize that they can interest their readers in the same way. No life is so prosaic that it is not full of incidents that make one laugh or cry, and when these stories can be told in a way that will make any reader feel the same emotions, they have news value that will carry them a long distance. Obviously their success depends very largely upon the way they are told.

**9. Personal Appeal** - Another element that may give a story news value is that of personal appeal or application to the reader's own daily life. Men are primarily egoistic and selfish and nothing interests them more than things that affect them personally. They can read complacently and without interest of the misfortunes and joys of others, but just as soon as anything affects their own daily lives, even a little, they want to hear about it. Perhaps the price of butter has gone up a few cents or the gas company has reduced its rates from eighty cents to seventy-seven. Every reader is interested at once, for the news affects his own daily life. Sometimes this personal appeal is due merely to the reader's familiarity with the persons or places mentioned in the story; sometimes it is due to the story's application to his business life, his social or religious activities, or to any phase of his daily existence. That is the reason why political news interests every one, for we all feel that the management of the government has an influence on our own lives. The story of any political maneuver - especially if it is one that may be looked upon as bad or good - carries farther than any other story. Show that your story tells of something that has even the slightest effect on the lives of a large number of people and it needs no other element to give it news value.

**10. Local Reasons** - These factors and many others give news stories a news value that will carry them a long distance and make them interesting in communities far from their source. Many local reasons may enhance the value of a story for local papers. A paper's policy or some campaign that it is waging may give an otherwise unimportant event a tremendous significance. If an unimportant person is slightly injured while leaving a trolley car the story is hardly worth a line of type. But if such an item should come to a newspaper while it is carrying on a campaign against the local street railway company, the story would probably be written and printed in great detail. Any slight occurrence that may be in line with a paper's political beliefs would receive an amount of space far out of proportion with its ordinary news worth. News value is a very changeable and indefinite thing, and there are countless reasons why any given story should be of interest to a large number of readers. And the possibility of interesting a large number of readers is the basis of news value.

**11. The Feature** - In connection with the study of news values the question of feature is important. In editorial offices one is constantly hearing the word "feature," and reporters are constantly admonished to "play up the feature" of their stories. Feature is the word that editors use to signify the essence of news value. Every story that is printed is printed because of some fact in it that makes it interesting - gives it news value. The element in the story that makes it interesting and worth printing is the feature. The feature may be some prominent name, a large list of fatalities, a significant amount of property destroyed, or merely the unusualness of the incident. This feature is the element that makes the story news; therefore it is used to attract attention to the story. Every newspaper story displays like a placard in its headlines the reason why it was printed--the element in it that makes it interesting. "Playing up the feature" is simply the act of bringing this feature to the front so that it will attract attention to the story. Just how this is done we shall see later. But when, as a reporter, you are looking for a feature to play up in your lead, remember that the feature to be played up is the thing in the story that gives the story news value. And few stories have more than one claim to news value, more than one feature.

# 3
# NEWSPAPER TERMS

The newspaper vernacular that is used in the editorial and press rooms of any daily paper is a curious mixture of literary abbreviations and technical printing terms. It is the result of the strange mingling of the literary trade of writing with the mechanical trade of setting type. For that reason a green reporter has difficulty in understanding the instructions that he receives until he has been in the office long enough to learn the office slang. It would be impossible to list all of the expressions that might be heard in one day, but a knowledge of the commonest words will enable a reporter to get the drift of his editor's instructions.

When a young man secures a position as reporter for a newspaper he begins as a *cub reporter* and is usually said to be on the *staff* of his paper. His sphere of activity is confined to the *editorial* room, where the news is written; his relations with the *business office*, where advertising, circulation, and other business matters are handled, consists of the weekly duty of drawing his pay. His chief enemies are in the *printing office* where his literary efforts are *set up* in type and printed. His superiors are called *editors* and exist in varying numbers, depending upon the size of his paper. The man who directs the reporters is usually called the *city editor*, or perhaps the *day* or *night city editor*; above him there are managing editors and other persons in authority with whom the cub is not concerned; and the favored mortals who enjoy a room by themselves and write nothing but editorials are called editors or *editorial writers*. There may also be a *telegraph* editor, a *sporting* editor, a *Sunday* editor, and many other editors; or if the paper is small and poor all of these editors may be condensed into one very busy man. On a city daily of average size there are *desk*

## NEWSPAPER REPORTING AND CORRESPONDENCE

*men*, or *copyreaders*, who work under editorial direction but feel superior to the reporter because they correct his literary efforts.

The reporter's work consists of gathering and writing news. In the office this is called *covering* and writing *stories*. He is ordinarily put on a *beat*, or *run*; this is simply a daily route or round of news sources which he follows as regularly as a policeman walks his beat. The reporter's work on a special story outside his beat is called an *assignment*. Any hint that he may receive concerning a bit of news is called a *tip*. Any bit of news that he secures to the exclusion of his paper's rivals is called a *beat*, or a *scoop*.

Everything that is written for the paper, whether it be a two-line personal item or a two-column report, is called a *story*, or a *yarn*, and from the time the story is written until it appears in the printed paper it is called *copy*. If the story is well written and needs few corrections it is called *clean copy*. After the story is written it is turned over to the copyreader to be *edited*. The copyreader corrects it and writes the headlines or *heads*; then he sends it to the composing room to be set in type by the *compositor*. The story itself is usually set up on a linotype machine and the heads are set up by hand. For the sake of keeping the two parts of the copy together the reporter or the copyreader ordinarily gives the story a name, such as "Fire No. 2"; the bit of lead on which the name is printed is called a *slug* and the story is said to be *slugged*. If at any time in its journey from the reporter's pencil to the printed page, the editor decides not to print the story, he *kills* it; otherwise he *runs* it, or allows it to go into the paper. When the story is in type, an impression, or *proof*, is taken of it, and this proof, still called copy, comes back to the copyreader or the proofreader for the correction of typographical errors. The gathering together of all of the day's stories into the form of the final printed page is called *making up* the paper; this is usually done by some one of the editors. In like manner, the finished aspect of the paper is called the *make-up*.

Some stories are said to be *big stories* because of unusual news value. When any news comes unexpectedly it is said to *break*; and when any story comes in beforehand and must be held over, it is said to be *released* on the day on which it may be printed. The first paragraph of any story is called the *lead* (pronounced "leed"); the word *lead* is also used to designate several introductory paragraphs that are tacked on at the beginning of a long story, which may be of the nature of a *running story* (as the running story of a football game), or may be made up of several parts, written by one or more reporters.

In general, that part of a story which presents the gist or summary of the entire story at the beginning is called the *lead*. The most interesting thing in the story, the part that gives it news value, is called the *feature*, and *playing up the feature* consists in telling the most interesting thing in the first line of the lead or in the headline. An entire story is said to be *played up* if it is given a prominent place in the paper. A *feature story* is either a story that is thus played up or a story that is written for some other reason than news value, such as human interest. When a story is rewritten to give a new interest to old facts it is called a *rewrite story*; when it is rewritten to include new facts or developments, it is called a *follow-up, second-day,* or *follow story*.

Because of the close relation between the editorial room and the printing office many printing terms are commonly heard about the editorial room. All copy is measured by the *column* and by the *stickful*. A column is usually a little less than 1,500 words and a stickful is the amount of type that can be set in a compositor's *stick*, the metal frame used in setting type by hand - about two inches or 100 words. A bit of copy that is set up with a border or a row of stars about it is said to be *boxed*. Whenever copy is set with extra space between the lines it is said to be *leaded* (pronounced "leded")--the name is taken from the piece of lead that is placed between the lines of type. The reporter must gradually learn the names of the various kinds of type and the various proofreader's signs that are used to indicate the way in which the type is to be set, for the whole work of writing the news is governed and limited by the mechanical possibilities of the printing office. The commonest signs used by the proofreader or the copyreader, together with instructions for preparing copy, are given in the Style Book at the end of this volume. (A complete list of proofreader's signs can be found in the back of any large dictionary.) *Style* is a word which editors use to cover a multitude of rules, arbitrary or otherwise, concerning capitalization, punctuation, abbreviation, etc. A paper that uses many capital letters is said to follow an *up* style, and a paper that uses small letters instead of capitals whenever there is a choice is said to follow a *down* style. Every newspaper has its own style and usually prints its rules in a Style Book; the Style Book given in this volume has been compiled from many representative newspaper style books. It sets forth an average style and the beginner is advised to follow it closely in his practice writing - for, as editors say, "uniformity is better than a strict following of style."

# 4
# THE NEWS STORY FORM

When we come to the writing of the news we find that there are many sorts of stories that must be written. In the newspaper office they are called simply stories without distinction. For the purpose of study they may be classified to some extent, but this classification must not be taken as hard and fast. The commonest kind of story is the simple news story. Practically all newspaper reports are news stories, but as distinguished from other kinds of reports the simple news story is the report of some late event or occurrence. It is usually concerned with unexpected news, and is the commonest kind of story in any newspaper. It is to be distinguished from reports of speeches, interview stories, court reports, social news, dramatic news, sporting news, human-interest stories, and all the rest. The distinction is largely one of form and does not exist to any great extent in a newspaper office where all stories are simply "stories."

The simple news story is probably the most variable part of a newspaper. Given the same facts, each individual reporter will write the story in his individual way and each editor will change it to suit his individual taste. No two newspapers have exactly the same ideal form of news story and no newspaper is able to live up to its individual ideal in each story.

But there are general tendencies. Certain things are true of all news stories; whether the story be the baldest recital of facts or the most sensational featuring of an imaginary thrill in a commonplace happening, certain characteristics are always present. And these characteristics can always be traced to one cause--the effort to catch and hold the reader's interest. When a busy American glances over his newspaper while he sips his breakfast coffee or while he clings to a strap on the way to his office, he reads only the stories that catch his interest - and he reads down the column in any one story only so long as his interest is maintained. Hence the ideal news story is one which will catch the reader's attention by its beginning and hold his interest to the very end. This is the principle of all newspaper writing.

The interest depends, in a large measure, on the way the facts are presented. True, certain facts are in themselves more interesting to a casual reader than others, but just as truly other less interesting facts may be made as interesting through the reporter's skill. The most interesting of stories may lose its interest if poorly presented, and facts of the most commonplace nature may be made attractive enough to hold the reader to the last word. The aim of every reporter and of every editor is to make every story so attractive and interesting that the most casual reader cannot resist reading it.

In the old days news stories were written in the logical order of events just like any other narrative, but constant change has brought about a new form, as different and individual as any other form of expression. Unlike any other imaginable piece of writing, the news story discloses its most interesting facts first. It does not lead the reader up to a startling bit of news by a tantalizing suspense in an effort to build up a surprise for him; it tells its most thrilling content first and trusts to his interest to lead him on through the details that should logically precede the real news. Therefore every editor admonishes his reporters "to give the gist of the news first and the details later."

There are other reasons for this peculiar reversal of the logical order of narrative. Few readers have time to read the whole of every story, and yet they want to get the news - in the shortest possible time. Therefore the newspaper very kindly tells the important part of each story at the beginning. Then if the reader cares to hear the details he can read the rest of the story; but he gets the news, anyway. Again, if the exigencies of making up the stories into a paper of mechanically limited space require that a story be cut down, the editor may slash off a paragraph or two at the end without depriving the story of its interest. Imagine the difficulty of cutting down a story that is told in its logical order! If the real news of the story were in the last paragraph it would go in the slashing, and what would be left? Whereas, if the gist of the story comes first the editor may run any number of paragraphs or even the first paragraph alone and still have a complete story.

## NEWSPAPER REPORTING AND CORRESPONDENCE

The arrangement of news stories in American newspapers is thus a very natural one, resulting from the exigencies of the business. Just how to fit every story to this arrangement is a difficult task. However, there are certain rules that the reporter may apply to each story, and these are very simple.

In the first place, almost every story has a feature - there is some one thing in it that is out of the ordinary, something that gives it interest and news value beyond the interest in the incident behind it. No two stories have the same interesting features; if they had, only one of them would be worth printing and that would be the first. This extraordinary feature the reporter must see at once. If a building burns he must see quickly what incident in the occurrence will be of interest to readers who are reading of many fires every day. If John Smith falls off a street car the reporter must discover some interesting fact in connection with Mr. Smith's misfortune that will be new and attractive to readers who do not know John and are bored with accounts of other Smiths' accidents. The accident itself may be interesting, but the part of the accident that is out of the ordinary - the thing that gives the accident news value - is the feature of the story, and the reporter must tell it first.

Thoroughly determined to tell the most interesting part, the gist, of his story in the first paragraph, the reporter must remember that there are certain other things about the incident that the reader wants to know just as quickly. There are certain questions which arise in the reader's mind when the occurrence is suggested, and these questions must be answered as quickly as they are asked. The questions usually take the form of *when? where? what? who? how? why?* If a man falls off the street car we are eager to know at once who he was, although we probably do not know him, anyway; where it happened; when it happened; how he fell; and why he fell. If there is a fire we immediately ask what burned; where it was; when it burned; how it burned; and what caused it to burn. And the reporter must answer these questions with the same breath that tells us that a man fell off the car or that there was any fire at all.

The effort to answer these questions at once has led to the peculiar form of introduction characteristic of every newspaper story. Newspaper people call it the lead. It is really nothing but the statement of the briefest possible answers to all these questions in one sentence or one short paragraph. It tells the whole story in its baldest aspects and aims to satisfy the reader who wants only the gist of the story and does not care for the details. When all his questions have been answered in

# GETTING THE SCOOP

one breath he is ready to read the details one at a time, but he won't be satisfied if he must read all about how the fire was discovered before he is told what building burned, when it burned, etc. For example:

| Fire of unknown origin caused the | |practical destruction of the famous old | |"Crow's Nest," at Tenth and Cedar | |streets, perhaps the best known and | |oldest landmark in the Second ward, | |yesterday afternoon.--*Milwaukee Free* | |*Press.* |

This is the lead of an ordinary news story - a newspaper report of a fire. The lead begins with "Fire" because the story has no unusual feature - no element in it that is more interesting than the fact that there was a fire. The reporter considers "Fire" the most important part of his story and begins with it. As soon as we read the word "Fire" we ask, "When?" - "Where?" - "What?" - "Why?" - "How?" The reporter answers us in the same sentence with his announcement, "yesterday afternoon" - "at Tenth and Cedar Streets" - "the famous old 'Crow's Nest,' perhaps the best known and oldest landmark in the Second ward" - "unknown origin." *How* is not worth answering, in this case, beyond the statement that the destruction was practically complete. Thus the reporter has told us his bit of news and answered our most obvious questions about it at the very beginning of his story - in one sentence. According to newspaper rules this is a good lead. The order of the answers will be considered later. For the present we are concerned only with the facts that the lead must contain.

# 5
# THE SIMPLE FIRE STORY

The simplest news story is the story which has no feature - which has no fact in it more important than the incident which it reports - e.g., the fire at the end of the last chapter. If we recall the various elements of news value we note that any incident may be given greater news value by the presence of some unusual or interesting feature - a great loss of life, an unusual time, a strikingly large loss of property, or simply a well-known name. Such a story is called a story with a feature, because its interest depends not so much on the incident itself as upon the unusual feature within the incident. On the other hand, many news stories do not have features. Many stories are worth printing simply because of the incident which they report, without any unusual feature within them. For example, a building may burn with no loss of life, no great loss of property, and no striking occurrence in connection with the burning. Such a fire is worth reporting, but there is no fact in the story more interesting than the fact that there was a fire; the story has no feature.

The leads of these two kinds of stories are different. When a story has a feature it is customary to play up that feature in the first line of the lead. If the story has no feature, is simply the record of a commonplace event, the lead merely announces the incident and answers the reader's questions about it.

The commonest of featureless stories is the simple fire story in which nothing out of the ordinary happens, no one is killed, no striking rescues take place, and no tremendous amount of property is destroyed. This may be taken as typical of all featureless stories. The reporter, in writing a report of such a fire, merely answers in the lead the questions *when*, *where*, *what*, *why*, and perhaps *how*, that the reader asks concerning the fire. The most striking part of the story is that there was a fire; hence the story begins with "Fire." For example:

> | Fire today wrecked the top of the | |six-story warehouse at 393 to 395 | |Washington street, used by the United | |States army as a medical supply | |storeroom for the Department of the | |East. Capt. Edwin Wolf, who is in charge | |of the warehouse, says the loss on tents, | |blankets, cots, and other bedding stored | |on the floors of the building was | |large. - *New York Mail.* |

As one reads down through the rest of the story he finds nothing more striking than the fact that there was a fire. Therefore there is no particular feature. No one was killed; no one was injured; the loss was not extraordinary for a New York fire - nothing in the story is of greater interest than the mere fact that there was a fire. Hence the story begins with the word "Fire." Notice that it does not begin "A fire" or "The fire" - for the simple reason that the word *fire* does not need an article before it. The editor will also tell you that it is not considered good to begin a story with an article, for the beginning is the most important part of a story and it is foolish to waste that advantageous place on unimportant words.

The first word tells the reader that there has been a fire. He immediately asks where? - what burned? - when? - how much was lost? And the reporter proceeds to answer his questions in their order of importance. The reporter who wrote this story apparently thought that the time was of greatest importance and slipped it in at once - "today." He might just as well have left the time until the end of the sentence because it is not of very great interest. He considers the question "*Where*" of next importance, and answers with "the top of the six-story warehouse at 393 to 395 Washington Street." The question "what?" he answers with a clause, "used by the United States army as a medical supply store-room for the Department of the East." He does not try to answer the question "*why?*" because, as the rest of the story tells us, no one knew exactly what caused the fire. And as for the "*How?*" there is nothing extraordinary in the way that it burned beyond the fact that it burned. Thus, in one sentence, he has answered all four questions about the fire, except a little query concerning the amount of the loss. That he considers worth a separate sentence of details.

This is not a perfect lead. Many editors would consider it faulty, but it illustrates one way of writing the lead of a featureless fire story. Obviously there are faults; for instance, the time is given an undue amount of emphasis and the cause is omitted.

Suppose that we construct another lead from the same story - a lead which would be more in accordance with the logic of newspaper writing. We shall begin with the word "fire," but after it we shall slip in a little mention of the cause since to the reader not directly acquainted with the property that point is always of the greatest importance. Then we shall tell where the fire was and after that what was burned. And last of all we shall give the time since that is of least importance to the average reader. This would be the result:

| Fire of unknown origin wrecked the top | | of the six-story warehouse at 393-395 | | Washington street, used by the United | | States army as a medical supply | | store-room for the Department of the | | East, destroying a large number of tents, | | blankets, cots, and other bedding, today. |

We might as well have put the *what* before the *where* or altered the lead in any other way. But we would always begin with the word "fire" and answer all the questions that the reader might ask - in one short simple sentence. This constitutes our lead. We have told the casual reader what he wants to know about the fire. We give him more details about the fire if he wants to read them, but after we have stated the case clearly in the lead we no longer reckon his time so carefully and allow ourselves some latitude in the telling. After the lead we begin the story from the beginning and tell it in its logical order from start to finish, always bearing in mind that the editor may chop off a paragraph or two at the end.

Hence the second paragraph of the story as it appeared in *The Mail* begins:

| John Smith, a man employed in the | | stock-room on the sixth floor, saw smoke | | rolling out of one corner and notified | | other employees in the building, while | | Patrolman Hogan turned in an alarm. |

We are back at the beginning now and telling things as they came. The next paragraph of the story tells us how they fought the fire, and the third tells us how they finally brought it under control. The last paragraph of the story reads:

| There are three such warehouses in the | | country, one at St. Louis, another at San | | Francisco, but the one in this city is by | | far the largest. In it are kept supplies |

# GETTING THE SCOOP

|for the Departments of the East, Gulf, | |Cuba, Porto Rico, and the Philippines. |

The editor of *The Mail* had plenty of space that day and saw fit to run this last paragraph, but we should not have lost much had he chopped it off. Perhaps the reporter's copy contained still another paragraph telling about Captain Wolf, but that did not pass the editorial pencil. Even more of the story might have been slashed without depriving us of much of the interesting news.

Judging from the above story a newspaper account is divided into two separate and independent parts: the lead and the detailed account. The lead is written for the casual reader and contains all the necessary facts about the fire; it may stand alone and constitute a story in itself. The detailed account is written for the reader who wants to hear more about the incident, and is written in the logical order of events - with an eye to the danger of the editor's pencil threatening the last paragraphs. In other words, the reporter tells his story briefly in one paragraph and then goes back and tells it all over again in a more detailed way. If the story is of sufficient importance the second telling may not be sufficient and he may go back a third time to the beginning and tell it again with still greater detail - but that is another matter. For the present we shall consider only the lead and the first detailed account.

There are certain other points to be noticed in the report of a featureless fire. Under no condition should it begin with the time. Why? Because, unless the time is of extreme interest, no one cares particularly when the fire occurred. And if the time is of great interest - as, for instance, if a church should burn while the congregation is in it - then the time becomes a feature to be played up and the story is no longer a featureless story. We are now considering stories in which nothing is of greater interest than the mere fact that there was a fire.

The same is true of the location. Who cares what street the fire was on until he knows more about the fire? If the location were of such significant importance as to be played up, the story would no longer be a featureless story.

The paragraphing is also important. Since the lead is in itself a separate part of the story it should always be paragraphed separately. Do not let the beginning of the detailed account lap over into the lead, and do not introduce into the first paragraph any facts which are not absolutely a part of the lead--that is, facts that are absolutely essential to a general knowledge of the fire. When once you begin to tell the story in detail tell it logically and paragraph it logically. Do not tell us that John Smith discovered the fire and that the loss is $500 in the same paragraph. Take up each point separately and treat it fully before you leave it - then begin a new paragraph for the next item.

* * * * *

To take a hypothetical case, suppose that misfortune visits the home of John H. Jones, who lives at 79 Liberty Street. A defective flue sets his house on fire and it burns to the ground. By inquiry we find that the house is worth about $4,000 and is fully insured.

There is nothing particularly striking about the story. We are sorry for Mr. Jones, but many houses worth $4,000 are set on fire by poor chimneys and many more houses burn down. No one was hurt, no one was killed; the most striking part of it all is that there was a fire. We would begin with the word "Fire." Perhaps our readers would be most interested in the cause of the fire and we shall tell them that first. Then we shall tell them what burned, when it burned, and where it stood. There is nothing else that a casual reader would want to know and the lead would read:

> | Fire starting in a defective chimney | |destroyed the residence of John H. Jones, | |79 Liberty street, at midnight last | |night, causing a loss of $4,000, covered | |by insurance. |

Our casual reader is satisfied. For the reader who wishes to know more about the fire we add a paragraph or two of detail. First, we may tell him who discovered the fire; then how the Jones family managed to escape; and after that how the fire was extinguished, and we might slip in a paragraph explaining just what trouble in the chimney made a fire possible. The editor may chop off any number of paragraphs or cut the story down to the lead, and yet our readers will get the facts and know just exactly what was the reason for the fire bell and the red sky at midnight last night.

# 6
# THE FEATURE FIRE STORY

A fire story without a feature begins with "Fire" because there is nothing in the story more interesting than the fact that there has been a fire. Such was the case in the burning of John Jones's house in the last chapter. But just as soon as any part of the story becomes more interesting than the fact that there was a fire, the story is no longer featureless - it is a fire story with a feature, or, for the purposes of our study, *a feature fire story*. This feature may be related to the story in one of two ways. In the first place, the answer to some one of the reader's questions may be the feature - e.g., the answer to *when, where, what, how, why, who*. On the other hand, the feature may be in some unexpected attendant circumstance that the reader would not think of; for instance, loss of life, an interesting rescue, or something of that sort. Such a distinction is entirely arbitrary and would not be considered in a newspaper office, but it will make the matter simpler for the purposes of study.

## A. FEATURES IN ANSWERS TO READER'S CUSTOMARY QUESTIONS

### (*When, Where, What, How, Why, Who*).

Suppose that John Jones's house did not burn in the usual way--suppose that there is some striking incident in the story that makes it different from other fire stories. The story has a feature. Perhaps the answer to some one of the reader's customary questions is more interesting than the answers to the others--so much more interesting that it supersedes even the fact that there was a fire. Then it would be foolish to begin with the mere word "fire" when we have something more interesting to tell. The fire takes a second place and we begin with the interesting fact that supersedes it. For the present we shall consider that this interesting fact is the answer to one of the questions that the reader always asks; for instance, why the house burned or when it burned.

**1. Why** - Perhaps Mr. Jones's house was set on fire in a very unusual way. There was a little party in session at the Jones's and some one decided to take a flash-light picture. The flash-light set fire to a lace curtain and before any one could stop it the house was afire. Few fires begin in that way, and our readers would be very interested in hearing about it. The story has a feature in the answer to the reader's *Why?* And so we would begin our lead in this way:

> | A flashlight setting fire to a lace | |curtain started a fire which destroyed | |the residence of John H. Jones, 79 | |Liberty street, at 11 o'clock last night | |and caused a loss of $4,000. |

In this way the feature is played up at the beginning of the sentence, and yet the rest of the reader's questions are answered in the same sentence and he knows a great deal about the fire. Or, leaving Mr. Jones to his fate, we may give another example of an unusual cause taken from a newspaper. This was a big fire, and yet the unusual cause was of greater interest than the fire itself or the amount of property destroyed:

> | A tiny "joss stick," the lighted end of| |which was no larger than a pinhead, is | |thought to have been responsible for a | |fire that destroyed the White City | |Amusement Park at Broad Ripple last | |night. The loss to the amusement company | |is $161,000.--*Indianapolis News.* |

**2. Where** - To return to Mr. Jones, there may have been some other incident in the burning of his house aside from the cause that was of exceptional interest. Let us say that his house stood in a part of the town where a fire was to be feared. Perhaps it stood within twenty feet of the new First Congregational Church. The burning of Jones's house would then be insignificant in comparison to the danger to the costly edifice beside it, and our readers would be more interested in an item concerning their church. The answer to *Where?* is more interesting than the fire itself. Hence we would bury, so to speak, Mr. Jones's misfortune behind the greater danger, and the story would read:

> | Fire endangered the new First | |Congregational Church on Liberty street, | |erected at a cost of

# GETTING THE SCOOP

> $100,000, when the | |home of J. H. Jones, in the rear of the | |church, was destroyed at midnight last | |night. |

Or:

> | The First Congregational Church, | |recently built at a cost of $100,000, was| |seriously threatened by a fire which | |destroyed the residence of John H. Jones,| |78 Liberty street, within twenty feet of | |the church, at midnight last night. |

Turning again to the daily papers, we can find many fire stories in which the location of the burned structure is important enough to take the first line of the lead. Here is one:

> | The Plaza Hotel had a few uncomfortable| |moments last night when flames from a | |building adjoining at 22 West Fifty-ninth| |street were shooting up as high as the | |tenth story of the hotel and the fire | |apparatus which responded to the delayed | |alarm was looking for the blaze several | |blocks away.--*New York Sun.* |

**3. When** - Sometimes the time of the fire is very interesting. John H. Jones's house may have caught fire from a very insignificant thing and its location may have been unimportant, but the fire may have come at an unusual time. Perhaps Mr. Jones's daughter was being married at a quiet home wedding in her father's house and in the midst of the ceremony the roof of the house burst into flames. The unusual time would be interesting; the answer to *When?* would be the feature. We might write the lead thus:

> | During the wedding of Miss Mary Jones | |at the home of her father, John H. Jones,| |78 Liberty street, last night, the house | |suddenly burst into flames and the bridal| |party was compelled to flee into the | |street. |

Or:

> | Fire interrupted the wedding of Miss | |Mary Jones at her father's home, 78 | |Liberty street, last night, when the | |house caught fire from a defective | |chimney during the ceremony. |

The daily papers furnish many illustrations of fires at unusual times - here is one:

> |When the snowstorm was at its height | |early this morning, a three-story brick | |building at Nos. 4410-18 Third Avenue, | |Brooklyn, caught fire, and the flames | |spread rapidly to an adjoining tenement, | |sending a

small crowd of shivering tenants into the icy street.--*New York Post.*

**4. What** - (a) *The Burned Building.*--Many fire stories have their feature in the answer to the reader's *What?* Not infrequently the building itself is of great importance. Naturally "The residence of John H. Jones" would not make a good beginning, if John Jones is not well known, because people would be more interested in reading about a mere fire than in reading about the residence of John H. Jones, whom they do not know. For it must be remembered that it is the first line that catches the reader's eye and the interest or lack of interest in the first line determines whether or not the story is to be read. Now, suppose that a building that is very well known burns - the City Hall, the Albany State House, the Herald Square Theater - the mere mention of the building will attract the reader's attention. Therefore the reporter begins with the answer to *What?* the name of the building, as in the following cases:

> GLENS FALLS, N. Y., Aug. 17.--The Kaatskill House, for many years a popular Lake George resort, was completely destroyed by fire this forenoon.--*New York Times.*

> The First M. E. Church of Chelsea, familiarly known as the Cary avenue church, was damaged last night to the amount of $7,000 by fire.--*Boston Herald.*

(b) *The Amount of Property Destroyed.* - The answer to *What burned?* is not necessarily a building, for the building itself may not be worth featuring. The contents of the building may be more interesting, especially if the amount of property destroyed can be put in striking terms, such as $2,000,000 worth of property, or two thousand chickens, or fifty-three automobiles, or 7,000 gallons of whisky. These figures printed at the beginning of the first paragraph catch the reader's eye, thus:

> Five automobiles, valued at $5,800, and property amounting to $6,200 were destroyed last evening when fire broke in the repair shop of the G. W. Browne Motor company, 228-232 Wisconsin street, near the North-Western station.--*Milwaukee Sentinel.*

**5. How** - Very rarely the manner in which a fire burns is quite unique and deserves featuring. It is inconceivable that John Jones's house could burn in any very unusual way--"with many explosions," "with a glare of flames that aroused the whole city," "with vast clouds of oily smoke" - but some fires do burn in some such a way and are interesting only for the way they burned. The following story begins with the answer to *How?* although the manner might be described more explicitly:

> | Stubborn fires have been fought in the | |past, but one of the hardest blazes to | |conquer that the local department ever | |contended with gutted the plant of N. | |Drucker & Co., manufacturers of trunks | |and valises, at the northwest corner of | |Ninth and Broadway, last | |night.--*Cincinnati Commercial Tribune.* |

**6. Who** - Just as it would be foolish to begin with "the residence of John Jones," since the building is not well known, it would not be advisable to begin with John Jones's name, no matter what part he played. John Jones is not well known and so to the newspaper he is just a man and is treated impersonally regardless of what he does or what happens to him. Our interest in him is entirely impersonal, and all we want to know about him is what he has done or what has happened to him. Therefore few reporters would begin a story with John Jones's name. However, let some man who is well known do or suffer the slightest thing and his name immediately lends interest to the story - and therefore commands first place in the introduction. If John D. Rockefeller should even witness a fire, or if President Taft should be in the slightest way connected with a fire, the mere fire story would shrink into significance behind the name. And so, very often it is advisable to begin a fire story with a name, if the name is of sufficient prominence. It is not necessary that the well-known man's property be destroyed or even endangered for his name to have the first place in the first sentence of the lead; if the well-known man has anything whatever to do with the fire his name should be featured because to the average reader the interest in his name overshadows any interest in the fire. In this example, the name overshadows a striking loss of property and the story begins with the answer to *Who?*

> | NEW YORK, Nov. 6.--While Clendenin J. | |Ryan, son of Thomas F. Ryan, the traction| |magnate, and a band of volunteer fire | |fighters--many of them | |millionaires--fought a blaze which | |started in the garage of young Ryan's | |country estate near Suffern, N. Y., early| |in the morning, three valuable | |automobiles, seven thoroughbred horses | |and several outbuildings were totally | |destroyed.--*Milwaukee Sentinel.* |

It will be seen that in each of the above feature fire stories some incident in the fire, or connected with the fire, overshadows the mere fact that there was a fire and makes it advisable to begin the story of the fire with the fact or incident of unusual interest. Furthermore, in each of these stories the unusual feature in the story is a direct answer to one of the reader's questions - *when? where? how? what? why? who?* In other words, the reporter in answering these questions, as he must in the lead of every story, finds the answer to one question so much more interesting than the answer to any of the other questions that he puts it first. In every fire story, however, the feature is not so easily discovered.

## B. FEATURES IN UNEXPECTED ATTENDANT CIRCUMSTANCES

There are other things in the day's fire stories, besides the answers to the reader's questions, that may overshadow the rest of the story and deserve to be featured. Very often there are unexpected attendant circumstances occurring simultaneously with the fire or resulting from the fire to command our interest. Perhaps a number of people are killed or injured; then we want to know about them first, and the reporter neglects to answer our questions for the moment while he tells us the startling attendant circumstances that we had not expected. Even so, while giving first place to the feature, he does not forget our questions but answers them in the same sentence. Hence the introduction of a fire story with significant attendant circumstances begins with the startling fact resulting from the fire and then goes on to answer the reader's questions - in the same sentence.

This is not so difficult as it may sound. Suppose that when John Jones's house burns there is a stiff breeze blowing and the chances are that all the other houses in the block will go with it. All of his neighbors become frightened and work with feverish haste to move their household goods out into the street. In the end the fire department succeeds in confining the fire to Mr. Jones's house and his neighbors promptly carry their chattels back indoors thanking the god of good luck. Now the mere fact that John Jones's house burned down is rather insignificant beside the fact that a dozen families were driven from their homes by the fire. Therefore the reporter would begin thus:

| Twelve families were driven from their | |homes by a fire which destroyed the | |residence of John H. Jones, 78 Liberty | |street, at 11 o'clock last night. The | |fire

was at length kept from spreading | |and the neighboring residences were | |reoccupied. |

Or to take an incident from the daily press in which the neighbors were not so fortunate; although they might have entirely lost their homes:

| Twenty-two families in the six-story | |tenement at 147 Orchard street were | |routed out of the house twice early today| |by fires which caused a great deal of | |smoke, but little real damage.--*New York*| |*Mail*. |

**1. Death** - (a) *Number of Dead.* - The most usual attendant circumstances that will come to our notice is death in the fire. Let us say that Mr. Jones's three children were alone in the house and burned to death. Their death would be of more interest to us than the burning of their father's house - and our story would necessarily begin in this way:

| Three children were burned to death in | |a fire which destroyed the home of their | |father, John H. Jones, 78 Liberty street,| |last night. |

So common is death in connection with fire that almost every day's paper contains one or more stories beginning "Ten persons were cremated----" or "Four firemen were killed----" And in every case the loss of human life is considered of greater importance than any other incident in the story, and the number of dead always takes precedence over many another startling feature. Here are a few examples:

| JOHNSTOWN, Pa., Jan. 18.--Seven men | |were cremated in a fire that burned to | |the ground three double houses near | |Berlin, Somerset County, early this | |morning.--*New York Sun*. |

| Three children of Mr. and Mrs. Bernard | |Lindberg, 3328 Nineteenth avenue south, | |were cremated in a fire which destroyed | |their home shortly after 12 o'clock | |yesterday. The children had been left | |alone in the house, shut up in their | |bedroom, etc.--*St. Paul Pioneer Press.* |

| One fireman was killed, another fireman| |and a woman were injured and eight people| |escaped death by a narrow margin Saturday| |night in a fire which destroyed the, | |etc.--*Milwaukee Sentinel.* |

| NEW YORK, March 27.--One hundred and | |forty-one persons are dead as a result | |of the fire which on Saturday afternoon | |swept the three upper floors of the | |factory loft building at the northwest | |corner of

# NEWSPAPER REPORTING AND CORRESPONDENCE

Washington place and Greene street. More than three-quarters of this number are women and girls, who were employed in the Triangle Shirt Waist factory, where the fire originated.--*Boston Transcript.*

(b) *List of Dead.* - When the number of dead or injured reaches any very significant figure it is customary to make a table of dead and injured. This table is usually set into the story close after the lead, but very often the list is put in a "box" and slipped in above the story. In writing the story, however, the reporter disregards the table and begins his lead as if there were no table: e.g., "Twelve firemen were killed and fourteen injured in a fire----" The list usually gives the name, address (or some other identification), and the nature of the injury, thus:

> =Injured Firemen:= Capt. Frank Makal, Engine Co. No. 4, cut by glass. Acting Captain W. E. Brown, fire boat No. 23, cut by glass. Peter Ryan, No. 15, flying glass.--*Milwaukee Free Press.*

Or:

> =The Dead:= Mrs. Charles Smith, 14 W. Gorham street. John Johnson, 1193 Chatham street. =The Injured:= Thomas Green, 1111 Grand street; face cut by flying glass. James Brown, 176 Orchard avenue; internal injuries; may die.

(c) *Manner of Death* - A number of fatalities at the beginning always attracts attention. Not infrequently the manner or the cause, especially in the case of a single death, is worth the first place in the lead - not as "One man killed----" but as "Crushed beneath a falling wall, a man was killed." If a man burns to death in a very unusual way, or for an unusual reason, we are more interested in the way he was burned, or the reason that he burned, than in the mere fact that he was burned to death. The first line then tells us how or why he was burned. Thus:

> To save his money, which he hoped would some day raise him from the rank of a laborer to that of a prosperous merchant, Hing Lee, a Chinese laundryman, ran back into his burning laundry at 3031 Nicollet avenue today, after he was once safe from the flames, and was so badly burned that physicians say he cannot live.--*Minneapolis Journal.*

**2. Injuries** - Very often no one is killed in a fire but some one is injured. For example, five firemen are overcome by ammonia fumes or two men are seriously injured by a falling wall. This then becomes the feature. Injuries to human beings, if serious or in any considerable number, take precedence over other features, just as loss of human life does. Here is an example from the press in which all the injuries are gathered together at the beginning:

| Six firemen and two laborers were | |overcome by smoke, while three other | |firemen received minor injuries by flying| |glass in a fire which broke out yesterday| |morning at 10:30 o'clock in the | |Wellauer-Hoffman building, at, | |etc.--*Milwaukee Free Press.* |

**3. Rescues** - (a) *Number of People Rescued* -When people are rescued from great danger in a fire their escape makes a very good feature. If many of them are rescued or escape very narrowly, the mere number of people saved deserves the first place, as:

| More than 150 men and women were saved | |from death today in a fire at 213-217 | |Grand street by toboganning from the roof| |of the burning structure on a board chute| |to the roof of an adjoining five-story | |building.--*New York Mail.* |

(b) *Manner of Rescue* - But more often the manner of their escape interests us most. If a man slides down a rope for four stories to escape death by fire we are more interested in how he saved himself than in the fact that he didn't burn, and so we tell how he escaped, in the first line. In the same way, if unusual means are used to save one or more persons, the means of rescue is usually worth featuring. For example:

| Overcoats used as life nets saved the | |lives of a dozen women and children in a | |fire of incendiary origin in the | |three-story frame tenement house at 137 | |Havemeyer avenue, Brooklyn, to-day, | |etc.--*New York Mail.* |

**4. Property Threatened** - Death and injury are the commonest unexpected circumstances in fire stories, but they are not the only ones that may be worth featuring. There is an inconceivable number of things that may happen at a fire and overshadow all interest in the fire itself. A good feature may be found in the property that is threatened. Often the fire in itself is insignificant, but because of a high wind or other circumstances it threatens to spread to neighboring buildings or to devastate a large area. In such a case the amount of property threatened or endangered deserves a place in the very first line, especially if it exceeds the amount of property actually destroyed and if it can be put in a striking way; *ie.*, the entire waterfront district, or twenty-five dwelling houses, or $5,000,000 worth of property. When contrasted with the small amount of damage actually done, the amount that is threatened becomes more important. Thus:

> | Fire that for a time threatened | |$2,000,000 worth of property destroyed | |$15,000 worth of lumber owned by the | |Milwaukee Lumber Company, 725 Clinton | |street, yesterday.... | | | |The territory between Mitchell street | |and the Kinnickinnic river and Reed | |street, to the lake, containing | |manufactories, dwellings and stores, was | |menaced.--*Milwaukee News.* |

**5. Fire Fighting** - Not unusually a serious fire results from the fact that it was not checked for some reason or other during its earlier stages. Perhaps the whole thing might have been avoided, or, on the contrary, a big fire may be extinguished with unexpected ease or unusual skill. In rare cases this matter of very efficient or very inefficient fire fighting is of sufficient importance to take the first place in the lead. For example:

> | Almost total lack of water pressure is | |blamed for the big loss in a fire started| |by a firebug to-day in the five-story | |factory building of Lamchick Brothers, | |manufacturing company, 400-402 South | |Second street, Williamsburg.--*New York* | |*Mail.* | | | | Rotten hose, which burst as fast as it | |was put in use, imperiled the lives of | |more than a score of firemen to-day at a | |blaze which swept the three-story frame | |flat house at Third avenue and | |Sixty-seventh street, Brooklyn, from | |cellar to roof, etc.--*New York Mail.* |

**6. Crowd** - Not uncommonly in the city a tremendous crowd gathers to watch a fire and blocks traffic for hours. In the absence of other significant incidents - death, great loss, etc. - the reporter may begin his story with an account of the crowd present or the blockade of traffic. Such a beginning should always be used only as a last resort when a fire has no other interesting phase, for crowds always gather at fires and only a very serious blocking of traffic is worth reporting. Thus:

> | Fully 15,000 persons were attracted to | |the scene of the fire in the portion of | |the plant of the Greenwald

# GETTING THE SCOOP

> Packing | |Company, Claremont Stock Yards, which was| |discovered at 4:56 yesterday | |afternoon.--*Baltimore American.* | | | | Twenty-five thousand people jammed | |Broadway between Bleecker and Bond | |streets yesterday noon and had the | |excitement of watching 250 girls escape | |from a twelve-story loft building which | |was afire.--*New York Sun.* |

**7. Miscellaneous** - There is an infinite number of things that may happen at a fire and overshadow the mere fire interest. These are the things that make one fire different from another, and whenever they are of sufficient importance they become the feature to be played up in the first line of the introduction. It would be impossible to enumerate all the unexpected things that might happen during a fire. It is this element of unexpected possibilities that makes the reporting of fires interesting, and an alert reporter is ever on the lookout for a new and unusual development in the fire to be used as the feature of his story. Here are the leads of a few fire stories clipped from the daily newspapers:

> | With her home on fire and the smoke | |swirling around her head, Mrs. B. B. | |Blank, a well-known leader of the | |social set of Roland Park, bravely | |stood by her telephone and called upon | |the Roland Park Fire Company for aid | |shortly after 8 o'clock this | |morning.--*Baltimore Star.* | | | | Four charming young women attired in | |masculine apparel were the unexpected | |and embarrassed hosts of four companies | |of fire department "laddies" last night, | |when fire broke out, etc.--*Milwaukee* | |*Free Press.* | | | | For the first time since its | |installation the high-pressure water | |power system was relied upon solely last | |night to fight a Broadway fire, and | |Chief Croker said that he was well | |satisfied with its work. The fire began | |on the third floor of the six-story, | |etc.--*New York Times.* |

## C. FIRE STORIES WITH MORE THAN ONE FEATURE

It would appear from the foregoing examples that almost every fire story has a feature. And so it usually has. The great majority of fires that are worth reporting at all have some unusual incident connected with them that overshadows the mere fire itself. Sometimes the features are not of great significance, but it is only as a last resort that a reporter begins his story with "Fire" - only when the most ordinary of fires is to be covered.

Unusual features are so common in connection with fires that very often a single fire has more than one unusual feature. Perhaps the cause of the fire is exceptionally striking and at the same time the amount of property destroyed is of great news value in itself. Or the time and some unexpected attendant circumstance are both worth the first place. In that case the reporter has to choose between the two features and begin with the one that seems to him to be the more striking.

The other feature or features may often be arranged in the order of importance immediately after the most striking fact at the beginning, provided that this does not make the lead unduly complicated.

For instance, a cold storage warehouse burns and four firemen are overcome by the fumes from the ammonia pipes. Next door is a hospital and the flames frighten the patients almost into a panic. Either one of these incidents is worth the first line of the story. But which one is of the greater importance? Naturally the element of danger to human life must be considered first and the actual disabling of four firemen is of greater significance than a possible panic in the hospital. Following that line of logic our story would begin:

| Four firemen were overcome by ammonia | |fumes and a panic in the St. Charles | |Hospital was narrowly averted, as a | |result of a fire which destroyed the cold| |storage warehouse of, etc. |

Such a lead would not be too complicated for practical purposes. But suppose that around the corner from the cold storage warehouse is a livery in which fifty horses are stabled. The flames frighten the horses and they break loose and stampede in the streets. The story now has three features of striking interest. It would be possible to combine them all in the lead and to begin in this way:

| Four firemen were overcome by ammonia | |fumes, a panic was narrowly averted in | |the St. Charles Hospital, and fifty | |frightened horses stampeded in the | |streets as a result of a fire, etc. |

But see how far from the beginning the fire, the actual cause of it all, is placed. The fire is buried behind a mass of details and the reader is confused. The lead is not a happy one. The only thing to do is to break up the mass of details and put part of them immediately after the lead. The arrangement is a matter that must be left to the judgment of the reporter.

# GETTING THE SCOOP

This, however, is an extreme case because the various features are so disconnected and separate. The reporter would have little trouble if the several features were more alike. For instance, if one of the walls of the building had fallen and killed three firemen the case would have been simpler. The death of these men so far overshadows the other unusual incidents that it drives them out of the lead altogether. For we do not care about horses and frightened patients when men are crushed beneath falling walls. All that we are concerned with in our lead now is the dead and injured - with a feature like this we can trust our readers to go into the story far enough to pick up the other interesting features; we would begin in this way:

> | Three firemen were killed by falling | |walls and four others were overcome by | |ammonia fumes in a fire which destroyed | |the cold storage, etc. |

The combination of dead and injured makes a good beginning, and it is always advisable to begin with such an enumeration whenever it is possible. Where the features are not so significant as death and injuries the matter of arranging more than one striking detail at the beginning of the lead becomes a greater problem. It must be left to one's own judgment and common sense. The lead must not be too long or complicated, and one must hesitate before burying the really important facts of the story behind several lines of more or less unusual details. Just as soon as the lead becomes at all confusing take out the details and put them into the story later.

# 7
# FAULTS IN NEWS STORIES

Before we go on to the consideration of other kinds of news stories it will be well to consider in greater detail the facts we have learned from writing up fires. Our fire stories should have taught us a number of things about the form of the news story. Let us sum them up.

**Paragraph Length** - We have seen that newspaper writing has a characteristic style of its own. In the first place notice the length of a newspaper paragraph. Count the number of words in an average paragraph and compare it with the number of words in a literary paragraph. We find that the newspaper paragraph is much shorter. There is a reason for this. Imagine a 150-word literary paragraph set up in a newspaper. There are about seven words to the line in a newspaper column and one hundred and fifty words would make something over twenty lines. Try to picture a newspaper made up of twenty-line paragraphs; it would be extremely difficult to read. We glance over a newspaper hastily and our haste requires many breaks to help us in gathering the facts. Hence the paragraphs must be short; the very narrowness of the newspaper column causes them to be shortened. The average lead, you will find, contains less than fifty words and the paragraphs following it are not much longer.

**Sentence Length** - Notice sentence lengths as compared with literary sentences. You will find that newspaper sentences usually fall into two classes: the sentences in the lead and the sentences in the body of the story. The first sentence is usually rather long--thirty to sixty words. But the sentences in the body of the story are much shorter than most literary sentences. Why is this? It results from exactly the same thing that makes the newspaper paragraphs short - the need of many breaks. Thus, after we finish a lead, we must fall into short sentences. They need not be choppy sentences, but they must be simple and easy to read.

**THE LEAD AND THE BODY OF THE STORY**

Our study of the fire story has shown that newspaper stories always have two separate and distinct parts: the lead and the body of the story. In writing the story a reporter must consider each part separately, although the reader does not distinguish between the two parts. Before writing a word the reporter must decide exactly what facts and details he is to put in the lead and exactly what fact he is going to play up in the first line, taking care to begin with the most interesting part of the story. After the lead is finished he writes the main body of the story in accordance with the rules of ordinary English composition. Each part must be separate and independent of the other.

**The Lead** - The lead itself is always paragraphed separately. Usually it consists of a single sentence, although it is much better to break it into two than to make the sentence too long and complicated. As we have said before, the lead must not only tell the most interesting fact or incident in the story, but it must answer the natural questions that the reader immediately asks about this matter; i.e., when, where, what, why, who, and how. These questions must be answered briefly and concisely in their order of importance, and the most unusual answer or the most striking part of the story must precede all the rest. Beyond the answers to these questions there is no space for details in the lead. Every word must have a purpose and a necessary purpose or it must be cut out and relegated to the body of the story. No space should be given to explanations of minor importance. State the content of the news story as completely, accurately, and concisely as possible so that the reader may know just what happened, when it happened, where, to whom, and perhaps how and why it happened. Then begin a new paragraph and start the body of the story.

Many editors require that the lead consist of one long sentence and yet it must be grammatical. Many reporters forget all about English grammar in their attempt to crowd everything they know into one sentence. But mere quantity does not make the lead good; it must be grammatical and easy to read. The verb must have a grammatical subject and, if it is an *active* verb, it must have a grammatical predicate. Clauses and modifiers must be attached in a way that cannot be overlooked. Dangling participles and absolute constructions should be shunned. All of the modifying clauses must be gathered together either before or after the principal clause. Everything must be compact and logical. Many papers disregard this matter, as will be seen in some of the extracts quoted in this book, but the best papers do not.

Every lead should be so constructed that it may stand alone and be self-sufficient. Never should a reporter trust to headlines to enlighten his readers upon the meaning of the lead--the exact reverse of this must be true. The story is written first and the headlines are written from the facts contained in the lead--and usually by another man. In writing the lead disregard the existence of headlines, for many readers do not read them at all. This is but an amplification of the old rule of composition that any piece of writing should be independent of its title. The title may be lost, but the essay must be clear without it.

There are many ways of beginning a lead in order to embody the feature in the first line. At first glance the operation of putting the emphasis of a sentence at the beginning, rather than at the end, may seem difficult, but with a clear idea of the rules of dependence in English grammar a reporter may transpose any clause to the beginning and thus play up the content of the clause. For instance, in this lead,

> | Fire, starting in a moving picture | | theatre, 4418 Third avenue, drove the | | tenants of the building out into the icy | | street while the snowstorm was at its | | height shortly before 12 o'clock last | | night. |

the striking feature of the story is buried - we do not get the unusual picture of a little group of people shivering in the street during a blinding snowstorm while they watch their homes burn. A simple transposition of the *while*-clause puts the feature in the first line. Thus:

> | While the snowstorm was at its height | | shortly before 12 o'clock last night, | | fire, starting in a moving picture | | theatre, 4418 Third avenue, drove the | | tenants of the building out into the icy | | street. |

The lead is not perfect now; it might be greatly improved, but it is better than before.

A few of the possible beginnings for a lead are:

**1. Noun** - The simplest beginning of a lead is of course the use of a noun as subject of the principal verb. For example, "Fire destroyed the residence of----" or "A flashlight setting fire to a lace curtain started a fire----" or "The Plaza Hotel had a few uncomfortable moments last night----" etc. The subject of the verb may of course have its modifiers--adjectives and phrases-- but it should not be separated too widely from its verb. One point is to be noted in the use of a simple noun at the beginning; an article should not precede the noun if it can be avoided, for the very simple reason that an article is not worth the important space that it takes at the beginning of the lead. In the case of fire no article is necessary. In other cases it is usually possible to put in an adjective or some other word that will take the article's place. However, never begin a story like this: "Supreme Court of the United States decided----" or "Young man in evening dress was arrested last night----" or "House of John Smith was destroyed yesterday----". Obviously something is lacking and, if no other word will supply the lack, use the article, *the* or *a*. When the *noun*-beginning is used the reporter must never forget that two or more nouns, however different, if subject of the same verb, require a plural verb. The verb may be active or passive, whichever is more convenient, but rarely is the object of an active verb put first--simply because English cannot bear this transposition of subject and predicate.

**2. *Infinitive*** - Other parts of speech aside from nouns may be subjects of verbs and so other parts of speech as subjects of the principal verb of the lead may be placed at the beginning of the lead. An infinitive with its object and modifier may occupy the first line as subject of the main verb; e.g.:

> | To rescue his own son during the | | burning of his own house was a part of | | yesterday's work for Fireman Michael | | Casey, who, etc. |

Here the infinitive "to rescue" and its object are the subject of the verb "was," and the construction is perfectly grammatical. Unfortunately the English language has another infinitive which very much resembles a present participle - the infinitive ending in *-ing*; e.g., *rescuing*. Without an article this part of speech must, of course, be used only as an adjective, but with an article it becomes an infinitive, to be treated as a noun; e.g., *the rescuing of*. It would be perfectly grammatical to begin the above lead in this way: "The rescuing of his own son ... was the work, etc." But it would be ungrammatical to begin it thus: "Rescuing his own son was the work, etc." For in the second case the word "rescuing," if used with an object, is not an infinitive but a participle, and must be used only as an adjective, thus: "Rescuing his own son, Fireman Casey performed his duty, etc.," or "In rescuing his own son, Fireman Casey performed his duty." The two uses should never be confused.

**3. Clause** - Another expression that may be used as subject of the lead's principal verb is a clause - usually a *that*-clause. For instance, "That the entire wholesale district was not destroyed by fire last night is due to, etc." Here the *that*-clause is subject of the verb is and the expression is entirely grammatical as well as very useful as a beginning.

**4. Prepositional Phrase** - When the feature of a story is an action rather than a thing, a noun can hardly be used to express it. Very often this lead may be handled by means of a prepositional phrase at the beginning. For example, one of the stories in the last chapter begins: "With her home on fire and with smoke swirling around her head, Mrs. John, etc." In this case the prepositional phrase modifies the subject and should not be far from it. Another variation of this is the prepositional phrase of time, modifying the verb; e.g., "During the wedding of Miss Mary Jones, last night, the house suddenly caught fire, etc." This beginning is effective if it is not overworked, but the reader should never be held back from the real facts of the story by a string of complicated phrases, intended to build up suspense.

**5. Participial Phrase** - Very much like the prepositional phrase beginning is the participial beginning. "Sliding down an eighty-foot extension ladder with a woman in his arms, Fireman John Casey rescued, etc." It must be borne in mind that the participial phrase must modify a noun and there should be no doubt in the reader's mind as to the noun that it modifies. It would of course be absurd to say "Sliding down an eighty-foot extension ladder, fire seriously burned John Casey----," but such things are often said. Never should this participial phrase be used as the subject of a verb, as "Returning home and finding her house in ashes was the unusual experience of Mrs. James, etc." The phrase must always modify a noun just like an adjective.

**6. Temporal Clause** - A feature may often be brought to the beginning of the lead by a simple transposition of clauses. Should the time be important a subordinate *when* or *while* clause may precede the principal clause of the sentence; i.e., "When the snowstorm was at its height early this morning, a three-story brick building burned, etc.," or "While 15,000 people watched from the street below, 250 girls escaped from the burning building at, etc."

**7. Causal Clause** - Should the cause of an action or an occurrence be attractive enough for the first line, a *for* or a *because* clause may begin the lead. "Because a tinsmith upset a pot of molten solder on the roof of pier No. 19, two steamers were burned, etc."

\* \* \* \* \*

This does not exhaust the list of possible beginnings. There are a dozen possible constructions for the beginning of any story; these are merely the commonest ones. Anything unusual or of doubtful grammar should be avoided because of the many possible alternatives that present themselves. And in every lead correct grammar should be considered above all else. If a lead is ungrammatical no clever arrangement of details can make it effective or other than ludicrous. For instance, this lead, taken from a newspaper, illustrates an unfortunate attempt to crowd too many details into a short lead:

| Bitten by a rattlesnake, Myrtle Olson's| |leg was slashed with a table knife, | |washed the wound with kerosene, then | |covered the incision with salt by her | |mother. Myrtle still lives. |

Another paper tried to arrange it more happily, thus:

| Bitten by a rattlesnake, Myrtle Olson's| |mother slashed her daughter's leg with a | |table knife, washed the wound with | |kerosene, then covered the incision with | |salt. Myrtle still lives. |

There is evidently something wrong in this. It would be a good exercise to try to express the idea grammatically.

\* \* \* \* \*

Before we go on to the consideration of the body of this story a few *Don'ts* in regard to writing leads may be in order.

Don't begin a lead with a person's name unless the person is well known. We are always interested in anything unusual that a man may do or anything unusual that he may suffer, but unless we know the man we are not at all interested in his name. Suppose that a man performs some thrilling act or suffers some unusual misfortune in a city of 100,000 people. Probably not more than one hundred people know him, and of that number only one or two will read the story. Then why begin with his name when his action is of greater interest to all but a few of our readers? And yet every reader wants to know whether the victim is one of his friends. Therefore the man's name must be mentioned in the lead, although it should not come at the beginning. On the other hand, if the man is prominent in the nation or the community and well known to all our readers, his name adds interest to the story and we begin with the name. There is a growing tendency among American newspapers to begin all of their stories with a name. The tendency appears to be the result of an attempt to break away from the conventional lead and to begin in a more natural way - also an easier way. But the name beginning is after all illogical, and any reporter is safe in following the logical course in the matter. If the name is not important begin with something that is important.

Don't waste the main verb of the sentence on a minor action while expressing the principal action in a subordinate clause. This is a violation of emphasis. For example, "Fatally burned by an explosion in his laundry, Hing Lee was taken to the hospital." Naturally he would be taken to the hospital, but why put the emphasis of the whole sentence on that point?

Don't resort to the expression "was the unusual experience of----" "was the fate of----" or any like them. Every word in the lead must count, and here are five words that say nothing at all. Use their place to tell what the unusual experience was. For instance, don't say "To stand in a driving snowstorm and watch their homes burn to the ground was the unusual experience of two families, living at, etc."; say instead, "Standing in a driving snowstorm two families watched their homes burn to the ground." The latter says the same thing more effectively in less space. The use of this expression - "was the unusual experience of" - is always the mark of a green reporter.

Don't overwork the expression "Fire broke out." All fires "break out," but usually we are more interested in the result of the fire than in its "breaking out." Try to use some expression that will give more definite information.

Don't be wordy. Editors are always calling for shorter and more concise leads. If you can say a thing in two words don't use half a dozen. For example, "Four members of the local fire department were rendered unconscious by the deadly fumes from bursting ammonia pipes." This takes three times as much space as "Four firemen were overcome by ammonia fumes," and it does not express the idea any more effectively.

Don't introduce minor details into the lead. If the reader wants the details he may read the rest of the story. Take the following lead as an example:

| Rushing back into his burning laundry, | | a one-story brick building, to rescue | | from the flames his savings, amounting to| | $437, with which he hoped to raise | | himself from the rank of laborer to that | | of a prosperous merchant, and which was | | hidden under the mattress of his bed in | | the back room of the laundry, Hing Lee, a| | Chinaman, who lives at 79 Nicollett | | avenue and has been in this country but | | three months, was overcome by smoke and | | so seriously burned that he had to be | | removed to the St. Mary Hospital and may | | not live, when his establishment was | | destroyed by a fire which, starting from | | the explosion of the tank of the gasolene| | stove on which he was cooking his dinner,| | gutted his laundry, entailing a loss of | | $1,000, shortly before noon to-day. |

It is entirely grammatical, but if the reader succeeds in wading through it there is nothing left to tell about the fire. Why not begin the story in this way and leave something for the rest of the story?

| Because he rushed back into his burning| | laundry to rescue his savings, Hing Lee, | | a Chinese laundryman, 79 Nicollett | | avenue, was seriously burned to-day. |

Don't waste the first line of the lead on meaningless generalities. Get down to the facts at once. For instance, "The presence of mind and bravery of Fireman David Mullen saved Mrs. Daniel Looker from being burned to death in her flat, etc." We are willing to grant his bravery and presence of mind, but we want to know at once what he did: "By sliding down an eighty-foot extension ladder through flames and smoke with an unconscious woman in his arms, Fireman David Mullen rescued Mrs. Daniel, etc." Equally useless is the beginning, "A daring rescue of an unconscious woman from the fourth story of a blazing flat building was made by Fireman David Mullen today, etc." Tell what the daring rescue was and let the reader manufacture a fitting eulogy.

Don't exaggerate the facts to make a feature. When a few persons are frightened don't turn it into a dreadful panic. Every little fire is not a holocaust and the burning of a small barn does not endanger the entire city, unless your imagination is strong enough to guess what might have happened had there been a high wind and no fire engines. A narrow escape from death does not always excuse the beginning, "Scores killed and injured would have been the result, *if*----" All beginnings of this kind give a false impression and do not tell the truth. If a story has no striking feature be satisfied to tell the truth about it without trying to make a world-wide disaster out of it for the sake of a place on the front page. Exaggeration for a feature is one of the bad elements of sensational journalism. For example, seven lives were lost in this fire, but this is the way the story was written, for the sake of a three-column scare-head:

> | That 500 sleeping babes and 100 more | |who were kneeling in prayer in St. | |Malachi's Home, a Roman Catholic | |institution for the care of orphans at | |Rockaway Park, are alive to-day is due to| |the coolness of the nuns in charge and | |the children's remembrance of their | |teacher's fire drills. |

The suspense is built up in such a way that at the end of the lead we do not know what happened and read on with breathless interest to find that there was a small fire at the Home and seven children were burned.

**The Body of the Story** - "A good beginning is half done," according to the proverb. In writing a news story a good beginning is more than half done - two-thirds at least. The lead is the beginning, and when that has been written we are ready to go on to the body of the story with a clear conscience.

Our lead has told the reader the main facts of the case and the most unusual feature. If he reads further he is looking for details. In giving him these we return to the ordinary rules of narration. We start at the very beginning of the story and tell it logically and in detail to the end. We tell it as if no lead preceded it and repeat in greater detail the incidents briefly outlined in the lead. Never should the body of the story depend upon the lead for clearness. If the feature of the story is a rescue and you have briefly described the rescue in the lead, ignore the lead and describe the rescue all over again in the body of the story in its proper place. The number of details that are to be introduced into the story is limited only by the space that the story seems to be worth. But no point should be mentioned in the story unless space permits of its being made clear.

The ordinary rules of English composition apply to the writing of the body of the story. The copy must be paragraphed, cut up into paragraphs that are rather shorter than ordinary literary paragraphs, since the narrowness of the newspaper column makes the paragraph seem longer. Heterogeneous details must not be piled together in the same paragraph, but the facts must be grouped and handled logically. No paragraph should be noticeably longer than the others, and it is decidedly

# GETTING THE SCOOP

bad to paragraph one sentence alone simply because it does not seem to go in with any other sentence. If the fact is important expand it into a paragraph by the introduction of further details; if it is unimportant either cut it out of the story altogether or attach it to the paragraph to which it seems most logically to belong.

One fact, already stated, must be borne in mind as the body of the story progresses. The report should be built up in such a way that the editor can slash off a paragraph or two at the end without injuring the story - without sacrificing any important facts. To do this the reporter should bring the important parts of the story as near the beginning as the logical order will permit. The interest of a perfect news story is like an inverted cone. The interest is abundant at the beginning and gradually dwindles out until there is nothing more to say when the end is reached. Just how far the dwindling should be carried depends upon the amount of space that the story seems to be worth in the paper.

This may seem difficult. It may be hard to see how a story can be told in its logical order while at the same time the most interesting facts are placed at the beginning, even if they logically belong near the end. For example, we may take the story of an unusual robbery. A well-dressed man goes into a grocery store to get some butter and tries to rob the grocer. In the ensuing scuffle the would-be robber escapes. A young woman who happens to be passing sees the end of the fight and pursues the robber down the street until he runs into a saloon. She calls a policeman who is standing on the corner and the officer rushes into the saloon, up three flights of stairs and finds the robber on the roof behind a chimney. The officer shouts to another policeman, and together they arrest the robber.

Now, what is the most interesting thing in the story? Probably the pursuit--a young woman chasing a robber down the street. Our lead might be written in this way:

| After being chased down Sixth street by| |a young woman, a robber, who had | |attempted to rob the grocery store of | |Charles Young, 1345 Sixth street, was | |arrested on the roof of a saloon at 835 | |Sixth street, at 7 o'clock last night. |

The lead might be arranged in a different way, but these are the facts that it would contain. Before we consider the arrangement of the body of the story it may be well to go back to the interviews by which we secured the story. In getting the facts we would probably talk to Young, the groceryman, and to the saloonkeeper into whose establishment the robber fled. We could probably interview the policeman who made the arrest, but let us suppose that the young woman could not be found. The groceryman would tell us about the attempted robbery and the escape, with the girl in pursuit. The saloonkeeper would tell us how the man fled into his saloon and ran up the stairs to the roof; then how two policemen came and made the arrest. The policeman could tell us how a young woman ran up to him and told him that a robber had fled into the saloon; then he would describe the arrest. None of these stories is told just as we want the newspaper story - each one tells us only a part of the story. If the finished story were written by a green reporter it would probably tell the story in the order in which it was obtained. That is if the reporter saw the policeman first, then the saloonkeeper, and lastly the groceryman; his story would tell in the first paragraph what the policeman said, in the second paragraph what the saloonkeeper said, and in the last paragraph what the grocer said. At least that is the way in which green reporters in the classroom attempted to write the story.

But, obviously, that is not the logical way to tell the story. The finished account should be written in the order in which it happened: i.e., first the robbery, then the pursuit, and lastly the arrest. This would be the ideal way to tell the story - according to the rules of English composition - if we could be sure that the entire story would be printed. But if it were written in this way and the editor decided to slash off the last paragraph, what would go? Obviously the arrest would not be printed; and the arrest was quite interesting. We must find some way to bring the arrest nearer to the beginning. This may be done by selecting the most interesting parts of the story - by picking out the high spots, as it were. In this story the high spots are the attempted robbery, the pursuit, and the arrest. The details that fill in between are interesting, but not so interesting as these high spots. Hence these high spots of interest must be pushed forward toward the beginning. After the lead the story would begin at the beginning and tell the affair briefly by high spots in their proper order. It might be something like this:

> | As Charles Young was closing his | |grocery last evening a young man came in | |and asked for a pound of butter. Young | |turned to get it and his customer struck | |him over the head with a chair. The | |grocer grappled with his assailant and | |they fell through the front door. In the | |scramble, the robber broke away and

ran | |down Sixth street. A young woman who was | |passing screamed and ran after him until | |he disappeared into a saloon. | | | |The young woman called Policeman Smith, | |who was standing nearby on Grand avenue, | |and the latter found the would-be robber | |on the roof of the saloon. After a | |struggle, Smith arrested the man, with | |the aid of another policeman. |

The above account tells us briefly the most interesting parts of the story. A copyreader might not find it perfect, for the assault is allotted too much space and the pursuit too little, but it tells the story in its baldest aspect. This, with the lead, could be run alone. However, perhaps the story is worth more space; at any rate, many interesting details have been omitted. If so, go back to the most interesting part of the story - the assault, perhaps, or the pursuit - and tell it with more details. Then retell some other part with more details. If your readers are interested enough to read beyond the first three paragraphs they want details and will not be so particular about the order - for they already know how the story is going to end.

This is one way of meeting the requirements of logical order and dwindling interest. This is a particularly hard story to arrange in the conventional way since we must have the whole story to be interested in any single part--it has too many striking incidents in it. On the other hand, a story which contains only one striking incident is much easier to handle. Suppose that we are reporting a fire which is interesting only for its cause or for a daring rescue in it. Our lead would suggest this interesting element and the first part of our story would be devoted entirely to the cause or to the rescue, as the case might be. But it is better to sketch briefly, immediately after or very close to the lead, the entire story, for our readers want to know how it ends before they can be interested in any particular part. If we sketch the whole story and show them that there is only one important thing in the story, they will be satisfied to read about the one striking incident without wondering if there is not something more interesting further on. If we leave the conclusion of the story to the end of our copy the editor may cut it off and leave our story dangling in midair. Every story must be treated in its own way, according to its own incidents and difficulties; no two stories are alike in substance or treatment. In every one our aim must be to keep to the logical order and at the same time to put the most interesting parts of the story near the beginning.

The construction of the body of a story may be illustrated more clearly by a fatal fire story - since fire stories are more uniform, and hence easier to write than other news stories. Let us suppose that the story is as follows: At four o'clock in the afternoon a fire started from some unknown cause in the basement of a four-story brick building at 383-385 Sixth Street, occupied by the Incandescent Light Company. Before the fire company arrived the flames had spread up through the building and into an adjoining three-story brick building at 381 Sixth Street, occupied by Isaac Schmidt's second-hand store and home on the first and second floors and by Mrs. Sarah Jones's boarding house on the third. The Schmidts were away and Mrs. Jones's lodgers escaped via the fire escapes. Her cook, Hilda Schultz, was overcome by smoke and had to be carried out by Jack Sweeney, a lodger. Mrs. Jones fell from the fire escape and was badly bruised. Meanwhile the firemen were at work on the roof of the burning four-story building. Blinded by the smoke, one of them, John MacBane, stepped through a skylight and fell to the fourth floor. His comrades tried to rescue him by lowering Fireman Henry Bond into the smoke by the heels; they were unsuccessful and Bond broke his arm in the attempt. The fire was confined to the lower floors of the two buildings and extinguished. In searching for MacBane, the firemen found him suffocated on the fourth floor where he had fallen.

The feature of the story is evidently the one death and the three injuries. Our lead might be written as follows:

| One fireman was suffocated and three | |other persons were injured in a fire in | |the Incandescent Light Company's plant, | |383-385 Sixth street, and an adjoining | |three-story building, late yesterday | |afternoon. |

This lead would suggest to the reader many interesting details to come in the body of the story, and evidently the details are not all of equal importance. The story could be told in its logical order, but, since the death is more interesting than the origin of the fire and the injuries are more significant than how the fire spread, it is obvious that it would not be best to tell the story in the order in which it is told above.

Disregarding the lead, we must cover the following details in the body of our story:

Description of buildings and occupants. Origin of fire. Discovery of fire. Spread of flames. Injury of Mrs. Jones.

# GETTING THE SCOOP

    Rescue of Hilda Schultz. Death of MacBane. Injury of Bond. Fire extinguished.

This is the order in which things occurred at the fire. However, in our lead, we have drawn attention to our story by announcing that it concerns a fire in which a man was killed; the death therefore should have first place in the body of the story. Hence, in the second paragraph immediately after the lead, we must tell how MacBane fell through the skylight and was suffocated. Along with his death we may as well tell how Bond broke his arm trying to rescue MacBane. Our lead has also announced two other injuries and, hence, they must be included next - that is, our third paragraph must be devoted to the injury of Mrs. Jones and the rescue of the unconscious Hilda. But as yet our details are hanging in the air because we have not said anything about the buildings or the fire itself. In the next paragraph it would be well to describe the buildings and their occupants and to give a very brief account of the course of the fire - perhaps in this way:

    | Flames were first discovered in the | |basement of the Incandescent building and| |before the fire department arrived had | |spread through the lower floors and into | |the adjoining three-story building. The | |absence of elevator shafts and air-shafts| |enabled the firemen to extinguish the | |blaze before it reached the upper floors.|

This tells the main course of the fire, but there are some interesting details to add: first, the origin of the fire; next, the discovery; then more about how the fire spread; and lastly, how the fire was extinguished. Our story by paragraphs would read as follows:

1st Paragraph--The lead.

2d Paragraph--Death of MacBane and injury of Bond.

3d Paragraph--Mrs. Jones's injury and Hilda's rescue.

4th Paragraph--Buildings, occupants, brief course of fire.

5th Paragraph--Detailed account of origin of the fire.

6th Paragraph--How the fire was discovered.

7th Paragraph--More about the spread and course of the fire.

8th Paragraph--How the fire was extinguished.

9th Paragraph--Loss, insurance, extent of damage.

    Thus, while telling the story almost in its logical order, we have picked out the high spots of interest and crowded them to the beginning. Our readers will get the facts just about as fast as they wish to read them and in the order in which they wish them. Our story may be run in nine paragraphs or even more; or the editor may slash off anything after the fourth paragraph without taking away any of the essential facts of the fire. This method of telling would fulfill all the requirements of an ideal news story. A similar outline of the facts that any story must present will often help a reporter to tell his story as it should be told. After listing the details he may number them in their order of importance and check them off as he has told them.

\* \* \* \* \*

This idea of throwing the emphasis and interest to the beginning applies to the individual paragraphs and sentences of the story, as well. Each paragraph must begin strongly and display its most interesting content in the first line. The emphatic part of each sentence should be the beginning. A glance at any newspaper column shows why this is necessary.

The body of a news story is the place for the reporter's skill and style. He is given all the liberties of ordinary narration and should make the most of every word. His individual style comes into play here. If the interest can be increased by a bit of dialogue the reporter may put it in. If the facts can be presented more effectively by means of direct quotation, the words of any one whom the reporter has interviewed may be of interest. However, these things must not be overworked because every trick of writing loses its effectiveness when it is overworked.

Dialogue used only to give facts which might be told more clearly in simple direct form should seldom be used. Dialogue in a news story is used only to color the story and not to reproduce the interviews by which the facts were obtained. In gathering the facts of a story it is sometimes necessary to interview a number of people, but these interviews should not be quoted in the resulting story. Many a green reporter tries to give his story character by telling what the policeman on the corner, the janitor, and a small boy in the street told him about the incident. He succeeds only in dragging out the length of his story and confusing the reader. After all, the purpose of a newspaper is to give facts - and the clearer and the more direct the method the better will be the result.

In striving for clearness and interest a reporter must remember that one of his greatest assets is concreteness of expression. Of all forms of composition newspaper writing possesses probably the greatest opportunity for definiteness. Facts and events are its one concern; theories and abstractions are beyond its range. Hence the more definite and concrete its presentation of facts, the better will be its effect. The reporter should never generalize or present his statements hazily and uncertainly - a fact is a fact and must be presented as such. He must try to avoid such expressions as "several," "many," "a few" - it is usually possible to give the exact number. He must continually ask himself "how many?" "what kind?" "exactly when?" "exactly what?" Expressions like "about a dozen," "about thirty years old," "about a week ago," "about a block away," are never so effective as the exact facts and figures. Definite concrete details make a news story real and vivid. The real reporter of news is the one who can see a thing clearly and with every detail and present it as clearly and distinctly.

# 8
# OTHER NEWS STORIES

The fire story is obviously not the only news story that is printed in a daily newspaper, but a study of its form gives us a working knowledge of the writing of other news stories. The fire story is probably the commonest news story, and it is by far the easiest story to handle, for its form has become somewhat standardized. We know just exactly what our readers want to know about each fire, and within certain limits all fires, as well as the reports of them, are very much alike. There is seldom more than one fact or incident that makes one fire different from another and that fact we always seize as the feature of our report. However, the fire story has been taken only as typical of other news stories. Now we are ready to study the others, using the fire story as our model in writing the others.

There is a vast number of other stories that we must be able to write, and they lack the convenient uniformity that fires have. Not only does every story have a different feature, but it is concerned with a different kind of happening. One assignment may call for the report of an explosion, another the report of a business transaction, and another a murder. In each one we have to get the facts and choose the most striking fact as our feature. Never can we resort to the simple beginning "Fire destroyed," but we must find a different beginning for each assignment.

Just as in the fire story, the lead of any news story is the most important part. It must begin with the most striking part of the event and answer the reader's *Where? When? How? Why?* and *Who?* concerning it. All the rules that apply to the fire lead apply to the lead of any story.

# GETTING THE SCOOP

It would be impossible to classify all the news stories that a newspaper must print. The very zest of reporting comes from the changing variety of the work; no two assignments are ever exactly alike - if they were only one would be worth printing. Newspapers themselves make no attempt to classify the ordinary run of news or to work out a systematic division of labor; a reporter may be called upon to cover a fire, a political meeting, a murder, a business story, all in the same day. Each one is simply a story and must be covered in the same way that all the rest are covered - by many interviews for facts. For our study it may be well to divide news stories into a few large groups. The groups overlap and are not entirely distinct, but the stories in each group have some one thing in common that may aid us in learning how to write them. At most, the list is only a very incomplete summary of the more important kinds of news stories and is intended to be merely a suggestive way of supplying the student with necessary practice.

**1. Accidents** - Accident stories may be anything from a sprained ankle to a disastrous railroad wreck, but they all depend upon one element for their interest. They are all printed because people in general are interested in the injuries and deaths of other people - physical calamity is the common ground in all these stories.

The number of possible accidents is infinite, but there are some common types that recur most often. Among these are: railroad, trolley, railroad crossing accidents; runaways; electrocutions; explosions; collapse of buildings; marine disasters; cave-in accidents; elevator, automobile, aviation accidents.

The feature of any accident story is always, of course, the thing that made the story worth printing, and that is usually the human life element. The feature of an accident story is almost always the number of dead and injured. Most reports of railroad wrecks begin with "Ten persons were killed and seventeen were injured in a wreck, etc." The same is true of any accident story; if more than one person is killed it is usually safe to begin with the number of fatalities. In this connection it may be noted that the death of railroad employees seldom makes a story worth printing; they may be included in the total number, but if no passengers are killed, fatalities among trainmen seldom give a story any news value.

Accident stories of course have many other possible features; newspapers report many accidents in which no one is killed. In that case some other element gives the story news value and that element must be played up as the feature.

Perhaps it is the manner in which the accident happened or the manner in which a person was killed or injured, as in an automobile accident. The cause of the accident may be the most interesting part of the story: train-wreckers or a broken rail in a railroad wreck, or the cause of an explosion. Very often an accident is reported simply because some well-known person was connected with it in some way; the name then becomes the feature and comes into the first line. A story may be worth printing simply because of the unusual manner of rescue; such a feature is often played up in stories of marine accidents, cave-ins, etc. Not infrequently some of the unusual attendant circumstances give a story news value: e.g., a policeman dragged from his horse and run over by an automobile while he is trying to stop a runaway.

Here are some accident stories from the newspapers:

**Fatalities:**

| Six men were killed and a dozen | | seriously injured early to-day by an | | outbound Panhandle passenger train | | crashing into the rear end of a Chicago, | | Milwaukee and St. Paul stock train at | | Twelfth and Rockwell streets.--*Chicago* | | *Record-Herald.* |

**Manner:**

| Run down by her own automobile, which | | she was cranking, at First and G streets,| | northwest, Dr. Alma C. Arnold, a | | chiropractic physician, 825 Fifteenth | | street, northwest, was forced against the| | wheel of a passing wagon and seriously | | injured this morning.--*Washington* | | *Times.* |

**Cause:**

| Over-balanced by a granite stone | | weighing four tons, the entire cornice | | over the west portico of the new west | | wing of the capitol fell to the ground | | this afternoon, carrying with it Daniel | | Logan, foreman for the Woodbury Granite | | Company.--*Madison Democrat.* |

**Attendant Circumstances:**

| With a blast that shook the entire city| | and was believed by many to be an | | earthquake, three boilers in the new | | engine house of the Pabst brewery on | | Tenth street, between Chestnut street and| | Cold Spring avenue, exploded at about 4 | | o'clock this morning.--*Milwaukee Free* | | *Press.* |

**2. Robberies** - Another large class of news stories is concerned with robberies of various kinds. Unfortunately for the reporter, very few robberies are alike; beyond the common ground of the interest in the amount stolen and the cleverness of the robber's work, there is seldom any one thing that may be looked for as the feature of a robbery story. The reporter must decide what in the story makes it worth printing.

Robbery stories may include anything from petty thievery to bank defaulting. Some of the possibilities are horse and automobile stealing, burglary, hold-ups, train and street-car robbery, embezzlement, fraud, kidnapping, safe-cracking, shop and bank robbery. It is well for the reporter who has to cover a story of this class to acquaint himself with the distinctions that characterize the various kinds of robbery and the various names applied to the people who commit this sort of crime: e.g., robber, thief, bandit, burglar, hold-up man, thug, embezzler, defaulter, safe-cracker, pick-pocket.

In general the chief interest in robbery stories is in the result of the work - the amount taken - usually accompanied by a term to designate the sort of robbery. Just how the crime was committed is often the feature, as in a train robbery or a clever case of fraud. If the victim or victims are at all well known their names may become the most interesting thing in the story - or even the name of a well-known criminal or band of robbers. In some stories, especially if another paper has already covered the story, the pursuit or capture of the criminals is often interesting; the stories of bank robberies often begin in this way. Other attendant circumstances, such as the number of persons who witnessed the crime, may be the feature. In hold-ups, burglaries, and crimes of that sort, the death or wounding of the victim is often played up. Sometimes the reason for the crime, as in a kidnapping case, is of great significance. In the case of a robbery of a bank or any other institution which depends upon credit for its business, the story usually begins with, or at least mentions near the beginning, the present condition of the robbed institution. It is safe to say that in no case is the name of the criminal, the manner of his arrest (if it is not unusual), the police station to which he was taken, or the charge preferred against him worth a place in the lead.

Some robbery stories from the daily press:

**Amount taken:**

| Furs worth $40,000 were stolen in the | |early hours of yesterday morning within a| |stone's throw of Madison Square. | |Apparently a gang in which there was a |

## NEWSPAPER REPORTING AND CORRESPONDENCE

|woman expert in choosing only the best | |furs carried off the costly skins, | |etc.--*New York World.* |

**Manner of hold-up:**

| Seized by thugs in broad daylight as he| |was crossing the railroad tracks at the | |foot of First avenue east, Fred Butzer, a| |stonemason of Butler, Minn., was thrown | |to the ground, a gag placed in his mouth,| |his pockets were rifled of $36.--*Duluth* | |*News-Tribune.* |

Unusual sort of pickpocket:

| A young man in evening dress, who was | |going down into the subway station at | |Times Square with the theater crowd that | |filled the entrance just outside of the | |Hotel Knickerbocker early last night, | |paused, knocked a woman under the chin | |and took away her silver chatelaine purse| |containing $20 as deftly as he might have| |flicked the ash off his cigarette. Then | |he disappeared.--*New York Times.* |

**Unusual thieves:**

| Two girl thieves not more than twelve | |years old and small in stature for their | |age have been operating with great | |success in the different stores in the | |neighborhood of Amsterdam avenue and | |Seventy-ninth street. Five or six thefts,| |etc.--*New York Telegram.* |

**Pursuit and capture:**

| After a chase along Forty-second street| |and up the steps of the Hotel Manhattan, | |a woman, who said she was Sadie Brown, | |thirty-three years old, of No. 215 West | |Forty-sixth street, was arrested early | |today on suspicion of having picked the | |pocket of a man at, etc.--*New York* | |*Telegram.* |

Present conditions of robbed bank (second paragraph of an embezzlement story):

| Banking Commissioner Watkins this | |afternoon declared that he found the bank| |perfectly sound, that all commercial | |paper was found intact, that none of the | |accounts have been juggled and that no | |erasures of any kind were | |discovered.--*Philadelphia Inquirer.* |

**Unusual sort of burglar:**

- 77 -

# GETTING THE SCOOP

| Wearing a Salvation Army uniform, a | |burglar was caught early yesterday in the| |home of Walter Katte, a vice-president of| |the New York Central railroad, at | |Irvington-on-the-Hudson.--*New York* | |*World*. |

**3. Murder** - The reports of crimes of this sort can hardly be classified, for there are so many things that may be worth featuring in any murder case. The story itself is usually of such importance that the mere fact that a murder has been committed gives it news value even if there is nothing unusual in the crime--just as in the case of a featureless fire story that begins with "Fire." The handling of a crime depends upon the character and circumstances; the reporter must weigh the facts in each case for himself. However, we usually find a feature in the number of persons murdered, the manner in which the crime was committed, the name of the victim, if he or she is well known, the reason for the deed, or in some of the many attendant circumstances, such as arrest, pursuit, etc. One rule must always be followed in the reporting of a murder story: the reporter must confine himself to the necessary facts and omit as many of the gruesome details as possible. He must tell it in a cold, hard-hearted way without elaboration, for the story in itself is gruesome enough. Just as soon as a murder story begins to expand upon shocking details it becomes the worst sort of a yellow story.

Examples of murder stories from the newspapers:

**Manner:**

| After crushing in the head of his | |superior officer with an axe, James | |Layton, boatswain of the Liverpool | |sailing ship Colony, refused to submit to| |arrest, and, still waving the bloody | |weapon, committed suicide by jumping into| |the sea.--*New York Mail*. |

**Motive:**

| In revenge for a beating he received | |the day before, Gaetona Ambrifi yesterday| |shot and instantly killed Frank | |Ricciliano, a sub-section foreman on the | |Pennsylvania Railroad, while they were | |working on the roadbed near Peddle | |street, Newark.--*New York Sun*. |

**Prominent name:**

| Mayor William J. Gaynor of New York | |City was shot and seriously, perhaps | |fatally, wounded on board the

## NEWSPAPER REPORTING AND CORRESPONDENCE

steamer | |Kaiser Wilhelm der Grosse at 9:30 as he | |was sailing for Europe. |

**Resulting pursuit:**

| The police of Brooklyn have another | |murder mystery to unravel through the | |finding early today of the body of Peter | |Barilla on Lincoln road, near Nostrand | |avenue, Flatbush. There were two bullet | |wounds in the body and four stab wounds | |in the back.--*Brooklyn Eagle.* |

**Attendant circumstances:**

| A hundred or more persons who were | |about to take trains witnessed the | |shooting to death of a Jersey City | |business man in the Pennsylvania Railroad| |station there this afternoon.--*New York* | |*Mail.* |

**4. Suicide** - What is true of murder stories is also true of suicide. Each individual case has an unusual feature of its own. We ordinarily find a good beginning in the manner of the suicide, the name of the person who has killed himself if he is well known, the reason for the act, or some one of the attendant circumstances - often the manner of resuscitation if the crime is unsuccessful. For some unexplained reason many papers do not print accounts of ordinary suicides, except when the individual is prominent. At any rate the story must be told without gruesome details and as briefly as possible.

Examples from the press:

**Name:**

| William L. Murray of Rockview avenue, | |North Plainfield, paying teller of the | |Empire Trust Company of New York, | |committed suicide at Scotch Plains early | |this afternoon by shooting himself in the| |head. No reason is assigned for the | |act.--*New York Sun.* |

**Motive:**

| Driven insane by continued brooding | |over ill health, Miss Ada Emerson, a | |former teacher in the Beloit city | |schools, killed herself in a crowded | |interurban car Saturday afternoon by | |slashing her throat with a | |razor.--*Beloit Free Press.* |

Here the manner is the feature, but it is not played up in the first line because it is too horrible.

# GETTING THE SCOOP

**5. Big Stories** - The big stories of catastrophes are usually handled on a large scale - played up, as the newspaper men say. The story in itself is of sufficient importance to make it unnecessary to play up any single feature of the story. However, the reporter, in looking for a good beginning, often finds it in the most startling fact in the story. If he is reporting a riot he usually begins with the number of killed or injured, the amount of property destroyed, the character of the riot, or the cause, as in this example:

> | In an effort to bring about the | |reinstatement of one of their number who | |had been discharged for non-unionism, a | |hundred or more journeymen bakers wrecked| |the bakeshop of Pincus Jacobs, at No. | |1571 Lexington avenue, early this | |morning.--*New York Evening Post.* |

In the case of a storm the human life element is of greatest importance, then the damage to property, and last, the peculiar circumstances. For example:

> | CLEVELAND, Dec. 11.--Fifty-nine lives | |were the cost of a storm which passed | |over Lake Erie Wednesday night and | |Thursday, and more than $1,000,000 worth | |of vessel property was destroyed.--*New* | |*York Evening Post.* |

If the story is concerned with a flood the human-life element is first, then the damage, the cause, the freaks of the flood, or the present situation. For example:

> | PARKERSBURG, W. Va., March 10.--Three | |persons are known to have perished in a | |flood which swept down upon the city on | |Friday when two water reservoirs on | |Prospect Hill burst without warning. | |Forty houses were destroyed and many | |persons are missing. The property damage | |will be nearly $500,000. |

**6. Police Court News** - The ordinary run of police court news is in a class by itself. Usually the only news value in the story depends upon some unusual incident or circumstance that attracts the attention of the reporter. This is of course the source of many of the stories of crime, mentioned before, but many stories turn up at the police courts which are not concerned with crime, although in some cases they are concerned with criminals. In this field of reporting there are many opportunities for the human-interest story which will be taken up in a later chapter. When the incident is reported in an ordinary news story the feature is usually in some attendant circumstance and the story might well be classed with one of the above groups. Here are two examples from the daily press:

> | Because he did not have sufficient | |money to buy flowers for his sweetheart, | |Henry Trupke, aged 21 years, forged a | |check for $22.50 on a grocer, J. | |Sieberlich, 781 Third street, and after a| |week's chase was caught last night as he | |got off a Wisconsin Central | |train.--*Milwaukee Sentinel.* |

> | But a few hours before receiving a | |sentence of two years in the house of | |correction for stealing furs from the | |store of Lohse Bros., 117 Wisconsin | |street, John Garner, self-confessed | |thief, was married to Rose Strean, one | |of the witnesses in the case, which was | |tried yesterday in the municipal | |court.--*Milwaukee Free Press.* |

**7. Reports of Meetings, Conferences, Decisions, etc.** - This group includes all reports of meetings, or conferences, of bodies of any sort, political or otherwise, reports of judicial or legislative hearings or decisions, or announcements of resolutions passed. Such as:

> | WASHINGTON, Jan. 15.--Acquisition of | |the telegraph lines by the government and| |their operation as a part of the postal | |system is the latest idea of Postmaster | |General Hitchcock. Announcement was made | |today that a resolution to this effect | |will be offered to Congress at the | |present session.--*Wisconsin State* | |*Journal.* |

There is always one thing in these stories that gives them news value - the purpose or result of the conference, hearing, or announcement. This purpose or result, of course, must be played up. The one point that the reporter should remember is that a well-written lead begins with the result or purpose of the meeting or announcement rather than with the name of the meeting or the name of the body that makes the announcement. Never begin a story thus: "At a meeting of the Press Club held in the Auditorium last night it was resolved that----" Transpose the sentence and begin with a statement of what was resolved. In the following story the order is wrong:

> | The Supreme Court of the United States,| |through the opinion delivered by Justice | |Vandevanter, today

# GETTING THE SCOOP

declared | |constitutional the employers' liability | |law of 1908. |

The import of the decision is buried; it should be written thus:

| The employers' liability law of 1908 | |was today declared constitutional by the | |Supreme Court of the United States. | |Justice Vandevanter delivered the opinion| |of the court, made in four cases. |

In these stories, as in all other news stories, the lead must begin with the fact or statement that gives the story news value. Burying this fact or statement behind two or three lines of explanation spoils the effectiveness of the lead. A student of journalism may gain very good practice in the writing of news stories by looking over the leads that appear in the daily papers and transposing those leads which bury their news behind explanations. The first line of type in a lead is like a shop's show window and it must not be used for the display of packing cases.

**8. Stories on Other Printed Matter** - A large part of a newspaper's space, especially in smaller cities, is devoted to stories based on printed bulletins, announcements, city directories, legislative bills, and published reports of various kinds. Sometimes a news story is written upon a pamphlet that was issued for advertising purposes - because there is some news in it. In all of these stories the reporter must look through the pamphlet to find something of news value or something that has a significant relation to other news. Smaller papers often print stories on the new city directory; the increase or decrease in population is treated as news and a very interesting story may be written on a comparison of the names in the directory. In university towns the appearance of a new university catalog or bulletin of any sort is the occasion for a story which points out the new features or compares the new bulletin with a previous one. Reporters and correspondents in political centers, like state capitals, get out stories on committee and legislative reports and on new bills that are proposed or passed by the legislature. The writing of these stories is very much like the reporting of a speech, which will be discussed later. The newest or most interesting feature in the report or bill is played up in the lead as the feature of the story, followed by the source of the story, the printed bulletin upon which the story is based; thus:

| A new plan for placing the control of | |all water power in the state in the hands| |of the legislature was proposed in the | |minority report of Senators J. B.

Smith | |and L. C. Blake, of the special | |legislative committee on drainage, issued| |today. |

These eight classes of news stories do not include all the news stories that a newspaper prints, but they are in a way typical of all the others that are not mentioned. It will be noted from these that all news stories, just like the fire story, are usually written in about the same way. Each one has a lead which begins with the feature of the story - i.e., the fact or incident in the story which gives it news value and makes it of interest - and concludes by answering the reader's questions, when, where, who, how, why, concerning the feature. Each story begins again after the lead, and in one or more paragraphs explains, describes, or narrates the incident in detail and in logical order. This body of the story which follows the lead, while following in general the logical order, is so written that its most interesting facts are near the beginning and its interest dwindles away toward the end. This is to enable the editor in making up his paper, to take away from the end of any story, as we have seen before, a paragraph or more without spoiling the story's continuity or depriving it of any of its essential facts. The form of the conventional fire story may be used as a model in the writing of any news story.

In writing the body of a story to explain, describe, or narrate the incident mentioned in the lead, every effort should be directed toward clearness. This is particularly true of stories which are in the main narrations of action. The number of facts that may be included must depend upon the length of the story; if all of the facts cannot be included without overburdening the story, cut out some of the details of lesser importance, but treat those that are included in a clear readable way. Short sentences are always much better in newspaper writing than long involved sentences. Pronouns should always be used in such a way that there can be no doubt in regard to their antecedents. If a relative clause or participial expression sounds awkward make a separate sentence of it. In other words, be simple, concise, and clear--that is better in a newspaper than much fine writing.

# 9
# FOLLOW-UP AND REWRITE STORIES

The terms "rewrite story" and "follow-up, or follow, story," are names which newspaper men apply to the rehashed or revised versions of other news stories. A large newspaper office employs one or more rewrite men who spend their entire time rewriting stories. To be sure, a part of their work consists of rewriting, or simply recasting, poorly written copy prepared by the reporters. But the major part of their work, the part that interests us, involves something more than that. It involves the rejuvenation of stories that have been printed in a previous edition or in another paper, with the purpose of bringing the news up to the present moment.

News ages very rapidly. What may be news for one edition is no longer news when another edition goes to press an hour later. A feature that may be worth playing up in a morning paper would not have the same news value in an evening paper of the same day. The news grows stale so quickly because new things are continually happening and new developments are continually changing the aspect of previous stories. If a story has been run through two or three editions and new developments have changed it, the story is turned over to a rewrite man for consequent alteration. A story in a morning paper is no longer news for an evening paper of the same date, but a clever rewrite man, with or without new developments added to the story, can recast it so that it will appear to contain more recent news than the original story. The story of an arrest in a morning paper begins with the particulars of the arrest; but when the evening paper's rewrite man has rearranged it for his paper it has become the story of the trial or the police court hearing which followed the arrest. Perhaps the evening paper sends a man to get the later developments in the case, but every rewrite man knows the steps that always follow an arrest and he can rewrite the original story without additional information. His account of the later developments is called either a rewrite or a follow-up story, depending upon the method employed. The same fundamental idea of rejuvenating the former story governs the preparation of both the rewrite and the follow-up story, but while the rewrite story contains no additional news, the follow-up presents later facts in addition to the old news.

**1. The Rewrite Story** - The rewrite story is primarily a rehashing of a previous news story without additional facts. It attempts to give a new twist to old facts in order to bring them nearer to the present time. Without the aid of later facts the rewrite man can only select a new feature and revise the old facts. For example, suppose that a $100,000 grain elevator burns during the night. The fire would make a big story in a city of moderate size and the papers next morning would treat it at length. If no one were killed or injured the story would probably begin with a simple announcement of the fire in a lead of this kind:

| Fire destroyed the grain elevator of | |the H. P. Jones Produce Company, First | |and Water streets, and $50,000 worth of | |wheat at 2 o'clock this morning. The | |total loss is estimated at $150,000. |

Then the reporter would describe the fire at length, including all obtainable facts. By afternoon almost every one in the city has read the story - and yet the afternoon papers must print something about the big fire. If no new facts can be obtained the previous story must be rehashed and presented with a new feature that will make it appear to be a later story. It is useless to begin the evening story with a mere announcement of the fire, for that is no longer news, and the rewrite man must find a new beginning to attract the attention of his readers. Perhaps in looking over the morning story, he finds that the fire was the result of spontaneous combustion in the grain stored in the elevator. In the morning story this fact was rather insignificant in the face of the huge loss, and most readers passed over it hastily. The rewrite man, however, who has no later facts at his command, may seize it as a new feature. Instead of beginning his story with the fact of the fire, which is already known, he begins with the cause, which appears to be later news. His lead may be as follows:

| Spontaneous combustion in the wheat | |bins of the H. P. Jones Produce Company's| |elevator, First and Water

streets, | |started the fire which destroyed the | |entire structure with a loss of $150,000 | |this morning. |

Or if the rewrite man is not so fortunate as to discover a new feature as good as this, he may have to resort to beginning with a picture of the present results of the fire--thus:

| Smouldering ruins and a tangled mass of| |steel beams are all that remain of the H.| |P. Jones Produce Company's $100,000 | |grain elevator, First and Water streets, | |which was destroyed by fire this morning.|

It will be noticed that, while these new rewrite leads begin with a new feature, each new lead contains all the facts presented in the previous lead and is told with an eye to the man who has not read the earlier account. After the lead the rewrite man retells the whole story for the benefit of readers who did not see the morning papers and rearranges the facts so that they appear new to those who read the previous stories. Facts which the other papers buried he unearths and displays; details which appear to be later developments he crowds to the beginning. The whole story is sorted and rewritten in a new order and with a new emphasis. The result is a rewrite story which appears to be later, although it contains no new facts at all. It is seldom, of course, that such a rewrite story is used for local news, for very rarely is it impossible for a later paper to discover new facts. But in the case of news from the outside world, from other cities, the simple method of rehashing old facts must often be resorted to. If the story is based upon a single dispatch announcing an earthquake in Hawaii or a shipwreck in mid-ocean, many rewrite stories must be printed on the same facts before another message brings later news and additional details. An example of this is the treatment of the first few stories of the wreck of the White Star liner *Titanic*. The story was a big one, but the first dispatches were very meager and many rehashings of these few facts had to be printed before later and more definite news could be obtained.

The simple rewriting of an old story ordinarily involves a condensation of the facts. If a morning paper printed two thousand words on the grain elevator fire above, an afternoon paper of the same day would hardly treat the story at such length. For the story is no longer big news. If a story has run through the first editions of a morning paper it would be cut down, as well as rehashed, in the later editions of the same paper. The story of the fire loses its initial burst of interest after the first printing, and only the essential facts and the facts that can be rejuvenated can be reprinted. The 2,000-word version in the morning paper may be worth only five hundred words or less four hours later.

**2. The Follow-up Story** - If new facts are added to a story between editions the new version is no longer a simple rewrite story. It becomes a follow-up story, for it follows up the subsequent developments in the previous story and corresponds to the second or succeeding installments of a serial novel in which each installment begins with a synopsis of previous chapters. For example, if, in the grain elevator fire story, the body of a watchman were found in the ruins after the morning papers have gone to press, the story would immediately have a different news value for the evening papers. The story of the big fire is old, but the discovery of the body is new. Hence the rewrite man would begin with the later development - perhaps thus:

> | The body of a watchman was found this | |afternoon in the ruins of the H. P. Jones| |Produce elevator, which burned to the | |ground this morning with a loss of | |$150,000. |

The new story, while retelling the principal facts in the previous account, would give prominence to the latest news, the discovery of the body. As an example from a newspaper, let us take the follow-up of a murder mystery. The first stories on this murder simply said that a grocer had been found dead in the cellar of his store and murder had been suggested. The follow-up on the next day (printed here) deals with a new development--has a new feature - and carries the story one step further in the attempt to unravel the mystery:

> | Developments yesterday in the story of | |the killing of James White, the Park | |street grocer, tended to support the | |contention of Coroner Donalds and the | |police that White was not murdered, but | |died by his own hand. |

**3. Analysis** - So far we have treated the rewrite story and the follow-up story separately, but for the purposes of analysis and study they may be treated together, because the same fundamental idea governs both. Dissection of the follow-up story will also show us what the rewrite story is made of.

From the above clippings it will be seen that the lead of the follow-up story is very much like that of any news story. The lead has its feature in the first line and answers the reader's questions concerning that feature. It is simply a new story

# GETTING THE SCOOP

written on an old subject which has been given a new feature to make it appear new. Furthermore, it will be noticed that the lead of the follow-up story is complete in itself, without the original story that preceded it. Although the whole idea of the follow story is based on the supposition that all readers have read every edition of the paper and are therefore acquainted with the original story, yet for the benefit of those readers who have not read the previous story, the follow-up must be complete and clear in itself. New facts are introduced into the follow story, but its lead tells the main facts of the original story so that no reader will be at loss to understand what it is all about - in other words, it gives a synopsis of previous chapters. In many follow-up stories the new developments are supplemented by an entire retelling of the original story. This is especially true when one paper is rewriting a story which broke too late for its preceding edition and was covered by a rival paper. At any rate, every follow-up story, like every other news story, must be so constructed as to stand by itself without previous explanation.

> | Of the 142 bodies of victims of the | |Triangle Waist Company's fire on | |Saturday, that had been taken to the | |morgue up to noon yesterday when it was | |decided that all the dead had been | |recovered, all but 45 had been identified| |today. |

This is a follow-up of a story two days before. Every reader of the paper probably knew everything that had been printed previously about the fire, and yet this lead very carefully recalls the fire to the reader's mind. Later in the story the principal facts of the original story are retold as if they were new and unknown.

It is interesting to see what in any given newspaper story can be followed up for a later story. The would-be reporter may get good practice in writing follow-up stories from the mere attempt to study out the next step in any given new story. With this next step as his feature he may try to write a follow-up story without additional information, and then compare it with other follow-up stories. For every news story contains within it clues to what may be expected to follow.

When any serious fire occurs certain additional facts may always be expected to follow. The finding of more dead, the unravelling of a mysterious origin, the re-statement of the loss, and the present condition of the injured are some of the possibilities that a rewrite man considers when he tries to prepare a follow-up story on a fire. The Washington Place fire in New York on March 25, 1911, furnished admirable material for

# NEWSPAPER REPORTING AND CORRESPONDENCE

the study of the rewriting of fire stories. The fire occurred on Saturday afternoon too late for anything but the Sunday editions. The original story as it appeared in the Sunday papers and the Monday issues, of papers which had no Sunday editions, began like this:

> One hundred and forty-one persons are dead as a result of a fire which on Saturday afternoon swept the three upper floors of the factory loft building at the northwest corner of Washington place and Greene street. More than three-quarters of this number are women and girls, who were employed in the Triangle Shirt Waist factory, where the fire originated.--*Boston Transcript,* Monday.

The Monday stories on the fire followed up various phases as shown in the following. Each one while indicating that the story was a follow-up retold the principal incidents in the fire.

> The death list in the Washington place and Greene street fire was swelled today to 145, a majority of the victims being young girls.--*Monday morning--second story.*

> At dawn today it was estimated that 25,000 persons had visited the temporary morgue on the covered pier at the foot of East Twenty-sixth street, set aside to receive the bodies of those who perished in the Washington place fire on Saturday afternoon.--*Monday morning--second story.*

> The horror of the fire in the ten-story loft building at Washington place and Greene street late Saturday afternoon, with its heavy toll of human lives, grows blacker each succeeding hour.--*Monday afternoon.*

> Of the 142 bodies in the morgue as a result of the Triangle Shirt Waist factory fire, all but fifty had been identified this morning.--*Monday afternoon.*

On Tuesday other lines opened up for the rewrite man:

> Sifting down the great mass of testimony at their disposal, city and county officials hoped today to draw closer to the source of responsibility for Saturday's factory fire horror in which 142 persons lost their lives. Investigations started yesterday.--*Tuesday afternoon.*

> With all but twenty-eight of the victims of the Triangle Shirt Waist factory horror identified, District Attorney Whitman continues steadily compiling

# GETTING THE SCOOP

> evidence. Funerals for scores | | of victims are being held today, while | | the relief fund, etc.--*Tuesday* | |*afternoon.* |
>
> | Borough President McAneny of Manhattan,| | the district attorney's staff, the fire | | marshal, the coroner and the state labor | | department are bending every energy | | toward fixing the blame for the loss of | | the 142 lives in the, etc.--*Tuesday* | |*afternoon.* |
>
> | Union labor, horrified by the full | | realization that the waste of human life | | in the Triangle Waist factory fire might | | have been saved had existing laws been | | enforced, today arranged for a monster | | demonstration of protest, etc.--*Tuesday* | |*afternoon.* |

And so the stories ran for many days until newspaper readers had lost all interest in the fire. Most of the stories were simply retellings of the original story with a new bit of information in the lead. People were ravenous for more details about the fire and the follow stories supplied them until they were satisfied. Rarely is a fire worth so many retellings.

A serious accident is often followed up in one or more editions. If many people are killed or injured, the revised list of dead or the present condition of the injured always furnishes material for a follow-up. Sometimes the fixing of the blame, as in a railroad accident, or other resulting features are used as the basis of the rewriting.

In the case of a robbery the commonest material for a follow-up story is the resulting pursuit or capture. Very often a final report of the loss, the present condition of a robbed bank or public institution, or perhaps the regaining of the booty, makes a feature for a new story. But usually the follow-up is concerned with the pursuit, capture, or trial. This is especially true if the original story has been told by an earlier paper and another later paper wishes to print a more up-to-date story on the robbery, such as:

> | MINOCQUA, Wis., Oct. 22.--It now begins| | to look as if the bandits who robbed the | | State Bank of Minocqua early Tuesday | | morning would make their escape with the | | booty. (This is followed by a re-telling | | of the entire story of the robbery and an| | account of the pursuit.) |

The most usual follow-up of a murder story is interested in the pursuit, capture, or trial of the perpetrator of the deed. For example:

| Following the discovery of the body of | |Pietro Barilla, an Italian, of Woodhaven,| |Long Island, who was stabbed to death by | |four men, presumably Black Hand members, | |in Lincoln Road, near Flatbush, early | |yesterday morning, the police arrested | |three men yesterday. |

Very often the present condition of the victim of an attempted murder calls for a new story. The stories following the attempted murder of Mayor Gaynor of New York are good examples of the latter. If a mystery surrounds the crime a possible solution is grounds for a new story. The stories which might follow the unraveling of the mystery surrounding the fictitious death of the grocer, mentioned at the beginning of this chapter, would be second-day murder stories. The original story, let us say, was something like this:

| James White, a groceryman, was found | |dying yesterday with a bullet wound in | |his abdomen, in the cellar of his grocery| |store at 1236 Park street. |

The next story on the murder would be concerned with the unraveling of the mystery, thus:

| The preliminary inquiry yesterday by | |Coroner John F. Donalds, into the | |mysterious death of James White, the Park| |street grocer, resulted in the conclusion| |that White was murdered. |

And so the stories might run on day after day following the solution of the case like the succeeding chapters of a continued novel, and each one gives the synopsis of the preceding chapters in its lead, as every good follow-up story should do.

Suicide stories seldom offer material for follow-up stories unless there is some mystery surrounding the case. Sometimes the present condition of a resuscitated victim of attempted suicide or the disposition of the estate of a suicide offers material for rewriting.

Serious storms and floods are usually followed up for several days. Readers are always interested in the present condition of the devastated region. Very often the list of dead and injured is revised from day to day, and any attempt to lend aid to the unfortunate victims is always a reason for a later story.

Any meetings, conferences, trials, conventions, or the like must be followed up day by day with succeeding stories. Each story is complete in itself, but each one adds one more chapter to the report of the meeting. This method of following a continued proceeding calls for a series of follow-up stories; examples of the stories that follow a continued legal trial will be given later under Court Reporting.

\* \* \* \* \*

Many other illustrations might be given of follow-up stories that appear daily in the newspapers. In the last analysis, the follow-up or the rewrite story is nothing more than an ordinary news story, and as such must be written in the same way. It begins with a lead which plays up a feature and answers the reader's questions about the subject; the body of the story runs along like the body of any news story. But it is different in being a later chapter of a previous account; while complete in itself, it must not only indicate the previous story, but must tell its most important facts for readers who may have missed the previous story. It is simply a news story which is tied to a previous story by a string of cause and effect.

**4. Following Up Related Subjects** - In this connection it may be well to mention another kind of follow-up story that is usually written in connection with big news events. It is written to develop and follow up side lines of interest growing out of the main story. In its most usual form it is a statistical summary of events similar to the great event of the day - such as similar fires, similar railroad wrecks, etc., in the past. Any big story attracts so much attention among newspaper readers that the facts at hand are usually not sufficient to supply the public's demand for information on the subject. To satisfy these demands editors develop lines of interest growing out of the main event. They interview people concerning the event and concerning similar events; they describe similar events that have taken place in the past; they summarize and compare similar events in the past - in short, they follow up every line of interest opened up by the big story and write stories on the result. These stories are of the nature of follow-up stories in that they grow out of, and develop, the main story in its greatest extent.

For example, the wreck of the ocean liner *Titanic* called for innumerable side stories because the public's interest demanded more facts than the newspapers had at hand to supply. Hence, the papers wrote up similar shipwrecks in the past, gathered together summaries of the world's greatest shipwrecks, interviewed people who had been in any way connected with shipwrecks or with any phase of this shipwreck, described glaciers and icebergs, estimated the depth of the ocean where the *Titanic* sank, described the White Star liner and other liners, pictured real or imaginary shipwrecks, and developed every other related subject. The real news in all this mass of material was very meager, but the related stories satisfied the greedy public and helped newspaper readers to understand and to picture the real significance of the meager news.

In the same way a disastrous fire, like the burning of the Iroquois Theater, calls for innumerable outgrowing stories. Even when the event reported in the main news story is not sufficiently important to call for related stories, it is often accompanied by a list (usually put in a box at the head of the story) of other similar events and their results. These follow-up stories of related subjects are, in form, very much like feature stories, although they usually conform to the follow-up idea of mentioning in their leads the main news event to which they are related.

# 10
# REPORTS OF SPEECHES

Every profession has its disagreeable tasks; journalism has perhaps more disagreeable tasks than any other profession. All of a reporter's work is not concerned with running down thrilling stories and writing them up in a whirl of breathless interest. Our readers demand other kinds of news, and it is the reporter's task to satisfy them faithfully. There is probably no phase of the work that is quite so irksome as the reporting of speeches, lectures, sermons, etc., and there is probably no phase of the work about which most reporters have fewer definite rules or ideas. Read the reports of the same speech in two different papers and note the difference. They seldom contain the same things and more seldom do they tell what the speaker said, in the way and the spirit in which he said it. It is irksome work and difficult work to condense an hour's talk into three stickfuls, and few reporters know exactly how to go about it.

The report of a speech or a sermon or a lecture may come to a newspaper office in one of two ways. A copy of it may be sent to the paper or the reporter may have to go to hear the address and take notes on it. Very often the speaker kindly sends a printed or typewritten copy of his speech to the editor a few days in advance with the permission to release it - or print it - on a certain date, after the speech has been delivered in public. If the speech is to be printed in full, the task is a mere matter of editing and does not trouble the reporter. Very few speeches receive so much space. The others must be condensed and put in shape for printing.

After all, the usual way to get a speech is to go to the public delivery of the speech and bring back a report of it. At first sight this is a difficult task and green reporters come back

# NEWSPAPER REPORTING AND CORRESPONDENCE

with a very poor resumé. However, a word or two of advice from the editor or some bitter experience eases the way. Some advice may be given here to prepare the would-be reporter beforehand.

Some reporters who know shorthand prefer to make a stenographic report of the entire speech and rearrange and condense it in the office. This method is advisable only in the case of speeches of the greatest importance; it is too laborious for ordinary purposes, since the account includes at most only a part of the speech. The best way, doubtless, to get a speech is to take notes on it. And yet this must be done properly or there is a danger of misinterpretation of statements or of undue emphasis upon any single part of the speech. The report of a speech should be as well balanced and logical as the speech itself, differing from the original only in length and the omission of details. The speech report must be accurate and truthful or the speaker may appear at the office in a day or two with blood in his eye. A few rules may be suggested as an aid to accuracy and truthfulness.

In the first place, do not try to get all the speech; do not try to get more than a small part of it - the important part. There are two ways of doing this. If the speech is well arranged and orderly it is easy to tell when the speaker has finished one sub-division and is beginning another. Each division and subdivision will naturally contain a topic sentence. Watch for the topic sentences and get them down with the briefest necessary explanation to make them clear. Political speeches or impromptu talks are, on the other hand, not always so logically arranged. Sometimes it is possible to get the topic sentences, but more often it is not. Then watch for the interesting or striking statements. You will be aided in this by the audience about you. Whenever the speaker says anything unusually striking or of more than ordinary interest the audience will show it by signs of assent or dissent. Watch for these signs, even for applause - and take down the statement that was the cause. If the statement interested the original audience it will interest your readers. Naturally, mere oratorical trivialities must not be mistaken for striking statements.

When you get back to the office to write up the report of the speech you will feel the need of direct quotations - in fact, the length of your report will be determined by the number of direct quotations that you have to use in it - as well as by editorial dictum. It would be entirely wrong to quote any expressions of your own because they are somewhat like the speaker's statements, and it is impossible to quote anything less than a complete sentence in the report of a speech. Hence you will need complete sentences taken down verbatim in the exact words of the speaker. Make it a point to get complete sentences as you listen to the speech. Whenever a striking statement or an interesting part of the speech seems worth putting in your story get it down completely. You will find yourself writing most of the time because, while you are writing down one important sentence, the speaker will be uttering several more in explanation and may say something else of interest before you have finished writing down his first statement. Strict attention, a quick pencil, and a good memory are needed for this kind of work, but the reporting of speeches will lose its terrors after you have had a very small amount of practice.

Just as any news story begins with a lead and plays up its most striking fact in the first line, the report of a speech usually begins with the speaker's most striking or most important statement. As you are listening to his words watch for something striking for the lead - something that will catch the reader's eye and interest him. But you must exercise great care in selecting the statement for the lead. Theoretically and practically it must be something in strict accordance with the entire content of the speech and, if possible, it should be the one statement that sums up the whole speech in the most concise way. Somewhere in the discourse, at the beginning, at the end, or in some emphatic place, the speaker will usually sum up his complete ideas on the subject in a striking, concise way. Watch for this summary and get it down for the lead. However, there may be times when this summary, though concise, will be of little interest to the average reader and you will be forced to use some other striking statement. Then it is perfectly permissible to take any striking statement in the speech and use it for the lead, provided that the statement is directly connected with the rest of the discourse. But be fair to the speaker. Do not play up some chance remark as illustrative of the entire utterance; don't bring in an aside as the most interesting thing in his speech. If a preacher forgets himself to the extent of expressing a chance political opinion, it would obviously be unfair to him for you to play up that remark as the summary of his sermon. Your readers would get a false impression and the preacher would be angry. If he considers the chance remark of real importance in his sermon he will back it up with other statements that will give you an excuse for using it. In brief, watch for the most interesting and most striking statement in the entire speech, and in selecting this statement be fair and just and try to avoid giving a false impression of the speaker or of the speech. If you follow this

# NEWSPAPER REPORTING AND CORRESPONDENCE

rule you will never be in any danger of getting your paper into difficulties.

Another rule in reporting lectures, speeches, etc., applies to the writing of all newspaper stories. Write your report at once while the speech is still fresh in your mind. Your report must preserve the logic and continuity of the speech - it must be a fair resumé. Your notes will be at best mere jottings of chance sentences here and there. Do not allow them to get cold and lose their continuity. Write the report at once.

\* \* \* \* \*

The writing of the report of a speech, lecture, or sermon is the same whether it is taken from a printed or stenographic copy of the discourse or from notes. It is perhaps easier to write from your notes because you have the important parts of the speech picked out, ready for use, by the aid of the rest of the audience. Before you can resumé a printed copy of the speech you must go through it and pick out the important sentences which you wish to quote and decide upon the most striking statement for the lead. There is no definite rule that can be followed in this except to take the topic sentences whenever they are stated with sufficient clearness. When you have decided on the statements that you wish to quote you have really reduced the speech to a form practically identical with the notes taken from verbal utterance, and the writing in either case is the same.

The lead of the report is very much like the lead of any other news story - for the report of a speech is really a news story. As soon as the speech is mentioned, the reader unconsciously asks a number of questions about it and the reporter must answer them in the first sentence. As in any other news story the questions are: *What? Who? Where? When?* and perhaps *How?* and *Why?* Reduced to the case of the speech report, they amount to what did he say, who said it, where did he say it, when, and perhaps how and why did he say it. You may answer the *what* by giving the subject of the discourse or by giving a striking statement in it. In every report the answer to some one of the questions is of greater interest and must be placed in the first line. If the speaker is of more than ordinary prominence his name makes a good beginning. If an ordinary person makes a speech at some meeting of prominence the *when* or *where* takes precedence over his name. But in most cases the reporter will find that none of these things is of sufficient importance for the beginning. Most public utterances that he will be called upon to report will be made by ordinary men in ordinary places and at ordinary times, and the most interesting part of the story will be what was said. Sometimes it suffices to give the title of the speech, but more often a striking statement from the speech makes the best beginning. However, although the speaker, the time, the place, etc., are overshadowed in importance by the subject or content of what the speaker says, they must be included in the same sentence with the title or striking statement. That is, in short, we catch the reader's interest with a striking statement from the speech and then delay the rest of the report while we tell who said it, when, where, etc. The necessity of this is obvious.

In accordance with the foregoing there are several possible ways in which to begin the lead of the report of any speech. It would be wrong to say that any one is more common or better than the others; the choice of the beginning must rest with the reporter. And yet there are various things to be noted in connection with each of these beginnings.

**1. Direct Quotation Beginning.—Sentence** - The quotation that is to have the first line must of course be the most striking or the most interesting statement in the speech. If it consists of a single sentence - and it cannot be less than a sentence - the report may begin thus:

> | "Participation in government is not | |only the privilege, but the right, of | |every American citizen and should be | |considered a duty," said the Rev. | |Frederick W. Hamilton, president of Tufts| |College, who spoke on "The Political | |Duties of the American Citizen" at the | |monthly men's neighborhood meeting in the| |Roxbury Neighborhood House last | |night.--*Boston Herald.* |

Here the reporter has given us a sentence that is practically a summary of the speech, has told us who said it, when and where, and has completed the paragraph with the title of the speech. Sometimes the title of the speech is not of great importance and its place in the lead may be given to a little summary as in the following:

> | "The modern man isn't afraid of hell," | |was the concise explanation which W. | |Lathrop Meaker gave in Franklin Union | |Hall yesterday afternoon and evening of | |the fact that the churches are losing | |their grip on the average man.--*New York*| |*Sun.* |

# NEWSPAPER REPORTING AND CORRESPONDENCE

A question which embodies the content of a speech may often be quoted at the beginning; thus:

| "Will the Baptist church continue to | | maintain an attitude of timidity when | | John D. Rockefeller of Standard Oil is | | mentioned?" asked the Rev. R. A. Bateman, | | from East Jaffrey, N. H., of the | | ministers assembled in Ford Hall last | | evening at the New England Baptist | | conference.--*Boston Herald.* |

The opening quotation may sometimes be made an excuse for a brief description of the speaker or his gestures as in the following. This is good at times but it may easily be overworked or become "yellow" in tone.

| "There is no fire escape," remarked | | Gypsy Smith, the famous English | | evangelist, yesterday before the | | fashionable audience of the Fifth Avenue | | Baptist Church. He held aloft a Bible as | | he made this declaration during an | | eloquent sermon on the possibility of | | losing faith and wandering from the | | narrow way.--*New York World.* |

**2. Direct Quotation Beginning. - Paragraph** - You notice that in each of the foregoing the quoted sentence is incorporated grammatically into the first sentence of the lead. It is followed by a comma and the words "said Mr. ----," "was the statement of ----," "declared Mr. ----," etc. This construction is possible only when the quoted sentence is short and simple. When it is long or complex, it is well to paragraph it separately and to put the explanations in a separate paragraph, thus:

| "If the United States had possessed in | | 1898 a single dirigible balloon, even of | | the size of the one now at Fort Myer, | | Virginia, which cost less than $10,000, | | the American army and navy would not have | | long remained in doubt of the presence of | | Cervera's fleet in Santiago harbor." | | | | This statement was made today by Major | | G. O. Squier, assistant chief signal | | officer of the army, in an address on | | aëronautics delivered before the American | | Society of Mechanical Engineers at 29 | | West Thirty-ninth street.--*New York* | | *Mail.* |

This same construction must *always* be used when the statement quoted in the lead consists of more than one sentence, as in the following:

| "The climate of Wisconsin is as good | | for recovery from tuberculosis as that of | | any state in the union. It is

not the | |climate, but the out-of-doors air that | |works the cure." | | | |So said Harvey Dee Brown in his | |tuberculosis crusade lecture in Kilbourn | |park last night.--*Milwaukee Free Press.*|

It is to be noted that the statement quoted in the lead is never split into two parts, separated by explanation. The quotation is always gathered together at the beginning and followed by the explanation.

**3. Indirect Quotation Beginning** - This method is best adapted to the playing up of a brief resumé of the content of the speech. It is sometimes called the "*that*-clause beginning" because it always begins with a *that*-clause which is the subject of the principal verb of the sentence - "was the statement of," "was the declaration of," etc. The *that*-clause may contain a resumé of the entire speech or only the most striking statement in it. Here is one of the latter:

| That the cruise of the battleship fleet| |around the world has taught the citizens | |of the United States that a powerful | |fleet is needed in the Pacific was the | |statement of Rear Admiral R. C. Hollyday,| |chief of the bureau of yards and docks of| |the navy, at a luncheon given to him by | |the board of trustees of the Chamber of | |Commerce at the Fairmont Hotel | |yesterday.--*San Francisco Examiner.* |

It is not always necessary to use the phrase "was the statement of." A variation from it is often very good:

| That it is the urgent mission of the | |white people of America, through their | |churches and Sunday-schools, to educate | |the American negro morally and | |religiously, was the sentiment of the | |twelfth session of the International | |Sunday-school Convention last night, | |voiced with special power and eloquence | |by Dr. Booker T. Washington, the chief | |speaker of the evening.--*Louisville* | |*Courier-Journal.* |

| That the Irish race has a great destiny| |to fulfill, one greater than it has | |achieved in its glorious past, was the | |prophecy of Prof. Charles Johnston of | |Dublin university in his lecture at the | |city library Sunday | |afternoon.--*Wisconsin State Journal.* |

It is perfectly good usage to begin such a lead with two *that*-clauses or even with three. The two clauses in this case are of course treated as a singular subject and take a singular verb. It is usually best not to have more than three clauses at the beginning and even three must be handled with great care. Three clauses at the beginning, if at all long, bury the speaker's name too deeply and may become too complicated. Unless the clauses are very closely related in idea, it is usually better not to use more than two. Naturally when more than one *that*-clause is used in the lead, all of the clauses must be gathered together at the beginning; never should one precede and one follow the principal verb. Here is an example of good usage:

> | NEW YORK, Feb. 25.--That America is | |entering upon a new era of civic and | |business rectitude and that this is due | |to the awakening of the moral conscience | |of the whole people was the prophecy made| |here tonight by Governor Joseph W. Folk | |of Missouri.--*Chicago Record-Herald.* |

**4. Summary Beginning** - This is a less formal way of treating the indirect quotation beginning. It is simply a different grammatical construction. Whereas in the *that*-clause beginning the principal verb of the sentence is outside the summary (e. g., "That ... was the statement of"), in the summary beginning the principal verb of the sentence is the verb of the summary and the speaker is brought in by means of a modifying phrase; thus:

> | MINNEAPOLIS, Oct. 1.--Both the free | |trader and the stand-patter are back | |numbers, according to Senator Albert J. | |Beveridge of Indiana, who delivered a | |tariff speech here tonight.--*Milwaukee* | |*Free Press.* |

> | Federal control of the capitalization | |of railroads is the solution of the | |railroad problem suggested by E. L. | |Phillipp, the well-known Milwaukee | |railroad expert, in the course of a | |speech at the third annual banquet of, | |etc.--*Milwaukee Free Press.* |

The summary beginning may be handled in many different ways and allows perhaps more grammatical liberty than any other beginning. The summary may even be given a sentence by itself as in the following. This kind of treatment may easily be overdone and should be handled with great caution:

> | If you have acute mania, it is the | |proper thing to take the music cure. Miss| |Jessie A. Fowler says so, and she knows. | |Miss Fowler discussed "Music | |Hygienically" before the "Rainy Daisies" | |at the Hotel Astor yesterday and | |prescribed musical treatment for various | |brands of mania.--*New York World.* |

**5. Keynote Beginning** - Very closely related to the summary beginning is the keynote beginning, in which the subject of the main verb is an indirect presentation of the content of the speech. Whereas the summary beginning displays its resumé in a complete sentence, the keynote beginning puts the content of the speech in a single noun and its modifiers. Thus:

| The ideal state university was the | |theme of a speech delivered by, etc. |

| The mission of the newspaper to tell | |the truth, to stand for high ideals, and | |to strive to have those ideals adopted by| |the public was the keynote of an address | |delivered by, etc. |

**6. Participial Beginning** - This is less common than the other kinds of indirect quotation beginnings but it is often very effective. The summary of the speech or the most striking statement is put into a participial phrase at the beginning and is made to modify the subject of the sentence (the speaker). It must of course be remembered that such a participial phrase can be used only to modify a noun, as an adjective modifies a noun, and can never be made the subject of a verb. Here is an example of good use of this beginning:

| Upholding the right of public criticism| |of the courts on the theory that there | |can be no impropriety in investigating | |any act of a public official, Judge | |Kennesaw M. Landis last night addressed | |the students of Marquette College of Law | |and many members of the Milwaukee | |bar.--*Milwaukee Free Press.* |

Just as it is perfectly possible to begin an indirect quotation lead with two *that*-clauses instead of one, it is also possible to use two participial phrases in the participial beginning; as:

| Pleading for justice and human | |affection in dealing with the delinquent | |child, and urging the vital need of | |legislation which shall enforce parental | |responsibility, Mrs. Nellie Duncan made | |an address yesterday which stirred the | |sympathies of an attentive audience in | |the First Presbyterian Church.--*San* | |*Francisco Examiner.* |

Although the participial phrase usually gives the summary of the speech, not infrequently the participial construction is used to play up the name of the speech or some other fact and the summary comes after the principal verb of the lead; thus:

> | Paying tribute to the memory of | |President William McKinley last night at | |the Metropolitan Temple, where exercises | |were held to dedicate the McKinley | |memorial organ, Judge Taft told in detail| |of his commission to the Philippine | |service and his subsequent intimate | |connection with the President.--*New York*| |*Tribune.* |

7. Title Beginning - There are two reasons for beginning the report of a public utterance with the speaker's subject or title. The title itself may be so broad that it makes a good summary of the speech, or it may be so striking in itself that it attracts interest at once. In the following examples the title is really a summary of the speech:

> | NEW YORK, Dec. 15.--"The Compensation | |of Employes for Injuries Received While | |at Work" was taken by J. D. Beck, | |commissioner of labor of Wisconsin, as | |the theme of his address before the | |National Civic Federation here | |today.--*Milwaukee Free Press.* |

> | "The Emmanuel Movement" was the subject| |of an address by Rabbi Stephen S. Wise of| |the Free Synagogue yesterday | |morning.--*New York Evening Post.* |

In the following stories the reporter began with the title evidently because it was so strikingly unusual and also because it was the title of a strikingly unusual speech by an unusual man. This kind of title beginning is always very effective:

> | "Booze, or Get on the Water Wagon," was| |the subject on which Rev. Billy Sunday, | |the baseball evangelist, addressed an | |audience of over 4,000 persons at the | |Midland Chautauqua yesterday afternoon. | |For two hours Sunday fired volley after | |volley at the liquor traffic.--*Des* | |*Moines Capital.* |

> | "If Christ Came to Milwaukee" was the | |subject of the Rev. Paul B. Jenkin's | |Sunday night in Immanuel Presbyterian | |Church.--*Milwaukee Sentinel.* |

**8. Speaker Beginning** - It is obvious that this is the easiest beginning that may be used in the report of a speech. But just

# GETTING THE SCOOP

as obviously it is the beginning that should be least used. Just as in writing news stories a green reporter always attempts to begin every lead with the name of some person involved, in reporting a public discourse he has a strong desire to put the name of the speaker before what the speaker said. But the same tests may be applied to both cases. Are our readers more interested in what a man does than in the man himself; do our readers go to hear a given speaker because they wish to hear what he has to say or because they wish to hear *him*? Whenever the public is so interested in a man that it does not care what he says, then you may feel safe in beginning the report of what he says with his name. This test may be altered, especially in smaller cities, by previous interest in the speech; if the speech has been expected and looked forward to with interest, then, no matter if the speaker is the President himself, his name is not as good news as what he has to say. Even if the lead does begin with the speaker's name, the reporter usually tries to bring a summary of the speech or the most striking statement into the first sentence after the name. For example:

> | Speaker Joseph G. Cannon placed himself| |on record last night in favor of a | |revision of the tariff in accordance with| |the promise of the Republican party | |platform and declared that so far as his | |vote was concerned he would see to it | |that the announced policy of revision | |would be written in the national laws as | |soon as possible. The words of the | |speaker came at a luncheon given to six | |rear admirals of the United States navy | |by Alexander H. Revell of Chicago in the | |Union League Club, at which the need of | |more battleships and increased efficiency| |of the fighting forces of the republic | |were the principal themes of discussion. |

This example was chosen because, while it is written in accordance with the rules of the speaker beginning, it is obviously too long and complicated - over 110 words. It would be better to gather it together and condense it as in the following:

> | Chief Forester Gifford Pinchot opened | |the second day's session of the national | |conservation congress yesterday by an | |address in which he expressed his entire | |satisfaction and his confidence in the | |attitude of President Taft toward | |conservating the national | |resources.--*Milwaukee Sentinel.* |
>
> | ST. PAUL, Minn., Feb. 10.--Booker T. | |Washington of Tuskegee, Ala., in an | |address at the People's Church

tonight | |predicted that within two years the | |liquor traffic would be driven out of all| |the southern states but two.--*Milwaukee* | |*Sentinel.* |

There are obviously other beginnings that cannot be classed under any of the above heads. Some of them, much like the "freak" leads that may be seen in many newspapers of the present day, may be called free beginnings for want of a better name. These free beginnings are quite effective when properly handled but the novice must use them with fear and trembling. They may be witty or they may be sarcastic, but they are usually dangerous. The difference in the eight beginnings discussed above is mainly one of grammatical construction; the same fundamental ideas govern them all. Their purpose is always to play up a striking statement or a summary of the speech report and to give at the very outset the necessary explanation concerning the speech.

**THE BODY OF THE REPORT**

The body of the report of a speech is not so distinct from the lead as the body of an ordinary news story. In the news story it is safe to assume that many readers will not go beyond the lead, but in the report of a speech this is not so true. It is less possible to give the main facts in the lead of a speech report and the rest of the story is more necessary. Hence it must be written with as great care as the lead.

The body of the report should consist of direct quotation in so far as possible. The reader is interested in what the speaker said and it is impossible to make a summary in indirect discourse as convincing as the actual quotation of his words. Be sure that the quotations are the speaker's exact words or very nearly his exact words, so that he cannot accuse you of misquoting him. The spirit of his words must be in the quotation, anyway.

In these quotations nothing less than a complete sentence should be quoted. Do not patch together sentences of indirect and direct quotation, like the following - He said that some of us are prone to let things be as they are, "because the philanthropic rich help in our times of trouble and in sickness." Such quotation is worse than no direct quotation at all. Of course, this does not mean that one cannot add "said the speaker" to a direct quotation, but it means that "said the speaker" can be added only to quotations that are complete sentences. Furthermore whenever it is necessary to bring in "said the speaker," or similar expressions, they should be added at the end of the quoted sentence - the least emphatic part of a newspaper sentence.

Obviously a condensed report of a speech can only quote sentences here and there throughout the speech - the high spots of interest, as we called them before. These must not be quoted promiscuously and disconnectedly. The original speech had a logical order and set forth a logical train of thought. These should be followed as far as possible in the report. Bring in the quotations in their true order and fill the gaps between them with indirect discourse to knit them together and to give the report the coherence of the original speech. But do not carry this indirect explanation to the extent of making your copy a report of the speech in indirect discourse with occasional bits of direct quotation to illustrate. Remember that, after all, the direct quotation is the truly effective part of the speech.

Whenever a paragraph contains both direct and indirect quotation, the direct quotation should always precede the indirect. But it is much better to paragraph the two kinds of quotation separately, making each paragraph entirely of direct, or entirely of indirect, quotation. If a paragraph must contain both, begin it with the direct so that as the reader glances down the column he will see a quotation mark at the beginnings of most, if not all, of the paragraphs. By the same sign, when your notes are lacking in direct quotations, bring in as many of the quotations as possible at the beginning of the report and let the indirect summary occupy the end where it may be cut off by the editor if he does not wish to run it.

Here is a good illustration of a part of the body of a good speech report - it is the second paragraph of one of the stories quoted under the "Speaker" beginning above:

> | "I can not account for the moral | |revolution that is sweeping over the | |South," he continued. "The sentiment | |against whisky is deeper than the mere | |desire to get it away from the black man.| |That same sentiment is found in counties | |that contain no negro population. People | |who say that the law will not be enforced| |have not been in the South.--B. T. | |Washington's speech, *Milwaukee* | |*Sentinel.* |

You will notice that although the above paragraph is composed entirely of direct quotation it has no quotation mark at the end. This is, of course, in accordance with the old rule of rhetoric which says that in a continuous quotation each paragraph shall begin with a quotation mark but only the last shall be closed by a quotation mark.

To illustrate the errors that may be made in reporting speeches we might write the above paragraph as follows:

| Mr. Washington continued by saying that| |he could not account for the revolution | |that is sweeping over the South. "The | |sentiment against whisky is deeper than | |the mere desire to get it away from the | |black man." He says that "the same | |sentiment is found in counties that | |contain no negro population." People who | |say that the law will not be enforced | |"have not been in the South," according | |to Booker T. Washington. |

The clumsiness of this mingling of direct and indirect quotation is very clear, as is the weakness of beginning with an explanation that is really subordinate.

Much more could be said about the reporting of speeches. Very few things will make a man so angry as the misquoting of his words. Therefore, whatever other faults your report of a speech may have, let it be accurate and truthful.

# 11
# INTERVIEWS

If you compare any interview story with any speech report in any representative newspaper, you will readily see how a discussion of interviews easily becomes an explanation of the differences between interview stories and speech-reports; that is, how the report of an interview differs from the report of a public utterance of a more formal kind. There are few differences in the written reports. Each usually begins with a summary or a striking statement and consists largely of direct quotation. Were it not for the line or two of explanation at the end of the introduction, it would be practically impossible to tell the one from the other, to tell which of the reports sets forth statements made in a public discourse and which gives statements made in a more private way to a reporter.

The difference lies behind the report, in the way the reporter obtained the statements and quotations. And the whole difference depends upon the attitude of the man who made the statements - whether his words were a conscious or an unconscious public utterance. When a man speaks from a platform he utters every sentence and every word with an idea of possible quotation - he is not only willing to be quoted but he wants to be quoted. But when he speaks privately to a reporter he usually dreads quotation. Of course, he expects that you will print a few of his remarks but he is constantly hoping that you will not remember and print them all. He speaks more guardedly, too, since he is not sure of the interpretation that may be given to his words. Hence it is a very different matter to report what a man says in public and to get statements for the press from him in private. Any one can report a speech but great skill is required to get a good interview - especially if the victim is unwilling to talk.

The first matter that a reporter has to consider is the means of retaining the statements until he is able to write his story. It is a simple matter to get quotations from a speech because it is possible to sit anywhere in the audience and write down the speaker's words in a notebook as they are uttered. But the notebook must be left behind when you try to interview. When a man is not used to being interviewed nothing will make him reticent so quickly as the appearance of a notebook and pencil; he realizes that his words are to appear in print just as he utters them and he immediately becomes frightened. Ordinarily so long as he feels that what he says is going into the confidential ear of the reporter - and out of the other ear just as quickly - he is willing to talk more freely and openly and to say exactly what he thinks. This, of course, does not apply to prominent men who are used to being interviewed and prefer to have their remarks taken down verbatim. Such an interview, however, is little more than a call to secure a statement for publication.

It might be well to settle the notebook question here and now when it assumes the greatest importance. The stage has hardened us to seeing a reporter slinking around the outskirts of every bit of excitement writing excitedly and hurriedly in a large leather notebook. So hardened are we to the sight that some new reporters buy a notebook just as soon as they get a place on a newspaper staff. But real reporters on real newspapers do not use notebooks. A few sheets of folded copy paper hidden carefully in an inside pocket ready for names and addresses and perhaps figures are all that most of them carry. Many people dread publicity and the appearance of a notebook frightens them into silence more quickly than the actual appearance of a representative of the press. This is true in the reporting of any bit of news, in the covering of any story - and it is ordinarily true in interviewing for statements that are to be quoted. Of course, an exception to this must be made in the case of some prominent men who prefer to issue signed written statements when they are interviewed.

The impossibility of using a notebook or writing down a man's words in an interview seriously complicates the task of interviewing. Some reporters train themselves until they are able to remember their victim's words long enough to get outside and write them down. Others are satisfied with getting the ideas and the spirit of what is said together with the man's manner of talking. A few characteristic mannerisms thrown in with a true report of his ideas will make any speaker believe that you have quoted him exactly. Whichever method is pursued, the reporter must always be fair and try to tell the readers of the paper the man's true ideas. The exigencies of the case give the reporter greater liberty than in quoting from a speech but he must not abuse his liberty.

The success of an interview depends very largely upon the way in which a reporter approaches the man whom he wishes to interview. It is never well to trust to the inspiration of the moment to start the conversation. The reporter must know exactly what he wishes to have the man say before he approaches him and must already have framed his questions so as to draw out the answers that he wishes. People are never interviewed except for a purpose and that purpose should suggest the reporter's first question. No matter how willing the man is to tell what he thinks he will seldom begin talking until the reporter asks him a definite question to help him in putting his thoughts into words. All of this should be considered beforehand. The reporter should have outlined a definite campaign and have a series of questions which he wishes to ask. If he has written the questions out beforehand, the task becomes an easier one - he merely fills in the answers on his list later and has the interview in better form than if he had tried to trust entirely to his memory. To be sure, the questions may open up unexpected lines of thought and he may get more than he went for, but he must have his questions ready for use as soon as each new line is exhausted. A skilled reporter frames the interview himself and keeps the result entirely in his own hands through the campaign that he has outlined beforehand. Unless he knows exactly what he wants to get, a wary victim may lead him off upon unimportant facts and in the end tell him nothing that his paper has sent him to get. A reporter must keep the reins of an interview in his own possession.

A good reporter takes great care in his manner of addressing a man whom he is to interview. A well-known newspaper follows the rule of asking its reporters never to do what a gentleman would not do. A reporter who is trying to interview must always be a gentleman and must not ask questions that a gentleman would not ask. If the victim is a prominent man of great personality it is not hard to follow this rule--in fact, it is impossible to get the interview by any other method of approach. But when one is trying to interview a person of humbler station, the case is different. It is very easy then to fall into a habit of demanding information and turning the interview into an inquisition. But the reporter who keeps his attitude as a gentleman gets more real facts even when his victim is of the most humble social status. Therefore, never approach your victim as if he were a witness and you a cross-questioning lawyer. Do not say: "See here, you know more about it than that," and thus try to force unwilling information from him. Go at him in a more round-about way and lead him to give you the facts unwittingly perhaps.

A young reporter often feels an impulse to become too personal with the man whom he is interviewing. He must always remember that he is not there for a friendly chat but as a representative of a newspaper, sent to get concise facts or opinions. This attitude must be maintained even with the humblest persons. Any desire to sympathize, criticize, or advise must be checked at the very start. The point of view must always be kept.

\* \* \* \* \*

Although the main difference between writing interview stories and reporting speeches lies in the very act of getting the quotations and words of the speaker, there are certain aspects in which the writing of an interview story is different. The actual form of the two stories is almost identical and yet there is a tone in the interview story that is lacking in the report of a speech. This may be called the personal tone.

The very name of the speaker obviously plays a much larger part in the interview story than in the speech report. We may be more interested in what a man says in a public discourse than we are in the man, but when we interview a man we want his opinions not for themselves so much as because they are his opinions. An interview with the President on the tariff is not necessarily interesting in the new ideas that it brings out, for we have many other ways of knowing the President's opinions on the tariff question; but the interview is worth printing because every one is interested in reading anything that the President says, although he may have read the same thing many times before. A man is seldom interviewed unless he is of some prominence - that is why he is interviewed, and so in the resulting story his name plays a very important part. In fact, his name is usually the feature of the story; most interview stories begin directly with the name of the man whose statements are quoted.

Although a man may be interviewed simply because of his prominence and popularity, there is usually another reason for the interview. We are interested not only in hearing him say something but we wish to hear him say something on a certain topic. The interview thus has a timeliness, a reason for existence. Since this timeliness is the reason for printing a certain man's statements, the reporter's account must indicate that timeliness near the beginning. That is, the first sentence of an interview story must not only tell who was interviewed and the gist of what he said, but it must tell why he said it. The interview must be connected with the rest of the day's news. This comes out very definitely in the custom which many newspapers have of printing the opinions of many prominent men in connection with any important event. Perhaps it is because we wish to know their opinions on the subject or perhaps it is simply because we are glad to have a chance to hear them talk - at any rate many editors make any great event an excuse for a series of interviews. This is illustrated by the opinions of the various labor leaders that were printed with the story of the recent confession of the McNamara brothers. In such a case, the reporter must make the reason for the interview his starting point in the report and must indicate very plainly why the man was interviewed.

This idea of timeliness is very often carried to the extent of making the interview merely a denial or an assertion from the mouth of a well-known man. There may be an upheaval in Wall Street. Immediately the papers print an interview in which some prominent financier denies or asserts that he is at the bottom of the upheaval. Naturally the report of the interview begins with the very words of the denial or the assertion. Very often a man when interviewed refuses to say anything on the subject. The fact that he has nothing to say does not mean that the interview is not worth reporting. In fact, that refusal to speak may be the most effective thing that he could say. The reporter begins by telling that his man had nothing to say on the subject and ends by telling what he should have said or what his refusal to speak probably means, - if the paper is not too scrupulous in such matters. At any rate, the denial or assertion or refusal to speak becomes the starting point of the report and furnishes the excuse for the interview story. The expanded remarks that follow the lead are of course important but they are not so important as the primary expression of opinion that the reporter went for.

The personal element in interviewing may be carried to an extreme extent. The man who is interviewed may so far overshadow the importance of what he says that the report of the interview becomes almost a sketch of the man himself. That is, the report is filled with human interest. The quotations are interspersed with action and description. We are told how the man acted when he said each individual thing. His appearance, attitude, expression, and surroundings become as important as his words and are brought into the report as vividly as possible. Such an interview may become almost large enough to be used as a special feature story for the Sunday edition, but when the human interest is limited to a comparatively subordinate position the report still keeps its character as an interview news story. Such a thing may be illustrated from the daily press:

> | "I would rather have four battleships | | and need only two than to have two and | | need four." | | | | Seated in the cool library of Colonel | | A. K. McClure's summer home at | | Wallingford, Rear Admiral Winfield Scott | | Schley, retired, thus expressed himself | | yesterday on the need of a larger and | | greater navy. |

After all has been said about interviewing, the one thing that a reporter must remember is that an interview story is at best rather dry and everything that he can do to increase the interest will improve the interview. But all of this must be done with absolute fairness to the speaker and great truthfulness in the quotation of his ideas and opinions.

\* \* \* \* \*

To come to the technical form of the interview story, we find that there are very nearly as many possible beginnings as in the case of the report of a speech. The interview story must begin with a lead that tells who was interviewed, when, and where, what he said (in a quotation or an indirect summary), and why he was interviewed. This is like the lead of a speech report in every particular except in the timeliness - the occasion for a speech is seldom mentioned in the lead, but a reporter usually tells at once why he interviewed the man whose words he quotes.

**1. Speaker Beginning** - The very purpose behind interviewing makes the so-called speaker beginning most common. It is almost an invariable rule that the report of an interview must begin with the man's name unless what he says is of greater importance than his name - which is seldom.

The simplest form of the speaker beginning is the one in which the speaker's name is followed directly by a summary of what he said, as:

# GETTING THE SCOOP

> | Dr. David Starr Jordan, president of | |Leland Stanford Junior University, said | |yesterday at the Holland House that in | |the development of American universities | |educators must separate the lower two | |classes from the upper two, the present | |freshman and sophomore classes to be | |absorbed by small colleges or | |supplemental high schools, making the | |junior year the first in the university | |training. He said the universities should | |receive only men, not boys.--*New York* | |*Tribune*. |

Another kind of speaker beginning may devote most of the lead to the explanation of the reason for the interview, giving the briefest possible summary of what was said: Thus:

> | Director Lang of the department of | |public safety is going to place a ban on | |the playing of tennis on Sunday. He | |doesn't know just yet how he is going to | |accomplish this, but yesterday he | |declared that he would find some law | |applicable to the case.--*Pittsburgh* | |*Gazette-Times*. |

One step further brings us to the entire exclusion of the result of the interview from the lead. In this case the reason for the interview occupies the entire lead and we must read part of the second paragraph to find what the man said; thus:

> | Charles F. Washburn, Richmond Hill's | |wizard of finance, promises to appear at | |his broker's office in Newark, N. J., | |this morning with a fresh bank roll, | |accumulated since the close of the market| |on Saturday. | | | | (The second paragraph tells what it is | |all about and the third quotes his | |words.)--*New York World*. |

It is to be noted that in each of the above leads the speaker's name is always accompanied by a word or two telling who he is and why he was interviewed. Furthermore the reporter himself has no more place in the lead than if he were reporting a speech - his existence and the part he played in getting the interview are strictly ignored.

**2. Summary Beginning** - There are two common ways of beginning an interview story with a summary. First, the lead may begin with a *that*-clause which embodies the gist of the interview; this is like the *that*-clause beginning of the report of a speech; thus:

> | That the apparent apathy among the | |voters of the country is merely | |contentment with the present |

> administration of affairs by the Republican party is the contention of ex-Senator John M. Thurston of Nebraska. Mr. Thurston was at Republican national headquarters today, etc.--*New York Evening Post.*

Secondly the summary beginning is used in the case of an interview that is a denial or an assertion by the man interviewed. The lead begins with a clause or a participial phrase embodying the substance of the interview, and the name of the speaker is made the subject of a verb of denying or asserting; thus:

> Declaring that his office is run as economically as possible, Sheriff H. E. Franke denied on Sunday that he had expended more than $688 for auto hire to collect $1,409.28 of alleged taxes. (The second paragraph begins with a direct quotation.)--*Milwaukee Sentinel.* Although he had sharply criticised Roosevelt's special message condemning some of the uses to which the possessors of large fortunes are putting their wealth, President Jacob Gould Schurman, Cornell University, declined to discuss Roosevelt or his policies in Milwaukee yesterday. He said that he was not talking politics. (The rest of the report is a quotation of his views on college athletics.)--*Milwaukee Free Press.*

**3. Quotation Beginning** - Many reports of interviews begin with a direct quotation. The logic of this is that the expression of opinion is, in some cases, of more interest than the name of the man who expressed the opinion. Sometimes the name of the speaker is not considered worth mentioning and in that case a direct quotation is the only advisable beginning; thus:

> "With the prices of food for hogs and cattle going up, it is natural that the food--beef and pork--for us humans should keep pace." This was the logic of an east-side butcher who discussed the probable rise in the prices of meat.--*Milwaukee Free Press.*

Sometimes a short quotation is used at the beginning of the lead very much as a title is used in a speech report; thus:

> NEW YORK, June 1.--"A business proposition which should have been put in effect nearly twenty years ago," was John Wanamaker's comment today on the adoption of 2-cent letter postage between the United

# GETTING THE SCOOP

States and Great Britain and Ireland.--*Milwaukee Free Press.*

If the quotation at the beginning consists of only one sentence the name of the speaker may be run into the same paragraph; thus:

"Judge McPherson's recent decision declaring Missouri's 2-cent fare confiscatory is an indication that vested interests are entitled to some protection and that legislatures must not go too far in regulating them," said Sir Thomas Shaughnessy, president of the Canadian Pacific road, on Sunday.--*Milwaukee Sentinel.*

However if the quotation at the beginning contains more than one sentence it is best to paragraph the quotation separately and leave the name of the speaker until the second paragraph; thus:

"The American Federation of Labor will enter the national campaign by seeking to place labor candidates on the tickets of the old parties. An independent labor party is eventually contemplated. But there is not time to get results in that way in the next national campaign." So said H. C. Raasch, national president of the tile-layers, upon his return yesterday, etc.--*Milwaukee Free Press.*

**4. Human Interest Beginning** - This is a designation devised to cover a multitude of beginnings. A human interest interview may begin with a quotation, a summary, a name, or an action. The aim is necessarily toward unconventionality and the form of the lead is left to the originality of the reporter. A few examples may illustrate what is meant by the human interest beginning:

"There goes another string. Drat those strings!" Only Joseph Caluder didn't say "Drat." "Say, do you know that I have spent pretty nearly $1,000 for strings for that violin? Well, it's a fact. Listen." Etc.--*Milwaukee Sentinel.*

Fire Marshal James Horan never bought a firecracker, but for many years he has celebrated Independence day in the thick of fires. He never owned a gun or revolver. His last prayer before trying to snatch a little needed sleep Friday night will be of the twofold form, etc.--*Chicago Post.*

After what has been said about the body of a speech report, there is little more to be said about the body of an interview story. The same rules apply in both cases. The body of the report should contain as much direct quotation as possible. However nothing less than a sentence should be quoted - that is, every quotation should be a complete sentence, with indirect explanation. Whenever "Said the speaker" or "Mr. Brown continued" or any similar expression is worked into the direct quotation it should always be placed at the end of the sentence; never begin a quotation in this way:- Mr. Jones continued, "Furthermore I would say, etc." In the same way, when a paragraph contains both direct and indirect quotation, the direct quotation should be placed at the beginning. Whenever it is possible, construct solid paragraphs of quotation, and solid paragraphs of summary. The report as a whole must have coherence and a logical sequence; for this a limited amount of indirect quotation may be used to fill in the gaps in the logic of the direct quotation.

According to the usage of the best newspapers of to-day the reporter must never be brought into the report of an interview. His existence must never be mentioned although every reader knows that some reporter secured the interview. In the old days reporters delighted in bringing themselves into their stories as "representatives of the press" or "a reporter for the Dispatch," but that practice has gone the way of the reporter's leather-bound notebook. The interview may be told satisfactorily without a mention of the reporter; hence newspaper usage has put a ban on his appearance in his story.

**GROUP INTERVIEWS**

We have said that a man is seldom interviewed without a reason; there is always a timeliness in interviewing. Any unusual event of broad importance becomes an excuse for the editor to print the opinion of some prominent man on some phase of the event. Sometimes the event is of such importance that the editor wishes to print the opinions of several men on the subject; or more than one prominent man may be involved in the affair and the public may wish to hear the opinions of every one involved. In such a case when several men are interviewed in regard to the same event it is considered rather useless and ineffective to print their interviews separately and the several interview stories are gathered together into one story and arranged in such a way that they may be compared. There are several ways of doing this.

# GETTING THE SCOOP

If the case or event is very well known, a lead or summary of the several interviews is considered unnecessary and the words of the various men are grouped together under a single headline. This may be illustrated by the interviews that were printed after the confessions of the McNamara brothers of Los Angeles in the recent dynamiting case. The *Wisconsin State Journal* may be taken as representative. This paper printed the statements of twelve prominent men interested in the case in a three-column box under a long head; thus:

> =Leaders Discuss the Case= Samuel Gompers, president American Federation of Labor--I am astounded; I am astounded; my credulity has been imposed upon. It is a bolt out of a clear sky. * * * * * * John T. Smith, president Missouri Federation of Labor--I can not believe it. But if the McNamaras blew up the Times building they should be fully punished. * * * * * * Gen. Harrison Grey Otis, publisher of the Times--The result may be and ought to be, etc.

If the case had not been of such broad interest a lead embodying a summary of the interviews might have preceded the individual statements. It might have been done in this way:

> Great surprise has been expressed by the prominent labor leaders of the country at the confession of the McNamara brothers in Los Angeles yesterday. That organized labor had no connection with the work of these men and that they should be fully punished is the consensus of opinion. Samuel Gompers, president American Federation of Labor--I am astounded; I am astounded; my credulity has been imposed upon. It is a bolt out of a clear sky. John T. Smith, president Missouri Federation of Labor--I can not believe it. Etc.

In such a story as the above, the statements are usually printed without quotation marks; each paragraph begins with a man's name, followed by a dash and what he said. The grouping together of several interviews is often done less formally. The whole thing may be written as a running story, and sometimes the names of the persons interviewed are omitted; thus:

> Proprietors of the big flower shops, the places from which blossoms are delivered in highly polished and ornate wagons, drawn by horses that might win blue ribbons, and where, in the proper season, a single rose costs three dollars, do not approve of the

> comments | |made by a dealer who recently failed. | |Among these sayings was one to the effect | |that young millionaires spend a thousand | |dollars a week on flowers for chorus | |girls who earn twelve dollars a week, and | |who sometimes take the flowers back to | |the shop to exchange them for money to | |buy food and clothes. | | | | "That's all nonsense," said one dealer. | |(This paragraph is devoted to his opinion | |on the matter.) | | | | "We have enough trouble in this | |business," said another dealer, "without | |having this silly talk given to the | |public." (This paragraph gives this | |dealer's opinion)--*New York Evening* | |*Post.* |

(Each paragraph is devoted to a single interview.)

The same paragraph may be done with more local color as in the following:

> | Chinatown feels deeply its bereavement | |in the deaths of the Empress Dowager and | |the Emperor of China. Chinatown mourns, | |but it does so in such an unobtrusive | |Oriental way that the casual visitor on | |sympathy bent may feel that his words of | |condolence would be misplaced. | | | | A reporter from this paper was assigned | |yesterday to go up to Chinatown and in as | |delicate a way as possible to gather some | |of the sentiments of appreciation of the | |merits of Kuang-hsu and his lamented aunt, | |Tzu-hsi. He was told that he might write a | |little about the picturesque though | |nevertheless sincere expressions of | |mourning that he might observe in Pell | |and Mott streets. | | | | Mr. Jaw Gum, senior partner in the firm | |of Jaw Gum & Co., importers of cigars, | |cigarettes, dead duck's eggs and Chinese | |delicatessen, of 7 Pell street, was at | |home. Mr. Gum was approached. | | | | "We would like to learn a little about | |the arrangements that are being made by | |the Chinese to indicate their sorrow at | |the deaths of their beloved rulers." | | | | "What number?" queried Mr. Gum. The | |question was repeated. | | | | "P'licyman, he know," remarked Mr. Gum | |sagely. | | | | (So on for a column with interviews and | |statements from several of Mr. Gum's | |neighbors.)--*New York Sun.* |

But this is very much like a human interest story - the reporter takes part in it - and we shall discuss that later.

# 12
# COURT REPORTING

Probably few classes of news stories present such a lack of uniformity and such a variety of treatments as the reports of court news. Legal stories belong to one of the few sorts of stories that do not tend to become systematized. But there is a reason for almost everything in a newspaper and there is also a reason for the freedom that reporters are allowed in reporting testimony. The reason in this case is probably in the fact that very rarely do two court stories possess the same sort of interest or the same news value.

We have seen that reports of speeches are printed in the daily press because our readers are interested in the content of the speech or in the man who uttered it. In the same way, our readers are interested in interviews because of the man who was interviewed, because of their content, or because of their bearing on some current event. On the other hand there is an infinite number of reasons why a court story is worth printing or why it may not be worth a line. Sometimes the interest is in the persons involved; sometimes in the significance of the decision. People may also be interested in a case because of its political or legal significance or merely because of the sensational testimony that is given. And again a very trivial case may be worth a large amount of space in the daily paper just because of its human interest - because of the pathos or humor that the reporter can bring into it. Thus the resulting reports are hard to classify. Each one depends on a different factor for its interest and each must be written in a different way so that its individual interest may be most effective. However there are general tendencies in the reporting of court news.

The news itself is comparatively easy to get. In a large city every court is watched every day by a representative of the press, either a reporter for an individual paper or for a city news gathering association. In some cities where there is no independent news gathering agency papers sometimes club together to keep one reporter at each court. The man who is on duty must watch all day long for cases that are of interest for one reason or another. Even with all this safeguarding sometimes an important case slips by the papers; often the reporter on duty considers of little interest a case that is worth columns when some paper digs into it. Every reporter however who is trying to do court reporting should learn the ordinary routine of legal proceedings; for example, the place and purpose of the pleas, the direct and cross examination of witnesses, and other legal business.

As we shall see when we begin to write court reports, it is necessary to exercise every possible trick to put interest into the story. In the actual court room all that relieves the dreary monotony of legal proceedings is an occasional bit of interesting testimony. And when the reporter tries to report a case he sometimes finds that interesting testimony is all that will lighten up the dull monotony of his story. Therefore while he is listening to a case he tries to get down verbatim a large number of the interesting questions and answers. Or if he is unable to be present he tries to get hold of the court stenographer's record to copy out bits of testimony for his account. Beyond this recording of testimony there is really little difficulty in court reporting except the difficulty of separating the interesting from the great mass of uninteresting matter.

As to the actual writing of the report of a legal trial, the one thing that the reporter must remember is that a case is seldom reported for the public's interest in the case itself. There is usually some other reason why the editor wants a half a column of it. That reason is the thing that the reporter must watch for and when he finds it he must make it the feature of his report to be embodied in the first line of the lead.

When we try to play up the most interesting feature of a court report we find that we must fall back upon the same beginnings that we used in reporting speeches and interviews. There are several possible ways of beginning such a story, depending upon the phase of the case or its testimony that is of greatest importance.

**1. Name Beginning** - The proper name beginning is very common. It is always used when any one of prominence is involved in the story or when the name, although unknown, can

# GETTING THE SCOOP

be made interesting in itself--as in a human interest story. The name is usually made the subject of the verb testified, as in this lead:

> | A. F. Law, secretary of the Temple Iron | |Company, a subsidiary company of the | |Reading Coal and Iron Company, called | |before the government investigation of | |the alleged combination of coal carrying | |roads, testified today in the Federal | |building that four roads had contributed | |$488,000 to make up the deficit of the | |Temple company during three years of coal | |strikes.--*New York Sun.* |

The name of a well-known company often makes a good beginning:

> | The Standard Oil Company sent a | |sweeping broadside into the Government's | |case yesterday at the hearing in the suit | |seeking to dissolve the Standard Oil | |Company of New Jersey under the Sherman | |anti-trust law, when witnesses began to | |tell of the character of a number of men | |the Government had placed upon the | |witness stand.--*New York Times.* |

The name of the judge himself may be used in the first line:

> | Judge Mulqueen of General Sessions | |explained today why he had sentenced two | |prisoners to "go home and serve time with | |the families." This punishment was | |imposed yesterday when both men pleaded | |drunkenness as their excuse for trivial | |offenses.--*New York Evening Post.* |

**2. Continued Case Beginning** - Many court reports begin with the name of the case when the case has been running for some time and is well known. Each individual story on such a case is just a continuation of a sort of serial story that has been running for some time and in the lead each day the reporter tries to summarize the progress that has been made in the case during the day's hearing. However each story, like a follow-up story, is written in such a way that a knowledge of previous stories is not necessary to a clear understanding:

> | The hearing yesterday in the | |Government's suit to dissolve the | |Standard Oil Company ended with a | |dramatic incident. Mr. Kellogg sought to | |show that the Standard compelled a widow, | |Mrs. Jones, of Mobile, Ala., to sell out | |her little oil business at a ruinous | |sacrifice.--*New York World.* |

In some cases this sort of a lead begins with the mere mention of the continuing of the trial:

> At the opening of the defence today in the sugar trials before Judge Martin of the United States Circuit Court, James F. Bendernagal took the witness chair in his own behalf, etc.--*New York Evening Post.*

**3. Summary Beginning** - The lead of a court report often begins with a brief summary of the result of the trial or of the day's hearing:

> What the Government has characterized as "unfair competition and discrimination" on the part of the Standard Oil Company continued to be the subject of the investigation of that corporation today before Franklin Ferris of St. Louis, referee, in the Custom House.--*New York Evening Post.*

The summary may be presented in as formal a way as the *that-*clause beginning which we used in reports of speeches:

> That the Adams' Express Company's business in New England in 1909 yielded a profit representing 45 per cent. on the investment, including real estate and, excepting real estate, a net income of more than 83 per cent., came out in the course of the hearing before the Interstate Commerce Commission, etc.--*New York Evening Post.*

**4. Direct Quotation Beginning** - A direct quotation of some striking statement made by the judge, by a lawyer, by a witness, or by any one connected with the trial may be used at the beginning of the lead. Here is a lead beginning with a quotation from the title of a case:

> "Captain Dick and Captain Lewis, Indians, for and on behalf of the Yokayo tribe of Indians, vs. F. C. Albertson, T. J. Weldon, as administrator of the estate of Charley, Indian, deceased, Minnehaha, Ollagoola, Hiawatha, Wanahana, Pocahontas, etc." So runs the title of as unusual a case as jurists, etc.--*San Francisco Examiner.*

**5. Human Interest Beginning** - The human interest beginning is a more or less free beginning which may be used in the reporting of rather insignificant cases which are of value only for the human interest in them. The beginning is capable of almost any treatment so long as it brings out the humor, beauty, or pathos of the situation. Sometimes the story begins with a rather striking summary of the unusual things that came out in the testimony, as in this case:

> | How suddenly and how radically a woman | |can exercise her inalienable prerogative | |and change her mind is shown in the | |testamentary disposition made of her | |estate by Mrs. Jennie L. Ramsay. She made | |a will on July 4 last, at 3 o'clock in | |the afternoon, leaving her property to | |her husband, and at 7 o'clock in the | |evening of the same day she made another | |will in which she took the property away | |from her husband.--*New York Times.* |

Here is an interesting illustration of the use of a trivial incident as the basis for a humorous lead:

> | Bang, an English setter dog, accused of | |biting 11-year-old Sophie Kahn, made an | |excellent witness in the City Court today | |when his owner, Hirman L. Phelps, a real | |estate dealer of the Bronx, appeared as | |defendant in a damage suit brought by the | |girl for $2,000.--*New York Evening* | |*Post.* |

The lead of a report of legal proceedings is very much like the lead of a report of a speech or an interview. It always begins with the most interesting fact in the case and briefly summarizes the result of the trial or the day's hearing. It is to be noted that the lead of such a story always includes a designation of the court in which the hearing was held and usually the name of the judge and of the case.

After the lead is finished a court report usually turns into a running story of the evidence as it was presented. This may be condensed into a paragraph, giving the reader merely the point of the day's hearing, or it may be expanded into several columns following the testimony more or less closely. In form, it is very much like the summary paragraphs in the body of a speech report. The result is usually more or less dry and reporters often resort to a means, similar to dialogue in fiction, to lighten it up. Some of the more important testimony is given verbatim interspersed with indirect summaries of the longer or less important speeches. Its presentation usually follows the ordinary rules of dialogue. Here is an extract from such a story:

> | After describing himself as a breeder | |of horses, Gideon said that he was a | |member of the Metropolitan Turf | |Association, the bookmakers' | |organization, but

had never been engaged in bookmaking. He did not know where "Eddie" Burke, "Tim" Sullivan (not the politician), or any of the other missing "bookies" could be found. "You are a member of the executive committee of the Metropolitan Turf Association?" asked Isidor J. Kresel, assistant counsel of the committee. "Yes." "Now, what did your committee do in 1908, when the anti-race track legislation was pending?" "I don't know." * * * * * "How much did you pay in 1908?" "Two hundred and fifty dollars." "To whom?" "Mr. Sullivan." "What for?" "Death assessments." Gideon said that the little he knew of the doings of the "Mets" was from conversation with the bookies. Etc., etc.--*New York Evening Post.*

Sometimes this direct testimony is given, not in the dialogue form, but as questions and answers. Thus:

In reply to other questions, Bendernagel said he ordered the office supplies, looked after the insurance on the sugar, and was responsible for the fuel, some 700 tons of coal a day. Question.--How much money was paid through your office in the course of a year? Answer.--Four million dollars. Q.--So yours was a busy office? A.--Exceedingly so. Q.--How long were the raw sugar clerks in your office? A.--About twenty years. Etc., etc.--*New York Evening Post.*

Some papers would arrange these questions and answers differently, paragraphing each speech separately as in dialogue:

Question.--Did you regulate their duties in any way? Answer.--No. Q.--Were you connected with the docks? A.--No; that was a separate department. It had its own forces, and they worked under Mr. Spitzer. He had entire charge. Etc., etc.

The court records take cognizance only of the actual words uttered in the testimony, but a newspaper reporter never fails to record any action or movement that indicates something beyond the words. Very often action is brought in merely for its human interest; thus:

"How long has it been since you have had a maid?" asked Mr. Shearn sadly. "Not for some time," she said. "Away back in 1907, I think." "What did it cost you for two rooms and bath at the Hotel Belmont, where you lived| |last year?" | | | | "About $300 a week altogether. The rooms| |cost $20 a day." | | | | There were tears in her eyes when she | |explained that she could no longer afford | |to keep up her own automobile. Etc., etc. | |--*Milwaukee Free Press.* |

This sort of dialogue is dangerous and may easily be overworked, but it is very often extremely effective. One word like "sadly," above, may convey more meaning than many lines of explanation.

\* \* \* \* \*

These quotations are usually interspersed with paragraphs which summarize the unimportant intervening testimony. The running story attempts to follow the progress of the hearing in greater or less detail, depending upon the space given to the story, just as a speech report attempts to follow a public discourse. Dry and unimportant facts are briefly summarized, interesting parts of the testimony are quoted in full. The running story is usually written while the hearing is in session or taken from a stenographic report of the hearing. After the running story has been completed, the reporter prepares a lead for the beginning to summarize the results or to play up the most significant part of the story. If the running story is short a lead of one paragraph is sufficient, but if it is long, the lead may be expanded into several paragraphs.

# 13
# SOCIAL NEWS AND OBITUARIES

The study of newspaper treatment of social news is a broad one. Every newspaper has its own system of handling social news and the general tendencies that are to be noted deal rather with the facts that are printed than with the manner of treatment. Every newspaper gives practically the same facts about a wedding but each individual newspaper has a method of its own of writing up those facts. One thing that is always true of social news reporting is that the amount of space given to social items varies inversely with the importance of the newspaper and the size of the city in which it is printed. A little country weekly or semi-weekly in a small town does not hesitate to run two columns or more on Sadie Smith's wedding. The report runs into minute details and anecdotes that all of the "Weekly's" readers know before the paper arrives. But the editor prints everything he can find or invent simply because all of his readers are more or less personally connected with the affair and are anxious to see their names in print and to read about themselves. The liberty that such an editor gives himself is of course impossible in a larger paper.

On the other hand, a daily in a city of average size would reduce such a story to a stickful and a metropolitan daily would run only a one-line announcement in the "List of marriages," unless the story was especially interesting. The same thing applies to all social stories. Some metropolitan newspapers do not run social news at all.

All of this is true because social news is governed by the same principles that regulate all news values. Unless a society event has some feature that is interesting impersonally - that is, of interest to readers who do not know the principals of the event - it is of value only as a larger or smaller number of the paper's readers are personally connected with the event. Hence in a small town where every one knows every one else, society news is of great value. In a large city a very small proportion of the readers are connected with the social items that the paper has to print and are therefore not interested in them - accordingly the newspaper either cuts them down to a minimum of space or does not run them at all.

Therefore in our study society news falls into two classes: social items that are of interest only in themselves to persons connected with the events; and big society stories or unusual social events that are of interest to readers who are not acquainted with the principals.

**1. Weddings** - The wedding story reduced to its lowest terms in a metropolitan paper consists of a one-line announcement in the list of "Marriages" or "Marriage Licenses"; thus:

| SMITH-JONES--Feb. 14, Katherine Jones | |to Charles C. Smith.--*New York Times.* |

If the paper runs a few columns of social news and the persons concerned in the wedding are of any importance socially, the wedding may be given a stickful. Such an account would confine itself entirely to names and facts and would be characterized by very decided simplicity and brevity. Usually nothing more would be given than the names and address of the bride's parents, the bride's first name, the groom's name, the place, and the name of the minister who officiated. Occasionally the name of the best man and a few other details are added, but never does the story become personal. It is interesting only to those who know or know of the persons concerned.

For example:

| SMITH-JONES | | | |The marriage of Miss Katherine M. Jones, | |elder daughter of Mr. and Mrs. Randolph | |Jones, 253 Ninth street, and Charles C. | |Smith was celebrated at 4 o'clock | |yesterday afternoon at the First Methodist| |Church, 736 Grand avenue. Rev. William | |Brown, rector of the church, performed the| |ceremony. |

It will be noted that in the above story the name of the bride is written out in full, "Miss Katherine M. Jones." Many newspapers, however, would simply give her first name, thus: "Katherine, elder daughter of Mr. and Mrs. Randolph Jones."

If the above wedding were of greater importance more details might be given. These would include the attendants, descriptions of the gowns of the bride and her attendants, the guests from out of town, music, decorations, the reception, and perhaps some of the presents. Sometimes the wedding trip and an announcement of when and where the couple will be at home are added. The above story might run on into detail something like this:

> Miss Jones, who was given in marriage by her father, wore a white satin gown trimmed with Venetian point lace, and her point lace veil, a family heirloom, was caught with orange blossoms. She carried a bouquet of white sweet peas and lilies of the valley. Miss Dorothy Jones, a sister of the bride, who was maid of honor, wore a gown of green chiffon over satin, with lingerie hat, and carried sweet peas. Douglas Jackson was the best man and the ushers were Dr. John B. Smith, Samuel Smith, Gordon Hunt, Rodney Dexter, Norris Kenny, and Arthur Johnston. A reception followed the ceremony at the home of the bride's parents.

This is probably as long a story as any average paper would run on any wedding, unless the wedding had some striking feature that would make the story of interest to readers who did not know the principals. Note in the foregoing story the simplicity and impersonal tone. There is a wealth of facts but there is no coloring. This tone should characterize every society story. A list of out-of-town guests might have been added, but as often that would be omitted. In some cases the last sentence might be followed by an announcement like this:

> The bride and bridegroom have gone on a wedding tour of the West; after April 1 they will be at home at 76 Kimbark avenue.

In this connection the young reporter should note the distinctions in meaning of the various words used in a wedding story. For instance, he should consult the dictionary for the exact use of the verbs "to marry" and "to wed" - he should know who "is married," who "is married to," and who "is given in marriage," etc. He should also know the difference between a "marriage" and a "wedding."

**2. Wedding Announcements** - Wedding announcements are run in the social columns of many papers. These items contain practically the same facts that we find in the story written after

# GETTING THE SCOOP

the wedding, except, of course, that the reporter cannot dilate on decorations, and must stick to facts. These facts usually consist of the names of the couple, the names of the bride's parents, and the time and the place of the wedding. Additionally the reporter may give the minister's name, the names of the maid of honor and of the best man, the reception or breakfast to follow, and where the couple will be at home.

> | The wedding of Miss Gladys Jones and | |Richard Smith will take place on | |Wednesday evening in All Angels' Church. | |The bride is a daughter of Mrs. Charles | |Jones, who will give a bridal supper and | |reception afterward at her home. |

There are of course many other ways to begin the announcement. "Miss Mary E. MacGuire, daughter of, etc."; "Invitations have been issued for the wedding of Miss, etc."; "One of the weddings on for Tuesday is that of Miss, etc."; "Cards are out for the wedding on Saturday of Miss, etc."; and many others. In each case the bride's name has the place of importance.

**3. Announcements of Engagements** - Announcements of engagements are usually even briefer than wedding announcements. The item consists merely of one sentence in which the young lady's mother or parents make the announcement with the name of the prospective groom.

> | Mrs. Russell D. Jones of 45 Ninth | |street announces the engagement of her | |daughter, Natalie, to John MacBaine | |Smith. |

The item may also begin "Mr. and Mrs. X. X. So-and-So announce, etc.," or simply "Announcement is made of the engagement of Miss Stella Blank, daughter of, etc."

**4. Receptions and Other Entertainments** - If a paper is to keep up in society news, it must report many social entertainments. However, such events are treated by large dailies as simply, briefly, and impersonally as possible. Such a story, like the report of a wedding, consists merely of certain usual facts. The name of the host or hostess, the place, the time, and the special entertainments are of course always included. Sometimes the occasion for the event, the guests of honor, and a description of the decorations are added, - also the names of those who assisted the hostess.

> | Mrs. James Harris Jones gave a | | reception yesterday at her home, 136 | | Fifth street, for her daughter, Miss | | Dorothy Jones. In the receiving line were | | Miss Marjorie Smith, Miss, etc. * * The | | reception was followed by an informal | | dance. |

If the event is held especially for débutantes, the fact is noted at the very start. "A number of débutantes assisted in receiving at a tea given by, etc."; "The débutantes of the winter were out in force, etc."

Such a story is usually followed by a list of guests, a list of out-of-town guests, a list of subscribers, or something of the sort. Ordinarily the list is not tabulated but is run in solid, thus:

> | The guests were: Miss Kathleen Smith, | | Miss Georgia Brown, etc. |

Very often the names are grouped together, thus:

> | The guests were: The Misses Kathleen | | Smith, Georgia Brown; Mesdames Robert R. | | Green, John R. Jones; and the Messrs. | | George Hamilton, Francis Bragg, etc. |

The number of variations in such stories is limited only by the ingenuity of the people who are giving such entertainments. But in each case the reporter learns to give the same facts in much the same order. And he gives them in an uncolored, impersonal way that makes the items interesting only to those who are directly connected with them. The story may vary from a single sentence to half a column, but it always begins in the same way and elaborates only the same details. Before trying to write up social entertainments, a reporter should always be sure of the use of the various words he employs - "chaperon," "patroness," etc. For instance, can we say that "Mr. and Mrs. Smith acted as chaperons"?

**5. Social Announcements** - Social announcements of any kind are usually, like the wedding and engagement announcements, confined to a single sentence. They tell only the name of the host and hostess, the name of the guest of honor or the occasion for the event, the time, and the place. Thus:

> | Mrs. Charles P. Jones will give a dance| | this evening at her home, 181 Nineteenth | | street, to introduce her sister, Miss | | Elsie Holt. |

A study of the foregoing sections on society stories shows how definitely a reporter is restricted in the facts that he may include in his social items - how conventional social stories have become. This very restraint in the matter of facts makes it the more necessary for a reporter to exercise his originality in the diction of social items. He must guard against the use of certain set expressions, like "officiating," "performed the ceremony," and "solemnized." While restricted in the facts that he may give, he must try to present the same old facts in new and interesting ways - he may even resort to a moderate use of "fine writing," if he does not become florid or frivolous.

**6. Unusual Social Stories** - Just as soon as any of these stories contains a feature that is of interest to the general public in an impersonal way it leaves the general class of social news and becomes a news story to be written with the usual lead. Even the presence of a very prominent name will make a news story out of a social item. For instance, the wedding of Miss Ethel Barrymore was written by many papers as a news story. On the other hand, an unusual marriage, an unusual elopement, or anything unusual and interesting in a wedding gives occasion for a news story. Here is one:

> | Because their 15-year-old daughter, | |Sarah, married a man other than the one | |they had chosen, who is wealthy, Mr. and | |Mrs. Markovits of 3128 Cedar street have | |gone into deep mourning, draped their | |home in crepe and announced to their | |friends that Sarah is | |dead.--*Philadelphia Ledger.* |

Or the story may be handled in a more humorous way, thus:

> | There is really no objection to him, | |and she is quite a nice young woman, but | |to be married so young, and to go on a | |wedding journey with $18 in their | |purses-- but Wallace Jones, student of the| |Western University, and Ruth Smith, | |student in the McKinley High School, | |decided it was too long a time to wait, | |and a nice old pastor gentleman in St. | |Joe has made them one.--*Milwaukee Free* | |*Press.* |

**7. Obituaries** - Like many other classes of newspaper stories, the obituary has developed a conventional form which is followed more or less rigidly by all the papers of the land. Every obituary follows the same order and tells the same sort of facts about its subject. It begins with a brief account of the deceased man's death, runs on through a very condensed account of the professional side of his life and ends with the announcement of his funeral or a list of his surviving relatives.

The lead is concerned only with his death, answering the usual questions about *where*, *how*, and *why*, and is written to stand alone if necessary. It ordinarily begins with the man's full name, because of course the name is the most important thing in the story, and then tells who he was and where he lived. This is followed, perhaps in the same sentence, by the time of his death, the cause, and perhaps the circumstances. Thus:

> | CAMBRIDGE, Mass., Nov. 25.--Dr. John H.| |Blank, professor of Greek at Harvard | |since 1887 and dean of the Graduate | |School since 1895, died at his home in | |Quincy street today from heart trouble. | |Professor Blank was an authority on | |classical subjects.--*New York Tribune.* |

This, as you see, might stand alone and be complete in itself. Many obituaries, however, add another paragraph after the lead in which the circumstances of the death are discussed in greater detail. Here is the second paragraph of another obituary:

> | At 8:30 tonight Mr. Blank was walking | |with his wife on the veranda of the | |Delmonte Hotel, when he suddenly gasped | |as if in great pain and fell to the | |floor. He was carried inside, but was | |dead before the physicians reached his | |bedside. Apoplexy is said to have been | |the cause. |

Next comes the account of the deceased man's life. It is told very briefly and impersonally and concerns itself chiefly with the events of his business or professional activities. It is but a catalogue of his achievements and the dates of those achievements. These facts are usually obtained from the file of biographies - called the morgue - which most newspapers keep. The account first tells when and where he was born and perhaps who his parents were. Next his education is briefly discussed. Then the chief events of his professional or business life. The date of his marriage and the maiden name of his wife are included somewhere in or at the end of this account. Usually a list of the organizations of which the man was a member and a list of the books which he had written are attached to this account. One of the foregoing obituaries continues as follows:

> | He was born in Urumiah, Persia, on | |February 4, 1852, being the son of the | |Rev. Austin H. Blank, a

missionary. He | |was graduated from Dartmouth in 1873, and| |that college awarded him the degrees of | |A. M. in 1876 and LL.D. in 1901. From | |1876 to 1878 he studied at Leipzig | |University. He was assistant professor of| |ancient languages at the Ohio | |Agricultural and Mechanical College from | |1873 to 1876, associate professor of | |Greek at Dartmouth from 1878 to 1880, | |and dean of the collegiate board and | |professor of classical philology at Johns| |Hopkins in 1886 and 1887. In 1906 and | |1907 he served as professor in the | |American School of Classical Studies in | |Athens. | | | (Then follows a list of the | |organizations of which he was a member | |and the periodicals with which he was | |connected.) | | | He married Miss Mary Blank, daughter of| |the president of Blank College, in 1879, | |and she survives him. | |-- *New York Tribune.* |

The obituary usually ends with a list of surviving relatives - especially children and very often the funeral arrangements are included. This is the last paragraph of another obituary:

| His first wife, Mary V. Blank, died in | |1872. Three years later he married Mrs. | |Sarah A. Blank, of Hightstown, N. J., who| |with four daughters, survives him. The | |funeral will be held tomorrow at 11:30 | |o'clock. The burial will be in the family| |plot in Greenwood Cemetery. |

This is the standard form of the obituary which is followed by most daily newspapers in fair-sized cities. The form is characterized by an extreme conciseness and brevity and an absolutely impersonal tone. Very rightly, an obituary is handled with a sense of the sanctified character of its subject. It offers no opportunity for fine writing or human interest; it simply gives the facts as briefly and impersonally as possible.

# 14
# SPORTING NEWS

Division of labor on the larger American newspapers has made the reporting of athletic and sporting events into a separate department under a separate editor. The pink or green sporting sheets of the big papers have become separate little newspapers in themselves handled by a sporting editor and his staff and entirely devoted to athletic news, except when padded out with left-over stories from other pages. Although on smaller papers any reporter may be called upon to cover an athletic event, in the cities such news is handled entirely by experts who are thoroughly acquainted with all phases of the athletic sports about which they write. The stories on the pink sheet enjoy the greatest unconventionality of form to be seen anywhere in the paper except on the editorial page. And yet, because athletic reporters are usually men taken from regular reporting and because the same ideas and necessities of news values govern the sporting pages, athletic stories follow, in general, the usual news story form.

One may expect to find under the head of sports almost any news that is any way connected with college, amateur, or professional athletics. The stories include accounts of baseball and football games, rowing, horse racing, track meets, boxing, and many other forms of sport, as well as any discussions or movements growing out of these sports. Many of the stories are only a few lines in length while others may cover a column or more. But in general each one has a lead which answers the questions *when? where? how? who?* and *why?* and runs along much like an ordinary news story. For, after all, even athletic stories are written to attract and to hold the reader's interest whether or not he is directly interested in the sport under discussion. Any reporter who is called upon to cover an athletic event is safe in writing his story in the usual news story form.

As it would be impossible to discuss all the various stories that come under the head of athletic news, the reporting of college football games will be taken as typical of the others. The rules that are suggested for the reporting of football games may be applied to baseball games, track meets, and other sporting events. The same principles govern all of them and the stories usually summarize results in about the same way. Football stories may be divided into three general classes: the brief summary story of a stickful or a trifle more; the usual football story of a half column or less; and the long story that may be run through a column or more, depending upon the importance of the game.

All three of these stories are alike in the general facts which they contain; they differ only in the number of minor details which they include in the elaboration of these general facts. Each one tells in the first sentence what teams were competing, the final score, when and where the game was played, and perhaps some striking feature of the game - the weather, the conditions of the field, the star players, or a sensational score. After that, with more or less expansion, each of the stories gives the essential things that the reader wants to know about the game. These consist usually of the way in which the scoring was done, a comparison of the playing of the teams, a list of the star players, the weather conditions, and the crowd. If the writing of the story includes a discussion of each of these points in more or less detail, the game will be covered in all of its essential phases. The three kinds of stories differ, from one another, not in the facts that they include, but in the length at which they expand upon these facts. One rule should be noted in the writing of all these stories or of any athletic story - avoid superlatives. To a green reporter almost every game seems to be "the most spectacular," "the most thrilling," "the hardest fought," "the most closely matched," but a broad experience is necessary to defend the use of any superlative about the game.

**1. The Brief Summary Story** - This is the little story of a stickful or less, which merely announces the result of some distant or unimportant game. Taken in its shortest form it gives only the names of the teams, the score, the time and place of the game, and perhaps a word or two of general characterization. As it is allowed to expand in length it takes up as briefly as possible the following facts in the order in which they are given: the scoring, the comparison of play, the star players or plays. It is a mere announcement of the result of the game and no more, for that is all the reader wants. The line-ups and other tables are usually omitted, and nothing is included that goes beyond this narrow purpose. Here are a few examples:

| IOWA CITY, Ia., Nov. 25.--Sensational | |end runs by McGinnis and Curry near the | |end of the final quarter of play gave | |Iowa a 6-to-0 victory over Northwestern | |here this afternoon. | | | | Fort Atkinson High School defeated | |Madison High today in the final moments | |of play when a punt by Davy, fullback | |for Madison, was blocked and the ball | |recovered behind the line, giving Fort | |Atkinson the game, 2 to 0. |

| INDIANAPOLIS, June 3.--Indianapolis | |started its at-home series today by | |defeating Kansas City, 3 to 2. Robertson | |was in fine form, striking out five men, | |permitting no one to walk and allowing | |only six hits. Score: (Tables.) |

| LAFAYETTE, Ind., June 1.--With the | |score 41 1-3 points, athletes | |representing the University of California| |won the twelfth annual meet of the | |Western Intercollegiate Athletic | |Conference Association today. | | | |Missouri was second with 29 1-3 points, | |Illinois third with 26, Chicago fourth | |with 15 and Wisconsin fifth with 12 1-2. |

**2. The Usual Football Story** - The usual report of a game is a story of a half column or less which is longer than the brief summary story and not so detailed as the long football story. This is the story that a correspondent would usually send to his paper. It is like them both in the facts that it includes and differs only in length and in manner of treatment. This story is usually divided into two parts: the introduction and the running account. The introduction, or lead, is very much like the brief summary story; in fact, the entire brief summary story might be used as the introduction of a story of this type. The second part, the running account, corresponds to the running account of the game as it will be taken up with the long football story.

The introduction of the usual athletic story always contains certain facts. The first sentence, corresponding to the lead of a news story, always gives the names of the teams, the score, the time, the place, and the most striking feature of the game. After this the plays that resulted in scores are described and the star plays or players are enumerated. Usually a comparison of the two teams, as to weight, speed, and playing, follows, and the opinion of the captain or of some coach may be included. The rest of the introduction may be devoted to the picturesque side of the game: the crowd, the cheering, the celebration, etc. All of this must be told briefly in 200 words or less. The introduction is simply the brief summary story slightly expanded. Here is a fair example (the paragraph containing the scoring has been omitted):

> Purdue triumphed over Indiana today, 12 to 5, recording the first victory for the Boilermakers over the Crimson in five years. (Omitted paragraph on scoring belongs here.) Purdue played a great game at all times Oliphant, right half-back on the Boilermaker eleven, played remarkably well and was the hardest man for the locals to handle. Baugh, Miller, Winston and Capt. Tavey also starred for Coach Hoit's men. The Lafayette rooters, 1,500 strong, rushed on the field at the close of the struggle and carried their players off the field.

This is ordinarily followed by a brief running account of the game. It does not attempt to follow every play or to trace the course of the ball throughout the entire game, as a complete running account would do. It is usually made from the detailed running account by a process of elimination so that nothing but the "high spots" of the game is left. Such an account may run from 200 to 300 words in length. At the end tables are usually printed to give the line-up and the tabulated results of the game, but these may sometimes be omitted. The following is an extract from a condensed running account:

> Again the cadets fought their way to the 10-yard line, runs by Rose and Patterson helping materially, but again Wayland held. The half ended after Wayland had kicked out of danger. In the second half St. John's outplayed Wayland throughout. The cadets by a succession of line plunges took the ball within striking distance several times, only to be held for downs or lose it on a fumble. Patterson electrified the crowd just before the third quarter ended by twice dodging through for 20-yard runs, placing the ball on the 15-yard line, where the cadets were held for downs.

**3. Long Football Story** - The third class of football story is the long detailed account. This is all that is left of the elaborate write-ups of the season's big games that were printed a few years ago and may be seen occasionally now. Ten or twenty years ago it was not unusual for an editor to run several pages, profusely illustrated, on a big eastern football game. The story was written up from every possible aspect - athletic, social, picturesque, etc. Every play was described in detail and sometimes a graphic diagram of the play was inserted. Each phase was handled by a different reporter and the whole thing was given a prominence in the paper out of all proportion with its real importance. Such a treatment of athletic news has now been very largely discarded.

The outgrowth of this elaborate treatment is the common one- or two-column account in the pink or green sporting pages. All of the various aspects of the big game are still to be seen, condensed to the smallest amount of space; and this brief account of the different aspects of the game is arranged as an introduction of a half column or less to head the running account of the game. This is the sort of story that is used to report the Yale-Harvard games and the more important middle western games. Its form has become very definitely settled and a correspondent can almost write his story of the big game by rule.

The first part of the story, called the introduction, consists of five or six general paragraphs. The material in this introduction is arranged, paragraph by paragraph, in the order of its importance. Following this is a running account of the game which may occupy a column or more, depending upon the importance of the contest. At the end is a table showing the line-up and a summary of the results.

The introduction of the big football or baseball story usually follows a very definite order. There are certain things which it must always contain: the result of the game; how the scoring was done; a characterization of the playing; the stars; the condition of the weather and the field; the crowd; etc. The reader always wishes to know these things about the game even if he does not care to read the running account. It is equally evident that the scoring is of greater interest than the crowd, and that a comparison of the teams is more important than the cheering. And so a reporter may almost follow a stereotyped outline in writing his account. A possible outline would be something like this:

**First Paragraph** - The names of the teams, the score, when and where the game was played, and perhaps some striking feature of the game. The weather may have been a significant factor, or the condition of the field; the crowd may have been exceptionally large or small, enthusiastic or uninterested; or the game may have decided a championship; some star may have been unusually prominent, or the scoring may have been done in an extraordinary way. Any of these factors, if of sufficient significance, would be played up in the first line just as the feature of an ordinary news story is played up. This paragraph corresponds to the lead of a news story and is so written. For example:

> | Playing ankle-deep in mud before a | |wildly enthusiastic gathering of football| |rooters, the gridiron warriors of Siwash | |College defeated the Tigers this | |afternoon on Siwash athletic field by the| |score of 5 to 0. |

**Second Paragraph** - Here the reporter usually tells how the scoring was done, what players made the scores, and how.

**Third Paragraph** - The next thing of importance is a comparison of the two teams. The reader wants to know how they compared in weight, speed, and skill, and how each one rose to the fight. A general characterization of the playing or a criticism may not be out of place here.

**Fourth Paragraph** - Now we are ready to tell about the individual players. Our readers want to know who the stars were and how they starred.

**Fifth Paragraph** - This brings us down near the tag end of the introduction. Very often this paragraph is devoted to the opinions of the captains and coaches on the game. Their statements, if significant, may be boxed and run anywhere in the report.

**Sixth Paragraph** - The picturesque and social side of the game comes in here. The size of the crowd, the enthusiasm, the celebration between halves or before or after the game, are usually told. This material may be of enough importance to occupy several paragraphs, but the reporter must always remember that he is writing a sporting account and not a picturesque description of a social event.

**Seventh Paragraph** - This paragraph usually begins the running account of the game.

\* \* \*

**N-th Paragraph** - This space at the end of the entire report is given to the line-ups and tabulated results of the game.

This arrangement may of course be varied, and any of the foregoing factors of the game may be of sufficient importance to be placed earlier in the story. Never, however, should the various factors be mixed together heterogeneously and written in a confused mass. Each element must be taken up separately and occupy a paragraph by itself.

The running account of the game, which follows the introduction, requires little rhetorical skill. Each play is described in its proper place and order and should be so clear that a reader could make a diagram of the game from it. It must also be accurate in names and distances as well as in plays.

Probably every individual sporting correspondent has a different way of distinguishing the players and the plays and of writing his running account. It is not an easy matter to watch a game from the press stand far up in the bleachers and be able to tell who has the ball in each play and how many yards were gained or lost. Familiarity with the teams and the individual players makes the task easier but few reporters are so favored by circumstances. They must get the names from the cheering or from other reporters about them unless they have some method of their own.

There is one method that may be followed with some success. Before the game the reporter equips himself with a table of the players showing them in their respective places as the two teams line up. It is usually impossible to tell who has the ball during any single play because the eye cannot follow the rapid passing, but it is always possible to tell who has the ball when it is downed. At the end of each play as the players line up, the reporter keeps his eye on the man who had the ball when it was downed and watches to see the position he takes in the new line-up. Then a glance at the table will tell him the man's name.

The running account is written as simply and briefly as possible. It follows each play, telling what play was made, who had the ball, and what the result was. It keeps a record of all the time taken out, the changes in players, the injuries, etc. A typical running account reads something like this:

> | Siwash advanced the ball two yards by a| |line plunge. Kelley carried the ball | |around left end for five yards to the | |Tigers' 50-yard line. The Tigers gained | |the ball on a fumble after a fake punt | |and lined up on their own 45-yard line. | |Time called. Score at end of first half, | |0 to 0. |

At the end of the running account are tables, usually set in smaller type, giving the line-up of the two teams and the tabulated results of the game. Some papers arrange the tables as follows:

|Siwash: Tigers: | | | |Smith...........left end.......Jones | | | |Brown.........left tackle......Green-Wood| | | |McCarthy.......left guard......Connor | | | |Hall (Capt.).....centre........Jacobs | | | |Etc. |

Other papers use this system which brings the opposing players together:

|Siwash: Tigers: | | | |l. e.........Smith : Williams........r. e. | | | |l. t........Brown : Jackson........r. t. | | | |l. g.....McCarthy : Cook (Capt.)...r. g. | | | |c....(Capt.) Hall : Jacobs............c. | | | |Etc. |

The tabulated results at the end may be something like this:

|Score by periods: | | | |Tigers....................0 2 1 3--6 | | | |Siwash...................0 0 0 0--0 | | | |Touchdown-- Brown. Goal from touchdown-- | |O'Brien. Umpire-- Enslley, Purdue. | |Referee--Holt, Lehigh. Field | |judge--Hackensaa, Chicago. Head | |linesman--Seymour, Delaware. Time of | |periods--fifteen minutes. |

Dispatches and stories on baseball games and track meets are usually accompanied by tables of results, similar to the above but arranged in a slightly different way. The form may be learned from any reputable sporting sheet.

# 15
# HUMAN INTEREST STORIES

In our study of newspaper writing up to this point we have been entirely concerned with forms, rules, and formulas; every kind of story which we have studied has had a definite form which we have been charged to follow. We have been commanded always to put the gist of the story in the first sentence and to answer the reader's customary questions in the same breath. Now we have come to a class of newspaper stories in which we are given absolute freedom from conventional formulas. In fact, the human interest story is different from other newspaper stories largely because of its lack of forms and rules. It does not begin with the gist of its news - perhaps because it rarely has any real news - and it answers no customary questions in the first paragraph; its method is the natural order of narrative. The human interest story stands alone as the only literary attempt in the entire newspaper and, as such, a discussion of it can hardly tell more than what it is, without any great attempt to tell how to write it. For our purposes, the distinguishing marks of the human interest story are its lack of real news value and of conventional form, and its appeal to human emotions.

The human interest story has grown out of a number of causes. Up to a very recent time newspapers have been content with printing news in its barest possible form - facts and nothing but facts. Their appeal has been only to the brain. But gradually editors have come to realize that, if many monthly magazines can exist on a diet of fiction that appeals only to the emotions, a newspaper may well make use of some of the material for true stories of emotion that comes to its office. They have realized that newsiness is not the only essential, that a story does not always have to possess true news value to be worth printing - it may be interesting because it appeals to the reader's sympathy or simply because it entertains him. Hence they began to print stories that had little value as news but, however trivial their subject, were so well written that they presented the humor and pathos of everyday life in a very entertaining way. The sensational newspapers took advantage of the opportunity but they shocked their readers in that they tried to appeal to the emotions through the kind of facts that they printed, rather than through the presentation of the facts. They did not see that the effectiveness of the emotional appeal depends upon the way in which a human interest story is written, rather than upon the story itself. Therefore they shocked their readers with extremely pathetic facts presented in the usual newspaper way, while the journals which stood for high literary excellence were able to handle trivial human interest material very effectively. Now all the newspapers of the land have learned the form and are printing effective human interest stories every day.

Another reason behind the growth of the human interest story is the curse of cynicism which newspaper work imprints upon so many of its followers. Every editor knows that no ordinary reporter can work a police court or hospital run day after day for any length of time without losing his sensibilities and becoming hardened to the sterner facts in human life. Misfortune and bitterness become so common to him that he no longer looks upon them as misfortune and misery, but just as news. Gradually his stories lose all sympathy and kindliness and he writes of suffering men as of so many wooden ten-pins. When he has reached this attitude of cynicism, his usefulness to his paper is almost gone, for a reporter must always see and write the news from the reader's sympathetic point of view. To keep their reporters' sensibilities awake editors have tried various expedients which have been more or less successful. One of these is the "up-lift run" for cub reporters - a round of philanthropic news sources to teach them the business of reporting before they become cynical. Another is the human interest story. If a reporter knows that his paper is always ready and glad to print human interest stories full of kindliness and human sympathy, he is ever on the watch for human interest subjects and consequently forces himself to see things in a sympathetic way. Thus he unconsciously wards off cynicism. The search for human interest material is a modification of the "sob squad" work of the sensational papers, on more delicate lines.

A human interest story is primarily an attempt to portray human feeling - to talk about men as men and not as names or things. It is an attempt to look upon life with sympathetic human eyes and to put living people into the reports of the day's news. If a man falls and breaks his neck, a bald recital of the facts deals with him only as an animal or an inanimate name. The fact is interesting as one item in the list of human misfortunes, but no more. And yet there are many people to whom this man's accident is more than an interesting incident - it is a very serious matter, perhaps a calamity. To his family he was everything in the world; more than a mere means of support, he was a living human being whom they loved. The bald report of his death does not consider them; it does not consider the man's own previous existence. But if we could get into the hearts of his wife and his mother and his children, we could feel something of the real significance of the accident. This is what the human interest story tries to do. It does not necessarily strive for any effect, pathetic or otherwise, but tries simply to treat the victim of the misfortune as a human being. The reporter endeavors to see what in the story made people cry and then tries to reproduce it. In the same way in another minor occurrence, he attempts to reproduce the side of an incident that made people laugh. Either incident may or may not have had news value in its baldest aspect, but the sympathetic treatment makes the resulting human interest story worth printing.

There are various kinds of human interest stories. The common ground in them all is usually their lack of any intrinsic news value. Many a successful human interest story has been printed although it contained no one of the elements of news values that were outlined earlier in this book. In fact, one of the uses of the human interest story is to utilize newspaper by-products that have no news value in themselves. Hence the human interest story has no news feature to be played up and, since it does not contain any real news, it does not have to answer any customary questions. In form it is much like a short story of fiction, since it depends on style and the ordinary rules of narration. The absence of a lead, more than any other characteristic, distinguishes the human interest story from the news story, in form. We have worked hard to learn to play up the gist of the news in our news stories; now we come to a story which makes no attempt to play up its news - in fact, it may leave its most interesting content until the end and spring it as a surprise in the last line. To be sure, most human interest stories have and indicate a timeliness. The story may have no news value but it is always concerned with a recent event and usually tells at the outset when the event occurred. Almost without exception, the examples quoted in this chapter show their timeliness by telling in the first sentence when the event occurred. So much for the outward form of the human interest story.

**1. Pathetic Story** - One of the many kinds of human interest stories is the pathetic story. Although it does not openly strive for pathos, it is pathetic in that it tells the story of a human misfortune, simply and clearly, with all the details that made the incident sad. It is the story that attempts to put the reader into the very reality of the pain and sorrow of every human life. Sometimes it makes him cry, sometimes it makes him shudder, and sometimes it disgusts him, but it always shows him misfortune as it really is. It looks down behind the outward actions and words into the hearts of its actors and shows us motives and feelings rather than facts. But just as soon as any attempt at pathos becomes evident, the story loses its effectiveness. Its only means are clear perception and absolute truthfulness. Here is an example of a pathetic human interest story taken from a daily paper:

> | Rissa Sachs' child mind yesterday | |evolved a tragic answer to the question, | |"What shall be done with the children of | |divorced parents?" | | | | She took her life. | | | | Rissa was 14 years old. The divorce | |decree that robbed her of a home was less | |than a week old. It was granted to her | |mother, Mrs. Mellisa Sachs, by Judge | |Brentano last Saturday. | | | | When the divorce case was called for | |trial Rissa found that she would be | |compelled to testify. Reluctantly she | |corroborated her mother's story that her | |father, Benjamin Sachs, had struck Mrs. | |Sachs. It was largely due to this | |testimony that the decree was granted and | |the custody of the child awarded to Mrs. | |Sachs. | | | | Then the troubles of the girl began in | |real earnest. She loved her mother dearly. | |But her father, who had been a companion | |to her as well as a parent, was equally | |dear to her. | | | | Both parents pleaded with her. Mrs. | |Sachs told Rissa she could not live | |without her. The father told the girl, in | |a conversation in a downtown hotel several | |days ago, that he would disown her unless | |she went to live with him. | | | | Every hour increased the perplexities of | |the situation for the child. She could not | |decide to give up either of her parents | |for fear of offending the other. So she | |sacrificed her own life and gave up both. | | | | Thursday evening, on returning from | |school to the Sachs home at 4529

> Racine | |avenue, Rissa talked long and earnestly | |with her mother. Then she retired to her | |room, turned on the gas and, clothed, lay | |down upon her bed to await death and | |relief from troubles that have driven | |older heads to despair. | | | | At the inquest yesterday afternoon the | |grief-stricken mother told the story of | |her daughter's difficulties. She said that | |Rissa had declared she could not live if | |compelled to give up either of her | |parents, but added that she never had | |believed it.--*Chicago Record-Herald.* |

This is a pathetic human interest story in that it attempts to give the human significance of an incident which in itself would have little news value. Perhaps, in the matter of words, there is a slight straining for pathos. The form, it will be noted, is decidedly different from that of a news story on the same incident and, although the timeliness is given in the first line, there is no attempt to present the gist of the story in a formal lead. The source of the news is indicated in the last paragraph.

**2. Humorous Story** - Another kind of human interest story is the humorous story. Its humor, like the pathos of a pathetic story, does not come from an attempt to be funny, but from the truthful presentation of a humorous incident, from the incongruity and ludicrousness of the incident itself. The writer tries to see what elements in a given incident made him laugh and then portrays them so clearly and truthfully that his readers cannot help laughing with him. The subject may be the most trivial thing in the world, not worth a line as a news story, and yet it may be told in such a way that it is worth a half-column write-up that will stand out as the gem of the whole edition. But after all the effectiveness depends upon the humor in the original subject and the truthfulness of the telling. The following humorous human interest story, which occupied a place on the front page, was built up out of an incident almost devoid of news value:

> | One of Johnnie Wilt's original ideas | |for entertaining his twin sister | |Charlotte is to build a big bonfire on | |the floor of their playroom. | | | | Johnnie, who is 4 years old, carried his | |plan into execution at the Wilt home, 2474 | |Lake View avenue, for the first time | |yesterday afternoon, with results that | |made a lasting impression upon his mind | |and the finishings of the interior of the | |house. | | | | The thing was suggested to him by a | |bonfire he saw a man build in the street. | |Charlotte hadn't seen the other fire. For | |some reason

> Charlotte's feminine mind | |refused to understand just what the fire | |was like. | | | | Consequently nothing remained for | |Johnnie to do but build a fire of his own. | |He piled all of the newspapers and | |playthings that could be found in the | |middle of the room and then applied a | |match. | | | | When the flames leaped to the ceiling, | |however, and a cloud of smoke filled the | |room, Johnnie began to doubt the wisdom of | |the move. While Charlotte ran to tell a | |maid he retreated to that haven of | |youthful fugitives--the space beneath a | |couch. | | | | The frightened maid summoned the fire | |engines and the fire was soon | |extinguished. But Mrs. Wilt discovered | |that Johnnie had disappeared. She | |telephoned to Charles T. Wilt, president | |of the trunk company that bears his name, | |and half hysterically told of the fire and | |the disappearance of Johnnie. | | | | Just then there was a scrambling sound | |from beneath the couch. Johnnie, looking | |as serious as a 4-year-old face can look, | |walked out. | | | | Mrs. Wilt seized him and, to an | |accompaniment of "I-won't-do-it-agains," | |crushed him to her bosom. Last reports | |from the Wilt home were that Johnnie had | |not yet been punished for his | |deed.--*Chicago Record-Herald.* |

The student will notice how all the facts of the story and the answers to the reader's questions are worked in here and there, how the content of a news story lead is scattered throughout the entire account.

**3. Writing the Human Interest Story** - It is one thing to be able to distinguish material for a human interest story and another to be able to write the story. The whole effectiveness of the story, as we have seen, depends upon the way it is written. Many a poorly written, ungrammatical news story is printed simply because it contains facts that are of interest, regardless of the way in which they are presented. But never is a poorly written human interest story printed; simply because the facts in it have little interest themselves and the story's usefulness depends entirely upon the presentation of the facts. Hence, the human interest story, more than any other newspaper story, must be well written. And yet there are no rules to assist in the writing of such a story. In fact, its very nature depends upon originality and newness in form and treatment.

In the first place, we cannot fall back upon the conventional lead for a beginning, because a lead would be out of place. As we have said before, the human interest story does not begin with a lead for the reason that it has no striking news content to present in the lead. In many cases the whole story depends upon cleverly arranged suspense; if the content is given in a lead at the beginning suspense is of course impossible. The human interest story has no more need of a lead than does a short story - in some ways a human interest story is very much like a short story - and a short story that gives its climax in the first paragraph would hardly be written or read. But, just like the short story, a human interest story must begin in an attractive way. In the study of short story writing almost half of the study is devoted to learning how to begin the story, on the theory that the reader is some sort of a fugitive animal that must be lassoed by an attractive and interesting beginning. The theory is of course a true one and it holds good in the case of human interest stories.

But no rules can be laid down to govern the beginning of human interest or short stories. Each story must begin in its own way - and each must begin in a different way. Some writers of short stories begin with dialogue, others with a clean-cut witticism, others with attractive explanation or description, others with a clever apology. The list is endless. This endless list is ready for the reporter who is trying to write human interest stories. But the choosing must be his own. He must select the beginning that seems best adapted to his story. As an inspiration to reporters who are trying to write human interest stories, a few beginnings clipped from daily papers are given here. Some are good and some are bad; the goodness or badness in each case depends upon individual taste. They can hardly be classified in more than a general way for originality is opposed to all classifications. They are merely suggestions.

A striking quotation or a bit of apt dialogue is commonly used to attract attention to a story. Here are some examples:

| "Burglars," whispered Mrs. Vermilye to | |herself and she took another furtive peek | |out of the windows of her rooms on the | |sixth floor of the, etc. |

| "Speaking of peanuts," observed the man | |with the red whiskers, "they ain't the | |only thing in the world what is small." | |Etc. |

| "Ales, Wines, Liquors and Cigars!" You | |see this sign in the windows of every | |corner life-saving station. But what | |would you say if you saw it blazing over | |the entrance to the Colony Club, that | |rendezvous for the little and big sisters | |of the rich at Madison avenue and | |Thirtieth street? Etc. |

# GETTING THE SCOOP

> WANTED--Bright educated lady as secretary to business man touring northwest states and Alaska: give reference, ability; age, description. Address E-640, care Bee. (7)-680 19x.
>
> The above innocent appearing want ad in *The Bee*, although alluring in its prospects to a young woman desiring a summer vacation, is the principal factor in the arrest of one M. W. Williams, etc.

A well-written first sentence in a human interest story often purports to tell the whole story, like a news story lead, and really tells only enough to make you want to read further. Here are a few examples:

> His son's suspicions and a can opener convinced Andrew Sherrer last Saturday that he had been fleeced out of $500 by two clever manipulators of an ancient "get-something-for-nothing" swindle. So strong was the victim's confidence, etc.

> There's a stubborn, unlaid ghost, a gnome, a goblin, a swart fairy at the least, who has settled down for the winter in a perfectly respectable cellar over in Brooklyn and whiles away the dismal hours of the night by chopping spectral cordwood with a phantom axe. Instead of going to board with Mrs. Pepper or another medium and being of some use in the world and having a pleasant, dim-lighted cabinet all its own, this unhappy ghost--or ghostess--is pestering Marciana Rose of 1496 Bergen street, who owns the cellar and the house over it--over both the ghost and the cellar. Etc.

> The gowk who calls up 3732 Rector today will get a splinter in his finger if he scratches his head. Nothing doing with 3732 Rector. From early morn till dewy eve Mr. Fish, Mr. C. Horse, Mr. Bass, Mr. Skate and other inmates of the aquarium will be inaccessible by 'phone. Etc.

> Under all the saffron banners and the sprawling dragons clawing at red suns over the roofs of Chinatown yesterday there was a tension of unrest and of speculation. It all had to do with the luncheon to be given to his Imperial Highness Prince Tsai Tao and the members of his staff at the Tuxedo Restaurant, 2 Doyers street, at noon to-morrow. Etc.

> | Man and wife, sitting side by side as | |pupils, was the interesting spectacle | |which provided the feature of the | |elementary night school opening last | |night. Etc. |
>
> | Two young Germans of Berlin, neither | |quite 18 years of age, had a perfectly | |uncorking time aboard the White Star | |liner Majestic, in yesterday. They were | |favorites with the smoke-room stewards. | |They learned later that man is born unto | |trouble as the corks fly upward. Etc. |
>
> | It was a long black overcoat with a | |velvet collar, big cuffed sleeves, and | |broad of shoulder, and looked decidedly | |warm and comfy. It stood in one of the | |large display windows of ----, and | |covered the deficiencies of a waxy dummy, | |who stared in a surprised sort of manner | |out into the street and appeared to be | |looking at nothing. Etc. |
>
> | The bellboys put him up to it and then | |Marcus caused a lot of trouble. Marcus is | |a parrot who has been spending the winter | |in one of the large Broadway hotels. Etc. |
>
> | Lame, old, but uncomplaining, | |remembering only his joy when a visitor | |came to him, and forgetting to be bitter | |because of the wrongs done him, meeting | |his rescuer with a wag of the tail meant | |to be joyful, a St. Bernard dog set an | |example, etc. |

Some human interest stories begin, and effectively, too, with a direct personal appeal to the reader; thus:

> | If you've never seen anybody laugh with | |his hands, you should have eased yourself | |up against a railing at the Barnum and | |Bailey circus in Madison Square Garden | |yesterday afternoon and watched a band of | |250 deaf mute youngsters, all bedecked in | |their bestest, signalling all over the | |Garden. Etc. |
>
> | If you've ever sat in the enemy's camp | |when the Blue eleven lunged its last yard | |for a touchdown and had your hair ruffled | |by the roar that swept across the | |gridiron, you can guess how 1,500 Yale | |men yelled at the Waldorf last night for | |Bill Taft of '78. Etc. |

A question is often used at the beginning of a human interest story:

> | A near-suicide or an accident. Which? | |Keeper Bean is somewhat puzzled to say | |which, but it is quite certain it will | |not be tried again. At least, Keeper Bean

| | does not think it will. | | | | But, it was a sad, sad Sunday for the | | little white-faced monkey. For hours he | | lay as dead, etc. |

Many of these stories, animal or otherwise, begin with a name:

| Long Tom, a Brahma rooster that had | | been the "bad inmate" of Jacob Meister's | | farm at West Meyersville, N. J., for | | three years, paid the penalty of his | | crimes Christmas morning when he was | | beheaded after his owner had condemned | | him to death. Bad in life, he was good in | | a potpie that day, etc. |

The beginning of a human interest story is always the most important part; just like a news story, it must attract attention with its first line. In the same way, a good beginning is something more than half done. But here the similarity between the two ends. The news story, after the lead is written, may slump in technique so that the end is almost devoid of interest; the human interest story, on the other hand, must keep up its standard of excellence to the very last sentence and the last line must have as much snap as the first. It is never in danger of losing its last paragraph and so it may be more rounded and complete; it must follow a definite plan to the very end and then stop. In this it is like the short story, although it seldom has a plot. There are no rules to help us in writing any part of the human interest story. Each attempt has a different purpose and must be done in a different way. Yet the reporter must know before he begins just exactly how he is going to work out the whole story. He must plan it as carefully as a short story. A few minutes of careful thought before he begins to write are better than much reworking and alteration after the thing is done. This applies to all newspaper writing.

Much of the effectiveness of the human interest story depends upon the reporter's style. When we try to write human interest stories we are no longer interested in facts, as much as in words. Our readers are not following us to be informed, but to be entertained. And we can please them only by our style and the fineness of our perception. Although we have been told to write news stories in the common every-day words of conversation, we are not so limited in the human interest story. The elegance of our style depends very largely upon the size of our vocabulary, and elegance is not out of place in this kind of story. Although we have been told to use dialogue sparingly in news stories, our human interest story may be composed entirely of dialogue. In fact, we are hampered by no restrictions except the restrictions of English grammar and literary composition. Although we have sought simplicity of expression before, we may now strive for subtlety and for effect; we may write suggestively and even obscurely. We are dealing with the only part of the newspaper that makes any effort toward literary excellence and only our originality and cleverness can guide us.

It is hardly necessary to repeat that one cannot write human interest stories in a cynical tone. They are a reaction against cynicism. They require one to feel keenly, as a human being, and to write sympathetically, as a human being. The reporter must see behind the facts and get the personal side of the matter - and feel it. Then he must tell the story just as he sees and feels it. Absolute truthfulness in the telling is as necessary as keen perception in the seeing. Humor must be sought through the simple, truthful presentation of an incongruous or humorous idea or situation; pathos must be sought by the truthful presentation of a pathetic picture. Just as soon as the reporter tries to be funny or to be pathetic he fails, for the reader is not looking to the reporter for fun or pathos - but to the story that the reporter is telling. That is, the story must be written objectively; the writer must forget himself in his attempt to impress the story upon his reader's mind. If the story itself is fundamentally humorous or sad and the story is clearly and truthfully told with all the details that make it humorous or sad, it cannot help being effective.

The best way to learn how to write human interest stories is to study human interest stories. Most papers print them nowadays - they can easily be distinguished by their lack of news value, and of a lead--and the finest example is just as likely to crop out in a little weekly as in a metropolitan daily.

**4. The Animal Story** - The examples printed earlier in this chapter are specimens of the truest type of human interest story because they deal with human beings. They derive their joy or sorrow from things that happen to men and women. But all the sketches that are classed as human interest stories are not so carefully confined to the limits of the title. From the original human interest story the type has grown until it includes many other things - almost any piece of copy that has no intrinsic news value. Every possible subject that may suit itself to a pathetic or humorous treatment and thus be interesting, although it has no news value, is roughly classed as a human interest story.

One of these outgrowths of the true human interest sketch is the animal story. In the large cities, the "zoo" and the parks have become a fruitful source of "news." Anything interesting that may happen to the monkeys, or the elephant, the sparrows or the squirrels in the parks, horses or dogs in the street, is used as the excuse for a human interest story. Sometimes the purpose is pathos and sometimes it is humor, but, whatever it may be, if it is clever and interesting it gets its place in the paper, a place entirely out of proportion to its true news value. The results sometimes verge very close upon nature faking, but after all they are only the result of the "up-lift" idea of looking at all life in a more sympathetic way. Several of the beginnings quoted earlier in this chapter belong to animal stories and the following is a complete one:

> | Smithy Kain was only a mongrel, | |horsemen will say, but in his equine | |heart there coursed the blood of | |thoroughbreds. | | | | Smithy Kain was killed yesterday | |afternoon, shot through the head, while | |thousands of Wisconsin fair patrons looked | |on in shuddering sympathy. | | | | It was a tragedy of the track. | | | | Owners, trainers and drivers always are | |quick to declare that no greater courage | |is known than that possessed and | |demonstrated by race horses in hard-fought | |battles on the turf, and the truth of this | |was never more strikingly brought home | |than in the death of Smithy Kain | |yesterday. | | | | With a left hind foot snapped at the | |fetlock, Smithy Kain raced around the | |track, his valiant spirit and unfaltering | |gameness keeping him up until he had | |completed the course in unwavering pursuit | |of the flying horses in front. Every jump | |meant intense agony, but he would not | |quit. Not until near the finish did his | |strength give out, and not until then was | |the pitiable truth discovered. Men used to | |exhibitions of gameness in tests that try | |the soul looked on in mute admiration as | |Smithy Kain shivered and stumbled from the | |pain that rapidly sapped his life. Women | |cried openly. | | | | Two shots from the pistol of a park | |policeman ended the life and sufferings of | |the horse that was only a mongrel, but | |who, in his equine way, was a thoroughbred | |of thoroughbreds. | | | | Smithy Kain gave to his master the best | |that his animal mind and soul possessed. | |No better memorial can be written even of | |man himself. |

**5. The Special Feature Story** - One step beyond the animal story is the special feature story. This kind of story is classed with the human interest story because it has no news value and because its only purpose is to entertain or to inform in a general way; and yet it rarely contains any human interest. There is no space in this book for a complete discussion of the special feature story - an entire volume might be devoted to the subject - but this form of story is often seen in the news columns of the daily papers and deserves a mention here. Ordinarily the special feature story is not written by reporters, although there is no reason why reporters should not use in this way many of the facts that come to them. The story usually comes from outside the newspaper office, from a contributor, from a syndicate, or from some other daily, weekly, or monthly publication; however a word or two here may suggest to the reporter the possibility of adding to his usefulness by writing such stories for his paper.

The special feature story may be almost anything. The name is used to designate timely magazine articles, timely write-ups for the Sunday edition, and timely squibs for the columns of the daily papers. The last use is the one that interests us and it interests us because it is very closely related to the human interest story. The editors usually call it a feature story because it is worth printing in spite of the fact that it has no news value. In this and in its timeliness it is like the human interest story. But it is not written for humor or pathos; its purpose is to entertain the reader. Its method is largely expository and its style may be anything; it may explain or it may simply comment in a witty way. The utilizing of otherwise useless by-products of the news is its purpose--in this it is very much like the animal story.

Subjects for feature stories may come from anywhere and may be almost anything. A very common kind of feature story is the weather story that many newspapers print every day. The weather is taken as the excuse for two or three stickfuls of print which explain and comment upon weather conditions, past, present and future. Growing out of this, there is the season story which deals with any subject that the season may suggest: the closing of Coney Island, the spring styles in men's hats, the first fur overcoat, Commencement presents, Easter eggs - anything in season. Further removed from the human interest story is the timely write-up which has no other purpose than to explain, in a more or less serious or sensible way, any interesting subject that comes to hand. The story purports not only to entertain but to inform as well. It has no news value and yet it is usually timely. Here are a few subjects selected at random from the daily papers: "He'll pay no tax on cake," explaining in a humorous way the customs methods that held up the importation of an Italian Christmas cake; "Clearing House for Brains," a description of the new employment bureau of the Princeton Club of New York; "Ideal man picked by the Barnard girl," a humorous resumé of some Barnard College class statistics; "Winning a Varsity Letter," telling what a varsity letter stands for, how it is won, and what the customs of the various colleges in regard to letters are; "Jerry Moore raises a record corn crop," telling how a fifteen-year-old boy won prizes with a little patch of corn.

These are just a few suggestions to open up to the reporter the vast field for special feature articles. To be sure, many of them are submitted by outsiders, but there is no reason why a reporter should not write these stories as well as human interest stories for his paper, since he is in the best position to get the material. Whenever a special feature story becomes too large for the daily edition there is always a possibility of selling it to the Sunday section or to a monthly magazine. The writing of special feature stories is directly in line with the reporter's work, because the ordinary method of gathering facts for a feature article and arranging them in an interesting, newsy way follows closely the method by which a reporter covers and writes a news story. Hence almost without exception the most successful magazine feature writers are, or have been, newspaper reporters.

# 16
# DRAMATIC REPORTING

Dramatic reporting is one of the most misused of the newspaper reporter's activities. To many reporters, as well as to their editors, it is just an easy way of getting free admission to the theater in return for a half column of copy. Hence it is treated in an unjustly trivial way; the reports of theatrical productions are printed most often as space fillers or as a small advertisement in return for free tickets. But after all the work is an important one and should be done only by skillful and expert hands. Dramatic reporting is included in this book, not because it is thought possible to give the subject an adequate treatment, but because theatrical reporting is a branch of the newspaper trade that may fall to the hands of the youngest reporter. In mere justice to the stage the reporter who writes up a play should know something about the real significance of what he is doing. It is much easier to tell the beginner what not to do than to tell him exactly what to do. The faults in dramatic reporting are far more evident than the virtues; and yet there are some positive things that may be said on the subject.

The first important question in the whole matter is "Who does dramatic reporting?" One would like to answer, "Skilled critics of broad knowledge and experience." But unfortunately almost anybody does it - any one about the office who is willing to give up his evening to go to the theater. To be sure, many metropolitan papers employ skilled critics to write their dramatic copy and run the theatrical news over the critic's name. Some editors of smaller papers have the decency to do the work themselves. But in most cases the work is given to an ordinary reporter - and not infrequently to the greenest reporter on the staff. Worse than that, the work is seldom given to the same reporter continuously, but is passed around among all the members of the staff. Even a green cub may learn by experience how to report plays, but if the work falls to him only once a month his training is very meager. It would seem in these days of much discussion of the theater that editors would realize the power which they have over the stage through their favorable or unfavorable criticism. But they do not, perhaps because they know little about the stage, and the appeal must be made to their reporters. Every reporter, except upon the largest papers, has the opportunity sooner or later to give his opinion on a play. In anticipation of that opportunity these few words of advice are offered.

The first requisite in dramatic criticism is a background of knowledge of the drama and the stage. To children, and to some grown people, too, the stage is a little dream world of absolute realities. Their imaginations turn the picture that is placed before them into real, throbbing life. They do not see the unreality of the art, the suggestive effects, the flimsy delusions; to them the play is real life, the stage is a real drawing room or a real wood, and they cannot conceive of the actors existing outside their parts. But the critic must look deeper; he must understand the machinery that produces the effects and he must weigh the success of the effects. He must get behind the play and see the actors outside the cast and the stage without its scenery; the dramatic art must be to him a highly technical profession. For this reason, he must know something about dramatic technique; he must have some background of knowledge. He must study the theater from every point of view, from an orchestra seat, from behind the scenes, from a peekhole in the playwright's study, and from the pages of stage history. All the tricks and effects must be evident to him. The only thing that will teach him this is constant, intelligent theater-going. He must be familiar with all of the plays of the season and with all of the prominent plays of all seasons. A child cannot criticize the first play that he sees because he has nothing with which to compare it. In the same way a reporter cannot justly judge any kind of play until he has seen another of the same kind with which to compare it. Hence he must know many plays and must know something about the history of the theater. Dramatic criticism is relative and the critic must have a basis for his comparison.

This background of knowledge may seem a difficult thing to acquire. It is; and it can best be acquired by watching many plays with an eye for the technique of the art. The critic may judge a play from its effect upon him, but his judgment will be superficial. He must try to see what the playwright is trying to do, how well he succeeds, what tricks he employs. He must judge the work of the stage carpenter and of the costumer. He must try to realize what problem the leading lady has to face and how well she solves it. The same carefulness of judgment must be given to each member of the cast. Only when the critic is able to see past the footlights and to understand the technique of the art, can he judge intelligently. And as his judgment can be at best only relative, he must have a background of many plays and much stage knowledge upon which to base his estimate of any one production.

The ideal criticism, based upon this background of knowledge, would be absolutely fair and unprejudiced. But unfortunately this ideal cannot always be followed. Much dramatic criticism is colored by the policy of the paper that prints it. Very few critics are so fortunate as to be able to say exactly what they think about a play; they must say what the editor wants them to say. Some theatrical copy, especially write-ups of vaudeville shows, is paid for and must contain nothing but praise. Sometimes it is necessary to praise the poorest production simply because the paper is receiving so much a column for the praise. In many other cases, when the copy is not paid for, the editor often considers it only fair to give the production a little puff in return for the free press tickets. And so a large share of any reporter's dramatic criticism is reduced to selecting things that he can praise. Yet, one cannot praise in a way that is too evident; he cannot simply say "The play was good; the staging was good; the acting was good; in fact, everything was good." He must praise more cleverly and give his copy the appearance of honest criticism. Perhaps the principle is wrong, but nevertheless it exists and happy is the dramatic critic whose paper allows him to say exactly what he thinks. However, whether one may say what he thinks or must say what his editor wants him to say, he must have as his background a thorough knowledge of the stage upon which he may base a comparison or a contrast and with which he may make intelligent statements. The following illustrates what may be done with a paid report of a mediocre vaudeville show in which every act must be praised - the report was written on Monday of a week's run and is intended to induce people to see the show:

> | This week's bill at ---- Vaudeville | |Theatre is dashed onto the boards by a | |very exciting act, "The Flying Martins," | |whose thrilling tricks put the audience | |in a proper state of mind for the | |sparkling and laughable program that | |follows--a state of mind that keeps its | |high pitch without a break or let-down to | |the very end of Dr. Herman's | |side-splitting electrical pranks.

> This man, who has truly "tamed electricity," does many remarkable things with his big coils and high voltage currents and plays many extremely funny tricks upon his row of "unsuspecting-handsome" young volunteers. The musical little playlet, "The Barn Dance," is very jokingly carried off by its Jack-of-all-Trades, "Zeke," the constable, and its pretty little ensemble song, "I'll Build a Nest for You." Many a young husband can get pointers on "home rule" from "Baseballitis;" it is a mighty good presentation of the "My Hero" theme in actual life. Hilda Hawthorne gives us some high-class ventriloquism with a good puppet song that is truly wonderful. There's a lot of good music, very good music in the sketch executed by "The Three Vagrants," as well as a lot of fun; one can hardly realize what an amount of melody an old accordion contains. Audrey Pringle and George Whiting have a hit that is sparkling with quick changes from Irish love songs to bull frog croaking with Italian variations.

For the purpose of a more complete study of the subject, however, we shall consider only dramatic criticism that is not restricted by editorial dictum or by the requirements of paid-space. That is, we shall imagine that we can praise or condemn or say anything we please concerning the dramatic production which we are to report. When we look at the subject in this way there are some positive things that may be said about theatrical reporting, but there are many more negative rules, that may be reduced to mere "Don'ts." The same principles hold good in dramatic criticism that is hampered by policy, but to a less degree.

    In the first place, the one thing that a dramatic reporter must have when he begins to write his copy after the performance is some positive idea about the play, some definite criticism, upon which to base his whole report. It is impossible to write a coherent report from chance jottings and to confine the report to saying "This was good; that was bad, the other was mediocre." The critic must have a positive central idea upon which to hang his criticism. This central idea plays the same part in his report as the feature in a news story - it is the feature of his report which he brings into the first sentence, to which he attaches every item, and with which he ends his report. To secure this idea, the reporter must watch the play closely with the purpose of crystallizing his judgment in a single conception, thought, or impression. Sometimes this impression comes as an inspiration, sometimes it is the result of hard thought during or after the play. It may be concerned with the theme of the play, the playwright's work, the lines, the staging, the effects, the tricks, the acting as a whole, the acting of single persons, the music, the dancing, the costumes - anything connected with the production - but the idea must be big enough to carry the entire report and to be the gist of what the critic has to say about the play. It must be his complete, concise opinion of the performance.

When, as the critic watches the play, some idea comes to him for his report he should jot it down. As the play progresses he should develop this idea and watch for details that carry it out. There is no reason to be ashamed of taking notes in the theater and the notes will prove very useful at the office afterward. Perhaps after the play is over the critic finds that his jottings contain another idea that is of greater importance than the first; then he may incorporate the second into the first or discard the first altogether. Even after one has crystallized his judgment into a concise opinion he must elaborate and illustrate it and the program of the play is always of value in enabling one to refer definitely to the individual actors, characters, and other persons, by name. But, however complete the final judgment and the notes may be, it is always well to write the report immediately. When one leaves the theater his mind is teeming with things to say about the play, thousands of them, but after a night's sleep it is doubtful if a single full-grown idea will remain and the jottings will be absolutely lifeless and unsuggestive.

This is the positive instruction that may be given to young dramatic critics. It is so important and is unknown to so many young theatrical reporters, that it may be well to sum it up again. A dramatic criticism must be coherent; it must be unified. It must be the embodiment of a single idea about the play and every detail in the report must be attached to that idea. It is not sufficient to state the idea in a clever way; it must be expanded and elaborated with examples and reasons and must show careful thought. It is well to outline the report before it is written and to arrange a logical sequence of thought so that the result may be well-rounded and coherent.

The following is an example of a dramatic criticism in which this course is followed. It neither praises nor condemns but it points out gently wherein the play is strong or weak - and every sentence is attached to one central idea:

| A POLITE LITTLE PLAY. | | | | Never raise your voice, my dear Gerald. | |That is the only thing left to |

| distinguish us from the lower classes. | | *Lord Wynlea in "The Best People".* |

| The new comedy at the Lyric Theatre is | | written in accordance with Lord Wynlea's | | dictum quoted above. It is mannerly, well | | poised, ingratiating and deft. As a minor | | effort in the high comedy style it is | | welcome, because it affords a respite | | from the "plays with a punch" and the | | prevalent boisterous specimens of the | | work of yeomen who go at the art of | | dramatic writing with main strength. | | | | "The Best People" is by Frederick | | Lonsdale and Frank Curzen, who manifestly | | know some of them. It was done at | | Wyndham's Theatre in London, and we think | | that in a comfortable English playhouse, | | with tea between acts and leisurely | | persons with whom to visit in the foyer, | | it would make an agreeable matinee. | | Certainly it is admirably acted here, and,| | as has been intimated, its quiet drollery | | and its polite maneuvering make it a | | relief. | | | | Whether American audiences, used to | | stronger fare than tea at the theatre, | | will find it sustaining is a question that| | would seem to be answered by the | | announcement, just received from the | | Lyric, that the engagement closes next | | Saturday evening. | | | | The fable relates how the Honorable Mrs.| | Bayle discovered that her husband and Lady| | Ensworth had been flirting with peril | | during her absence in Egypt, how she | | blithely threw them much together, with | | the result that they grew intensely weary | | of each other, and how at last everybody | | concerned was happily and sensibly | | reconciled. | | | | The spirit of the piece is sane and | | "nice," the decoration of it whimsical and| | graceful. | | | | Miss Lucille Watson, embodying the | | spirit of witty mischief, gives a very | | fine performance of the part of Mrs. | | Bayle, a "smart," good woman, and Miss | | Ruth Shepley is excellent in byplay and | | flutter as a silly, good woman. | | | | Cyril Scott is graceful and vigorous as | | a philandering husband, Dallas Anderson | | comical as a London clubman with a keener | | relish in life than he is willing to | | betray, and William McVey wise, paternal | | and weighty in that kind of a part. | | | | "The Best People" is a pleasant spring | | fillip. |

The first admonition in theatrical reporting is "Don't resumé the plot or tell the story of the play." This is almost all that many dramatic reporters try to do, because it is the easiest thing to do and requires the least thought. But, after all, it is usually valueless. The story of the play does not interest readers who

# NEWSPAPER REPORTING AND CORRESPONDENCE

have already seen the play and it spoils the enjoyment of the play for those who intend to see it. The usual purpose of any theatrical report is to criticize, but a report that simply resumés the story of the play is not a criticism; hence space devoted to the story is usually wasted. To be sure, this admonition must be qualified. If the development of the critic's judgment of the play requires a resumé of the story, there is then a reason for outlining the action. However, even then, the outline should be very brief.

The following is a typical example of the usual dramatic reporting which is satisfied when it has told the story of the play. In this, the first two sentences are a very bald attempt to repay the manager for his tickets. The resumé of the story, given very obviously to fill space, is not of any critical value. The only real criticism is at the end and is inadequate because the praise is given without reason.

| Grace George and her small but | |excellent company of artists added one | |more to their long list of successful | |performances last night in the production | |of Geraldine Bonner's clever comedy of | |modern life, "Sauce for the Goose," at | |the ---- Theatre. That the moody and | |sparkling Miss George has a good claim to | |the title of America's leading | |comedienne, no one who saw the | |performance last evening could deny. In | |this piece she is cast for the part of | |Kitty Constable, who is in the third year | |of her married life and living with her | |husband in New York City. Mr. Constable | |has been engaged in writing a book on the | |emancipation of woman and as a result has | |come to neglect his pretty little wife | |and seek the companionship of a certain | |woman of great intellect, Mrs. Alloway, | |who leads him on by an affected sympathy | |with his work. He chides his wife for her | |seeming negligence of the culture of her | |mind, telling her that she lacks grey | |matter. The climax comes when Mr. | |Constable tries to get away from his wife | |on the evening of their wedding | |anniversary to dine with Mrs. Alloway. | |Kitty tries the emancipated woman idea | |and goes to the opera with another man | |and has dinner with him in his | |apartments. She lets her husband know of | |her plans and he comes to the room in a | |rage. By thus playing first on his | |jealousy and then by ridiculing his | |ideas, she wins him back to herself. The | |company was made up of artists and there | |was not a crude spot in the whole | |performance. The part of Harry Travers, | |the friend of Mrs. Constable's,

was | |excellently done by Frederick Perry, as | |was that of Mr. Constable by Herbert | |Percy. Probably the most difficult | |character in the play to portray was that | |of the "woman's rights" woman, Mrs. | |Alloway, which was most admirably done by | |Edith Wakeman. |

The word criticism must not lead the reporter to think that, as a critic, his only function is to find fault. To criticize may mean to praise as well as to condemn. If the critic is not restricted by the policy of his paper, he should be as willing to praise as to condemn, and vice versa. But whichever course he takes he must be ready to defend his criticism and to tell why he praises or why he condemns. There is always a tendency to praise a play in return for the free tickets; this should be put aside absolutely. The critic owes something to the public as well as to the manager. If the play seems to him to be bad, he must say so without hesitation and he must tell why it is bad. Too many really bad plays are immensely advertised by a critic's undefended statement that they are not fit to be seen. Had the critic given definite reasons for his condemnation, his criticism might have accomplished its purpose. In the same way it is useless to say simply that a play is good. Its good points must be enumerated and the reader must be told why it is good.

However, criticism must be written with delicacy. If your heart tells you to praise, praise; if your heart tells you to condemn, condemn with care. Remember that your condemnation may put the play off the boards or at least hurt its success, and there must be sufficient reason for such radical action. The critic's debt to the public is large, but he owes some consideration to the manager. He must hesitate before he says anything that may ruin the manager's business. Critics very often condemn a play for trivial reasons; they feel indisposed, perhaps because their dinner has not agreed with them, the play does not fit into their mood and they turn in a half column of ruinous condemnation. Perhaps they like a certain kind of production--farces, for instance - and systematically vent their ire on every tragedy and every musical comedy. They do not use perspective; they do not judge the stage as a whole. No matter how poor a play is or how much a critic dislikes it, he must consider what the stage people are trying to do and judge accordingly. In many cases it is not the individual play that deserves adverse criticism, but the kind of play. All of these things must be considered; every dramatic critic must have perspective. He must be fair to the stage people and to the public; his influence is greater than he may imagine.

No matter how strong the occasion for condemnation may be, the dramatic critic is never justified in speaking bitterly. The poor production is not a personal offense against him nor against the public. It is simply a bad or an unworthy attempt and his duty is confined to pointing how or why it is not worthy. That does not mean that he is justified in using bitter, abusive, or even sarcastic language. It is great sport to make fun of things and to exercise one's wits at some one's else expense - it is also easy - but that is not dramatic criticism. The public asks the critic to tell them calmly and fairly, even coldly, the reasons for or against a production - the reasons why they should, or should not, spend their money to see it - bitter sarcasm overreaches the mark. Just as soon as a critic tries to be personal in his remarks on a play he is exceeding his prerogative and is open to serious criticism himself.

The necessary attributes of a dramatic reporter, as we have seen, are: fairness, logical thinking, and a background of stage knowledge. And of these three, the background is of the greatest importance; it is the stimulus and the check for the other two. The more a critic can know about every phase of the theatrical profession, contemporary or historical, the better will be his criticisms. The more knowledge of the stage that his copy shows, the more greedily will his readers look for his "Theatrical News" each day. However clear his idea of a play may be he cannot express it clearly and readably without a background of other plays to refer to. And, by the same sign, a wealth of allusions and a quantity of theatrical lore will often carry a critic past many a play concerning which he is unable to form a clear opinion. To develop your ability as a dramatic reporter, watch the theatrical criticisms in reputable dailies and weeklies and learn from them.

# 17
# STYLE BOOK

*Being a copy of the Style Book compiled for the Course in Journalism of the University of Wisconsin from the style books of many newspapers.*

**1. Capitalize:-**

All proper nouns: Smith, Madison, Wisconsin.

Months and days of the week, but not the seasons of the year: April, Monday; but autumn.

The first word of every quotation, enumerated list, etc., following a colon.

The principal words in the titles of books, plays, lectures, pictures, toasts, etc., including the initial "a" or "the": "The Merchant of Venice," "Fratres in Urbe." If a preposition is attached to or compounded with the verb capitalize the preposition also: "Voting *For* the Right Man."

The names of national political bodies: House, Senate, Congress, the Fifty-first Congress.

The names of national officers, national departments, etc.: President, Vice President, Navy Department, Department of Justice (but not bureau of labor), White House, Supreme Court (and all courts), the Union, Stars and Stripes, Old Glory, Union Jack, United States army, Declaration of Independence, the (U. S.) Constitution, United Kingdom, Dominion of Canada.

All titles preceding a proper noun: President Taft, Governor-elect Wilson, ex-President Roosevelt, Policeman O'Connor.

The entire names of associations, societies, leagues, clubs, companies, roads, lines, and incorporated bodies generally: Mason, Odd Fellow, Knights Templar, Grand Lodge of Knights of Pythias, Woman's Christian Temperance Union, Wisconsin University, First National Bank, Schlitz Brewing Company (but the Schlitz brewery), Metropolitan Life Insurance Company, Chicago and Northwestern Railway Company, the Association of Passenger and Ticket Agents of the Northwest, Clover Leaf Line, Rock Island Road, Chicago Board of Trade, New York Stock Exchange (but the board of trade and the stock exchange).

The names of all religious denominations, etc.: Catholic, Protestant, Mormon, Spiritualist, Christian Science, First Methodist Church (but a Methodist church), the Bible, the Koran, Christian, Vatican, Quirinal, Satan, the pronouns of the Deity.

The names of all political parties (both domestic and foreign): Republican, Socialism, Socialist, Democracy, Populist, Free Silverite, Labor party, (but anarchist).

Sections of the country: the North, the East, South America; southern Europe.

Nicknames of states and cities: The Buckeye State, the Hub, the Windy City.

The names of sections of a city and branches of a river, etc.: the East Side, the North Branch.

The names of stocks in the money market: Superior Copper, Fourth Avenue Elevated.

The names of French streets and places: Rue de la Paix, Place de la Concorde.

Names of automobiles: Peerless, the White Steamer, Pierce Arrow.

Names of holidays: Fourth of July, Christmas, New Year's day, Thanksgiving day.

Names of military organizations: First Wisconsin Volunteers, Twenty-third Wisconsin Regiment, Second Army Corps, second division Sixth Army Corps, National Guard, Ohio State Militia, First Regiment armory, the militia, Grand Army of the Republic.

The names of all races and nationalities (except negro): American, French, Spanish, Chinaman.

The nicknames of baseball clubs: the White Sox, the Cubs.

Miscellaneous: la France, Irish potatoes, Enfield rifle, American Beauty roses.

# GETTING THE SCOOP

**2. Capitalize when following a proper noun:-** Bay, block, building, canal, cape, cemetery, church, city, college, county, court (judicial), creek, dam, empire, falls, gulf, hall, high school, hospital, hotel, house, island, isthmus, kindergarten, lake, mountain, ocean, orchestra, park, pass, peak, peninsula, point, range, republic, river, square, school, state, strait, shoal, sea, slip, theatre, university, valley, etc.: South Hall, Park Hotel, Hayes Block, Singer Building, Dewey School, South Division High School, Superior Court, New York Theatre, Beloit College, Wisconsin University, Capitol Square.

**3. Do not capitalize when following a proper name:-** Addition, avenue, boulevard, court (a short street), depot, elevator, mine, place, station, stockyards, street, subdivision, ward, etc.: Northwestern depot, Pinckney street station, Third ward, Harmony court, Amsterdam avenue, Broad street, Wingra addition, Washington boulevard, Winchester place.

**4. Capitalize when preceding a proper noun:-** All titles denoting rank, occupation, relation, etc. (do not capitalize them when they follow the noun): alderman, ambassador, archbishop, bishop, brother, captain, cardinal, conductor, congressman, consul, commissioner, councilman, count, countess, czar, doctor, duke, duchess, earl, emperor, empress, engineer, father, fireman, governor, her majesty, his honor, his royal highness, judge, mayor, motorman, minister, officer, patrolman, policeman, pope, prince, princess, professor, queen, representative, right reverend, senator, sheriff, state's attorney, sultan: Alderman John Smith (but John Smith, alderman), Senator La Follette (but Mr. La Follette, senator from Wisconsin).

The same rule applies when the following words precede a proper noun as part of a name: bay, cape, city, college, county, empire, falls, gulf, island, point, sea, state, university, etc.: City of New York, Gulf of Mexico, University of Wisconsin, College of the City of New York, College of Physicians and Surgeons.

**5. Do not capitalize:-**

The names of state bodies, etc.: the senate, house, congress, speaker, capitol, executive mansion, revised statutes. (These are capitalized only when they refer to the national government: e.g., the capitol at Madison, the Capitol at Washington.)

The names of city boards, departments, buildings, etc.: boards, bureaus, commissions, committees, titles of ordinance, acts, bills, postoffice, courthouse (unless preceded by proper noun), city hall, almshouse, poorhouse, house of correction, county hospital, the council, city council, district, precinct: e. g., the fire department, the tax committee.

Certain other governmental terms: federal, national, and state government, armory, navy, army, signal service, custom-house.

Points of the compass: east, west, north, south, northeast, etc.

The names of foreign bodies: mansion-house, parliament, reichstag, landtag, duma.

Common religious terms: the word of God, holy writ, scriptures, the gospel, heaven, sacred writings, heathen, christendom, christianize, papacy, papal see, atheist, high church, church and state, etc.

The court, witness, speaker of the chair, in dialogues.

Scientific names of plants, animals, and birds: formica rufa.

a. m., p. m., and m. (meaning a thousand); "ex-" preceding a title.

The names of college classes: freshman, sophomore.

College degrees when spelled out: bachelor of arts; but B. A.

Seasons of the year: spring, autumn, etc.

Officers in local organizations (election of officers); president, secretary, etc.

Certain common nouns formed from proper nouns: street arab, prussic acid, prussian blue, paris green, china cup, india rubber, cashmere shawl, half russia, morocco leather, epsom salts, japanned ware, plaster of paris, brussels and wilton carpets, valenciennes and chantilly lace, vandyke collar, valentine, philippic, socratic, herculean, guillotine, derby hat, gatling gun.

### 6. Punctuation:-

Omit periods after nicknames: Tom, Sam, etc.

Always use a period between dollars and cents and after per cent., but never after c, s, and d, when they represent cents, shillings, and pence: $1.23, 10 per cent., 2s 6d.

Punctuate the votes in balloting thus: Yeas, 2; nays, 3.

Punctuate lists of names with the cities or states to which the individuals belong thus: Messrs. Smith of Illinois, Samson of West Virginia, etc. If the list contains more than three names, omit the "of" and punctuate thus: Smith, Illinois; Samson, West Virginia; etc. Where a number of names occurs with the office which they hold, use commas and semicolons, thus: J. S. Hall, governor; Henry Overstoltz, mayor; etc.

Never use a colon after viz., to wit, namely, e. g., etc., except when they end a paragraph. Use a colon, dash, or semicolon before them and commas after them, thus: This is the man; to wit, the victim.

"Such as" should follow a comma and have no point after it: "He saw many things, such as men, horses, etc."

Set lists of names thus without points:

Mesdames-- George V. King Charles C. Knapp Henry A. Lloyd John H. Cole Jr.

Do not use a comma between a man's name and the title "Jr." or "Sr." as John Jones Jr.

Use the apostrophe to mark elision: I've, 'tis, don't, can't, won't, canst, couldst, dreamt, don'ts, won'ts, '80s.

Use the apostrophe in possessives and use it in the proper place: the boy's clothes, boys' clothes, Burns' poems, Fox's Martyrs, Agassiz's works, ours, yours, theirs, hers, its (but "it's" for it is). George and John's father was a good man; Jack's and Samuel's fathers were not.

Do not use the apostrophe when making a plural of figures, etc.: all the 3s, the Three Rs.

Do not use the apostrophe in Frisco, phone, varsity, bus.

Use an em dash after a man's name when placed at the beginning in reports of interviews, speeches, dialogues, etc.: John Jones--I have nothing to say. (No quotation marks.)

In a sentence containing words inclosed in parentheses, punctuate as if the part in parentheses were omitted: if there is any point put it after the last parenthesis.

Use brackets to set off any expression or remark thrown into a speech or quotation and not originally in it: "The Republican party is again in power - [cheers] - and is come to stay."

Use the conjunction "and" and a comma before the last name in a list of names, etc.: John, George, James, and Henry.

Use no commas in such expressions as 6 feet 3 inches tall, 3 years 6 months old, 2 yards 4 inches long.

Punctuate scores as follows: Wisconsin 8, Chicago 0.

Punctuate times in races, etc.: 100-yard dash--Smith, first; Jones, second. Time, 0:10 1-5.

Peters carried the ball thirty yards to the 10-yard line.

### 7. Date lines:-

Punctuate date lines as follows:

MADISON, Wis., Jan. 25.--

Do not use the name of the state after the names of the larger cities of the country, such as New York, Chicago, Boston, Philadelphia, Baltimore, San Francisco, Seattle. Abbreviate the names of months which have more than five letters.

### 8. Quoting:-

Quote all extracts and quotations set in the same type and style as the context, but do not quote extracts set in smaller type than the context or set solid in separate paragraphs in leaded matter.

Quote all dialogues and interviews, unless preceded by the name of the speaker or by "Question" and "Answer":

"I have nothing to say," answered Mr. Smith. William Smith - I have nothing to say. Question - Were you there? Answer - I was.

Quote the names of novels, dramas, paintings, statuary, operas, and songs: "The Brass Bowl," "Il Trovatore."

Quote the subjects of addresses, lectures, sermons, toasts, mottoes, articles in newspapers: "The Great Northwest," "Our Interests."

Be sure to include "The" in the quotation of names of books, pictures, plays, etc.: "The Fire King"; not the "Fire King"; unless the article is not a part of the name.

Do not quote the names of theatrical companies, as Her Atonement Company.

Do not quote the names of characters in plays, as Shylock in "The Merchant of Venice."

# GETTING THE SCOOP

Do not quote the names of newspapers. In editorials put "The Star" in italics, but in "The Kansas City Star" put "Star" in italics and use no quotation marks.

Do not quote the names of vessels, fire engines, balloons, horses, cattle, dogs, sleeping cars.

**9. Compounds and Divisions:-**

Omit the hyphen when using an adverb compounded with -ly before a participle: a newly built house.

Use a hyphen after prefixes ending in a vowel (except bi and tri) when using them before a vowel: co-exist. When using such a prefix before a consonant do not use the hyphen except to distinguish the word from a word of the same letters but of different meaning: correspondent, but co-respondent (one called to answer a summons); recreation, but re-create (to create anew) reform, but re-form (to form again); re-enforced; biennial, etc.

Do not use the hyphen in the names of rooms when the prefix is of only one syllable: bedroom, courtroom, bathroom, etc. (except blue room, green room, etc.).

When the prefix is of more than one syllable use the hyphen. Follow the same rule in making compounds of house, shop, yard, maker, holder, keeper, builder, worker: shipbuilder, doorkeeper.

In dividing at the end of a line:

Do not run over a syllable of two letters. Do not divide N. Y., M. P., LL. D., M. D., a. m., p. m., etc. Do not divide figures thus: 1,-000,000; but thus 1,000,-000. Do not divide a word of five letters or less.

**10. Figures:-**

Use figures for numbers of a hundred or over, except when merely a large or indefinite number is intended: twenty-three, 123, about a thousand, a dollar, a million, millions, a thousand to one, from four to five hundred.

Use figures for numbers of less than 100 when they are used in connection with larger numbers: There were 33 boys and 156 girls; there were 106 last week and 16 this week.

Use figures for hours of the day: at 7 p. m.; at 8:30 this morning.

Use figures for days of the month: April 30, the 22nd of May.

Use figures for ages: he was 12 years old; little 2-year-old John. If the words "2-year-old John" begin a sentence or headline, spell out the age.

Use figures for dimensions, prices, degrees of temperature, per cents., dates, votes, times in races, scores in baseball, etc.: 3 feet long, $3 a yard, 76 degrees, Jan. 14, 1906. Time of race--2:27.

Use figures for all sums of money: $24, $5.06, 75 cents.

Use figures for street numbers: 1324 Grand avenue.

Use figures for numbered streets and avenues above 99th; spell out below 100th: 123 Twenty-third avenue, 10 East 126th street.

Use figures in statistical or tabular matter; never use ditto marks.

Use figures, period, and en quad for first, second, etc.: 1.--, 2.--.

Do not begin a sentence or paragraph with figures; supply a word if necessary or spell out: At 10 o'clock; Over 300 men.

Do not use the apostrophe to form plurals of figures: the 4s, rather than the 4's.

In all texts from the Bible set the chapters in Roman numerals and the verses in figures: Matt. xxii. 37-40; I. John v. 1-15. In Sunday school lessons say Verse 5.

Say three-quarters of 1 per cent.; not 3/4 of 1 per cent.

Set tenths, hundreds, etc., in decimals: 1.1; 2.03.

## 11. Abbreviations:-

Abbreviate the following titles and no others, when they precede a name: Rev., Dr., Mme., Mlle., Mr., Mrs., Mgr. (Monsignore), M. (Monsieur).

Do not put Mr. before a name when the Christian name is given except in society news and editorials: Mr. Johnson; but Samuel L. Johnson.

Supply Mr. in all cases when Rev. is used without the Christian name: Rev. Henry W. Beecher; but Rev. Mr. Beecher.

Never use "Honorable" or the abbreviation thereof except with foreign names, in editorials, or in documents.

# GETTING THE SCOOP

Abbreviate thus: Wash., Mont., S. D., N. D., Wyo., Cal., Wis., Colo., Ind., Id., Kan., Ariz., Okla., Me. Do not abbreviate Oregon, Iowa, Ohio, Utah, Alaska, or Texas.

Abbreviate thus: Madison, Dane County, Wis.: but Dane County, Wisconsin.

Use the abbreviations U. S. N. and U. S. A. after a proper name.

Y. M. C. A., W. C. T. U., M. E. are good abbreviations.

Abbreviate names of months when preceding date only when the month contains more than five letters: Jan. 20; but April 20. When the date precedes the month in reading matter spell it out: the 13th of January; the 26th inst.

Abbreviate "Number" before figures: No. 10.

Abbreviate contract, article, section, question, answer, after the first in bills, by-laws, testimony, etc.: Section 1., Sec. 2.; Question--, Answer--, Q.--, A.--.

Do not abbreviate railway, company, the names of streets, wards, avenues, districts, etc.: Madison Street Railway Company; State street, Monona avenue.

Street and avenue are sometimes abbreviated in want-ads: State-st, Monona-av.

Spell out numbered streets and avenues up to 100th: Thirty-fourth street, 134th street.

Use & in names of firms, but use the long "and" in names of railroads. Use Etc. and not &c.; use Brothers and not Bros. (except in ads); use & only when necessary to abbreviate in stocks.

Do not abbreviate the names of political parties except in election returns, then: Dem., Rep., Soc., Lab., Ind., Pro., Un. Cit.

Put in necessary commas in abbreviating railroad names: C., M. & St. P. Ry. (Chicago, Milwaukee and St. Paul Railway); C., C., C. & St. L. R. R. (Cleveland, Cincinnati, Chicago and St. Louis Railroad).

Abbreviate without periods in market review and quotations: 25c, bu, brls, tcs, pkgs, f o b, p t, etc. Spell out centimes except when given thus: 10f 20c.

Do not abbreviate Fort and Mount: Fort Wayne, Mount Vernon.

**12. Preparation of Copy:-**

# NEWSPAPER REPORTING AND CORRESPONDENCE

Use a typewriter or write legibly; some one must read your copy.

If you write with a typewriter, double or triple space your copy; never use single space.

Don't write on more than one side of the paper.

Leave sufficient margin for corrections and leave a space at the top of the first page for headlines; leave an inch at the top of each page.

Don't put more than one story on a single sheet of paper.

Don't trust the copy-reader to fill in blanks or to correct misspelled names. If you write by hand print out proper names as legibly as possible; underscore *u* and overscore *n*.

Don't assume that the copy-reader, the proofreader, or the editor will punctuate for you, or eliminate all superfluous punctuation.

Remember that uniformity is more to be desired than a strict following of style.

Don't turn in copy without re-reading carefully and verifying all names and addresses.

Use short paragraphs; always paragraph the lead separately; indent paragraphs distinctly.

Don't write over figures or words; scratch out and rewrite.

Number your pages; when pages are inserted use letters: pages 2, 3a, 3b, 4, 5.

A circle around an abbreviation or a figure indicates that the word or number is to be spelled out. A circle around a spelled-out word or number indicates that it is to be abbreviated or run in figures.

Mark the end of your story, thus: # # #

## 13. Don'ts:-

Don't use "Honorable" or abbreviations thereof, except in extracts from speeches or documents, in editorials, or before foreign names.

Don't add final s to afterward, toward, upward, downward, backward, earthward, etc.

Don't use "signed" before the signature of a letter or document; run signature in caps.

Don't begin a sentence or paragraph with figures; insert a word before the figures or spell out.

Don't use commas in dates or in figures which denote the number of a thing, as A. D. 1908, 2324 State street, Policy 33815; in other cases use the comma, as $5,289; 1,236,400 people.

Don't forget that the following are singular and require singular verbs: sums of money, as $23 was invested; United States; anybody, everybody, somebody, neither, either, none; whereabouts, as "His whereabouts is known."

Don't forget that things OCCUR by chance or accident, and that things TAKE PLACE by arrangement.

Don't "sustain" broken legs and other injuries.

Don't "administer" punishment.

Don't confound "audiences," "spectators," and casual "witnesses."

Don't say "party" for "person."

Don't use "suicide," "loan," "scare," as verbs.

Don't use "gotten"; it is questionable; use "got."

Don't use "burglarize."

Don't use "transpire" for "occur."

Don't use "locate" for "find"; to locate a thing is to place it.

Don't use "stopped" for "stayed": He stayed at the Central Hotel.

Don't "tender" receptions nor "render" songs; use simply "give" and "sing."

Don't "put in an appearance"; just appear.

Don't use "don't" for "doesn't."

Don't use "stated" for "said."

Don't say "per day" or "per year," but "a day," "a year"; per is a Latin word and can be used only before a Latin noun, as "per diem" or "per annum."

Don't say "the meeting convened"; members might convene but a single body cannot.

Don't "claim that" anything is so; you can "claim" a thing, however.

Don't say "Mrs. Dr. Smith," just "Mrs. Smith."

Don't say "between" when more than two are mentioned.

# NEWSPAPER REPORTING AND CORRESPONDENCE

Don't use "proven" for "proved."

Don't confound "staid" with "stayed."

Don't say "different than," but "different from."

Don't split infinitives or other verbs.

Don't use "onto."

Don't use "babe" or "tot" for "baby" or "child."

Don't use superlatives when you can help it.

Don't use trite expressions or foreign words and phrases.

Don't use "corner of" in designating street location.

Don't say "died from operation," but "died after operation"--to avoid danger of libel.

Don't get the *very* habit.

Don't use "couple of" instead of "two."

Don't use Mr. before a man's full name.

Don't use slang unless it is fitting - which is seldom.

Don't mention the reporters, singly or collectively, unless it is necessary. It rarely is.

Don't qualify the word "unique"; a thing may be "unique," but it cannot be "very unique," "quite unique," "rather unique," or "more unique."

Don't use the inverted passive: e. g., "A man was given a dinner," "Smith was awarded a medal."

Don't concoct long and improper titles: Justice of the Supreme Court Smith, Superintendent of the Insurance Department Jones, Groceryman Brown. If the title is long put it after the man's name; thus: George Smith, justice of the Supreme Court.

Don't use the verb "occur" with weddings, receptions, etc.; they take place by design and never unexpectedly.

Don't say "a number of," if you can help it. Be specific.

Don't use the word "lady" for "woman," or "gentleman" for "man."

Don't say "a man by the name of Smith," but "a man named Smith."

Don't use "depot" for "station" - railway passenger station.

# APPENDIX 1
## SUGGESTIONS FOR STUDY

These Suggestions for Study embody the method used in the course in News Story Writing in the Course in Journalism of the University of Wisconsin. The text of the several chapters corresponds to the lectures that are given in preparation for, and in connection with, the study of the various kinds of news stories. These Suggestions for Study correspond to the exercises by which the students learn the application of the principles embodied in the lectures. Hence these suggestions are given mainly from the instructor's point of view; however, a slight alteration will adapt them to home or individual study. Although they give very little practice in news gathering, they enable the student to gain practice in the writing of news - in accordance with the purpose of this book. The reporter who is studying the business in a newspaper office may use them to advantage in connection with his regular work.

### *EXERCISES FOR THE FIRST CHAPTER*

1. Collect clippings of representative news stories, printed in the daily papers, to be used as models.

2. Keep a book of tips of expected news in your town or city.

3. Study news stories in your local paper and try to determine from what source the original news tip came. Try to discover from the story the routine of news gathering which furnished the facts.

4. In the same stories try to determine what persons were interviewed; frame the questions that the reporter might have asked to secure the facts. The instructor may impersonate various persons in a given news story and have the students

# NEWSPAPER REPORTING AND CORRESPONDENCE

interview him for the facts; this is to assist the student in learning to keep the point of view and to keep him from asking ridiculous questions.

5. Try to discover what stories in any newspaper are the result of actual reporting by staff reporters--point out where the others come from.

6. Notice the date line on stories that come from the outside, and learn its form.

## EXERCISES FOR THE SECOND CHAPTER

1. Watch for local stories that seem to be worth sending out; determine what element in them makes them worth sending out; calculate how far from their source they would be worth printing.

2. Study the news value of stories that are printed in the local papers; determine why they were printed. Look for the same things in stories with date lines in the local papers.

3. Determine what class of readers any given news story would interest.

4. Notice the time element (timeliness) in newspaper stories.

5. Try to determine the radius of your local paper's personal news sources: how near the printing office one must live to be worth personal mention.

6. Watch for local stories whose news value depends upon the death element, upon a prominent name, a significant loss of property, mere unusualness, human interest, or personal appeal; see what the local papers do with these stories and whether the local correspondents send them out.

7. Analyze the nature of the personal appeal in stories that are printed only for their personal appeal.

8. Notice how local reasons change the news values of local stories.

9. In any or all of these stories determine what the feature is. Distinguish between the fundamental incident which the story reports and the additional significant feature which enhances the news value of the fundamental incident.

## EXERCISES FOR THE THIRD CHAPTER

1. Run over the Style Book at the end of this book; note the essential points in newspaper style.

2. Give the principal rules for the preparation of copy.

3. Glance over the "Don'ts" in the Style Book.

## *EXERCISES FOR THE FOURTH CHAPTER*

1. Study the form and construction of news stories, especially simple fire stories.

2. Pick out the feature of each story--the additional incident in the story which increases the news value of the story itself--and see if the striking feature has been played up to best advantage.

3. Notice how the reader's customary questions--what, where, when, who, how, and why--are answered in the lead. Make a list of the answers in any given story.

## *EXERCISES FOR THE FIFTH CHAPTER*

1. Collect good fire stories appearing in the newspapers. Study the construction of the lead and the order in which the facts are presented in the body of each story.

2. Write the leads of fire stories. The chances are that actual fires will seldom occur at the time when the student wishes to study the writing of fire stories, but the instructor may give his class, orally or in writing, the facts of a fire story. He may use imaginary facts or he may take the facts from a story clipped from a newspaper--the latter method is better because it enables the instructor to show the students, after they have written their stories, just how the original story was written in the newspaper office. The facts should be given in the order in which a reporter would probably secure them in actual reporting so that the student may learn to sort and arrange the facts that he wishes to use, and to select the feature. The instructor may even impersonate different persons connected with the story and have the class interview him for the facts. This method is to be followed throughout the whole study of news story writing. (In individual study, practice may be secured from writing up imaginary or real facts.)

3. In these first fire stories, use fires that have no interest beyond the interest in the fire itself--that is, no feature. Begin the story with "Fire" and devote the lead to answering the reader's customary questions.

4. Look for newspaper fire stories that are not correctly written and reconstruct the lead according to the logic of the fire lead. That is, strive for conciseness and cut out details that do not properly belong in the lead.

5. Make a list of the reader's customary questions concerning any fire and write out the briefest possible answers. Then construct a lead to embody these answers. Determine which answer should come first and which last, according to importance.

6. Write the bodies of some of these stories. First list the facts that are to be presented and determine the order of their importance.

7. Emphasize the separateness and completeness of the two parts of the story - the lead and the body of the story. Test the leads to see if they would be clear in themselves without further explanation.

8. Strive for brevity, conciseness and clearness; wage war on all attempts at fine writing.

## *EXERCISES FOR THE SIXTH CHAPTER*

1. Study fire stories which have features - an interest beyond the mere fire itself - and see how the newspapers write them.

2. In a feature fire story of Class I., make a list of the reader's customary questions concerning the fire, as if it were a simple fire story, and a list of the answers. See if any answer is more interesting than the fire itself, or if its presence makes the story more interesting. Show that such an answer is the feature.

3. Write fire stories with features in some one of the reader's customary answers. (Class I.)

4. Study a simple fire story and try to imagine what things - properly answers to the reader's customary questions - might happen to give the fire greater news value. This will show the student how to look for the feature of a story.

5. Write the lead of any fire story in as many different ways as possible, striving in each one to play up the same feature.

6. Study a simple fire story and try to imagine what unexpected things might occur in connection with the fire which would be of greater interest than the fire itself. Show that these would be features and that they do not fall within the answers to the reader's customary questions - i. e., they are unexpected.

7. Write fire stories with features in unexpected attendant circumstances.

8. Make up lists of dead and injured; notice how the newspapers arrange and punctuate these lists.

9. Study fire stories with more than one feature. Work out the possibilities in any given fire along these lines.

10. Write fire stories in which there is more than one feature worth a place in the lead. Try various combinations in the lead to discover the happiest arrangement. Show how one of many striking features may be of so much importance as to drive the other features entirely out of the lead.

## *EXERCISES FOR THE SEVENTH CHAPTER*

1. Count the number of words in the sentences and paragraphs of representative newspaper stories.

2. Practice writing fire leads that might be printed alone without the rest of the story.

3. Take a fire lead and experiment with various beginnings to show the possibilities:

a. Noun - experiment with and without articles. b. Infinitive-- Distinguish infinitives in "to" and in "-ing." c. *That* clause. d. Prepositional phrase. e. Temporal clause. f. Causal clause. g. Others.

Show that any of these beginnings may be used in the playing up of any one feature.

4. Study how a name may overshadow an interesting story; determine when a name is worth first place in a lead. Study the practice of representative papers in this - do not hesitate to show how a paper has been illogical in beginning certain stories with an unknown name, for everything one sees in a newspaper is not ipso facto good usage in newspaper writing.

5. In students' stories, notice what the principal verb says and point out any misplaced emphasis.

# NEWSPAPER REPORTING AND CORRESPONDENCE

6. Wage war on "was the unusual experience of" and "was the fate of" in leads.

7. Try to avoid "broke out" in fire leads. Devote the space to more interesting action.

8. Cut out all useless words in students' exercises; strive for brevity. Go through a student's story and weigh the value of each word, phrase, and sentence; cut out the useless ones or try to express them more briefly. Do the same to actual newspaper stories.

9. Weigh the value of every detail introduced into a lead and cut out the unnecessary ones; relegate them to the rest of the story.

10. Wage war on all meaningless generalities; demand exactness.

11. Refer the class to the Style Book in this volume and require them to follow a uniform style. Point out the differences in style of various papers.

12. See if the bodies of students' stories mean anything without the presence of the leads. Require the body of the story to be separate and complete in itself. This need not, of course, be carried to the point of repeating addresses given in the lead.

13. Try writing a story by simply elaborating and explaining the details mentioned in the lead of the story. Determine what facts must be added.

14. See if any story can stand the loss of its last paragraph. Determine how many paragraphs it can lose without sacrificing its interest.

15. In writing the body of a fire story, list the facts that are to be told, in their logical order; thus: origin, discovery, spread, death of firemen, escapes, injuries, rescues, explosion, extinguishing of fire. Number them in the order of their importance. Try to build a story out of these by following the logical order and at the same time crowding the most interesting facts to the beginning.

16. Practice getting the facts of a story by means of interviews. The instructor may have the students determine what persons they wish to interview for the facts and the instructor may impersonate these persons in turn. The class may then write the story from the facts gained in this way without reference to the interviews. This is for selecting and arranging facts in their logical order.

17. Practice the use of dialogue in stories. Judge its effectiveness and show that in most cases it is well to avoid dialogue.

18. Practice rewriting long stories into short press dispatches of 150 words or less, considering the different news value.

## *EXERCISES FOR THE EIGHTH CHAPTER*

1. Collect clippings of other kinds of news stories.

2. In writing these other stories use the fire story as a model; the facts may be presented as they were in the fire story.

3. Study the possible features in accident stories; write accident stories with various features; make lists of dead and injured.

4. Study and write robbery stories with various features; distinguish between the various names applied to robbery and to the people who rob.

5. Study and write murder and suicide stories with various features, striving in each case to give the facts without shocking the reader. Show how the featureless murder or suicide story is very much like a featureless fire story.

6. Study and write riot, storm, flood, and other big stories.

7. In the study of police court news have the class go to the local police courts and report actual cases.

8. Send the students to report meetings. Report conferences, decisions, etc. Insist that the story begin with the gist of the report in each case and never with explanations.

9. Write stories on bulletins, catalogues, city directories, etc. Study them with reference to their timeliness and try to discover what in them has the most news value. Require the student to begin with this element of news value and to give the source (the name and date of the bulletin, etc.) in the lead.

10. Look over the daily papers and pick out news stories which bury the gist of their news and have the students rewrite the leads to play up the real news or to give greater emphasis to buried features.

## *EXERCISES FOR THE NINTH CHAPTER*

1. Collect good examples of the follow-up and the rewrite story; follow one important story through several days' editions to see how it is rewritten day by day. Examine an afternoon paper's version of a story covered in a morning paper.

2. Take any news story and work out the follow-up possibilities; imagine what the next step in the story will be.

3. On this basis, write follow-up stories and rewrite stories.

4. Write a follow-up story which, while beginning with a new feature, retells the original story.

5. Study and write follow-up stories involving fires, accidents, robberies, murders, suicides, storms (present condition), etc.

## EXERCISES FOR THE TENTH CHAPTER

1. Collect good examples of speech reports.

2. Take notes on oral speeches and write reports of varying lengths. Practice taking notes in the proper way and write the report at once - perhaps as an impromptu in class. The instructor may send his students to public lectures or read representative speeches to them in class.

3. Write reports of speeches from printed copies of the speech; that is, edit them in condensed form.

4. Take one lead and experiment with different beginnings, playing up the same idea in each case.

5. Discuss speeches to determine the newsiest and timeliest thing in the speech - the statement to be played up in the lead.

6. In the body of the report try to use as much direct quotation as possible, use complete sentence quotations, do not mix quotation and summary in the same paragraph or sentence. Study the rules regarding the use of quotation marks.

7. Have the students write running reports of speeches - that is, have them write their report as they listen to the speech and submit their report in this form. Naturally the lead must be written later.

## EXERCISES FOR THE ELEVENTH CHAPTER

1. Collect representative interview stories.

2. Have students interview various people without the aid of a note book; have them bring back quoted statements by the use of their memory. Have them interview some one who will criticize their manner and method.

3. Have a definite reason or timeliness for every interview - have the student map out a definite campaign beforehand. Try writing out the questions beforehand in shape to fill in the answers.

4. Write interview stories from the results of these attempts.

5. Begin the same interview story in various ways.

6. Write an interview story in which the feature is a denial or a refusal to speak; tell what should have been said and what the denial or refusal signifies.

7. Study the form of the body of the report (see Speech Reports).

8. Write stories which are the result of several interviews on the same subject; arrange them informally and formally.

## *EXERCISES FOR THE TWELFTH CHAPTER*

1. Collect examples of good court reports.

2. Attend and report actual cases in the local courts (preferably civil courts).

3. Determine what is the most interesting thing in each.

4. From this, write court reports - reports of the cases which the students have heard.

5. Experiment with the various beginnings for the same report.

6. Try summarizing a case in one paragraph.

7. Practice getting down testimony verbatim.

8. Practice summarizing testimony in indirect form.

9. Practice writing out the testimony in full in the various ways.

10. Write testimony with action in it for the sake of human interest.

11. Show how all of these may be combined into one good court report.

## *EXERCISES FOR THE THIRTEENTH CHAPTER*

1. Notice how various newspapers treat social news; study the reason in each case; collect examples.

2. List the facts of a wedding story; write short and long wedding stories.

3. Write wedding announcements, beginning in various ways.

4. Write engagement announcements.

5. Write up receptions, banquets, dinners, etc.; report actual functions.

6. Write announcements for the same functions.

7. Write up some unusual social story as a news story.

8. Practice writing obituaries and simple death stories with accompanying obituary. Write sketches of the lives of prominent people.

9. In these exercises use actual events as subjects.

## EXERCISES FOR THE FOURTEENTH CHAPTER

1. Study sporting stories for their material and method.

2. Report a football game or some other sporting event.

3. Make a running account of a football or baseball game.

4. Write a brief summary of the game to be sent out as a dispatch, limiting it to 150 words.

5. Write up the same game in 200-300 words; attach a condensed running account of the same length.

6. Write a long story of the same game, following the outline given in the text; attach a detailed running account by periods or innings; compile tables of players and results for the end.

7. The study of sporting news may be taken out of its logical place and studied during the baseball or football season.

## EXERCISES FOR THE FIFTEENTH CHAPTER

1. Collect human interest and newspaper feature stories.

2. Watch for material for human interest stories; look at the facts in your other news stories in a sympathetic way and see how they could be made into human interest stories.

3. Write human interest stories on facts given by the instructor and on facts discovered by the students.

4. Write animal stories, and witty comments on the weather.

5. Write up some timely local subject as a 1500-word feature story.

## EXERCISES FOR THE SIXTEENTH CHAPTER

1. Gather good theatrical reports and watch for those in which the whole report is written around a single idea.

2. At the theater watch for things to comment on; try to bring away one definite idea about the play - with illustrations.

3. Write dramatic criticisms that are the embodiment of a single idea or criticism on the play.

4. Try to point out the bad things in a play without being bitter or personal.

5. Write a half-column of copy on a vaudeville show, supposing that the copy is paid for and must praise, not only the show as a whole, but each individual act.

## EXERCISES FOR THE SEVENTEENTH CHAPTER

1. Notice the form and punctuation of the date line: MADISON, Wis., Feb. 29.--

2. Notice the writing of street addresses: 234 Grand avenue, 4167 Twenty-sixth street; 3857 138th street; (without "at").

3. Notice in the use of figures--sums of money, hours of day, ages, figures at the beginning of sentence.

4. Notice use of titles; use of Mr. before a man's name - always give a man's initials or first name the first time you mention it in any story.

# APPENDIX II
## NEWS STORIES TO BE CORRECTED

(The following stories have been prepared to illustrate some of the most usual mistakes in newspaper writing. They may be rewritten or used as exercises in copy-reading. As a class exercise, the student may revise and correct these stories *without recopying*, just as a copy-reader revises poorly written copy.)

### I

Shortly after 2:30 this morning fire broke out in a pile of old papers in the basement of the Harmony Flat building, at 1356 Congress avenue, a four-story eight-apartment structure. Two firemen were killed by a falling wall.

The fire had a good start before the janitor, Michael Jones, who sleeps in the basement, awoke. He turned in an alarm and ran through the halls awakening the occupants. The people on the two lower floors escaped in their night clothing by the stairways, but the fire spread very rapidly, the occupants of the upper floors being forced to flee down the fire escapes in the rear.

When the firemen put in an appearance, Mrs. Jeanette Huyler appeared at a third story window and called for help. An extension ladder being hoisted, she was rescued without difficulty. During the fire the wall on the east side fell and killed Fireman John Casey and Jacob Hughes; Fireman Williams Jacobs was hit on the head by a brick and seriously injured. The fire was extinguished before it spread to an adjoining three-story flat building on the west.

The firemen in searching the ruins found the body of a man who was later identified as Rupert Smithers; he was 70 and occupied a lower flat by himself. The janitor said that he was deaf and probably did not hear the warning. The three dead and injured firemen belong to Hose Co. No. 24.

Loss $50,000, fully insured.

II

The police have arrested John Johnson, 23 years old, 2367 Sixth Street, charged with murdering Mrs. Laura Buckthorn, the well-known proprietor of the Duchess Restaurant, 438 High street. He is now in the county jail.

Mrs. Buckthorn was sixty years old and the widow of one of the oldest settlers in the city.

She lived in her small cottage at 2367 Sixth Street and supported herself by means of the restaurant. John Johnson, a street car motorman occupied a room in her cottage. Mrs. Buckthorn was found dead in her bed, in a pool of blood, with two bullet holes in her head this morning. Mrs. Grady, the restaurant cook said, "I became alarmed when Mrs. Buckthorn did not appear as usual at the restaurant this morning and went to her home to find her."

Inquiry showed that Mrs. Buckthorn had drawn $250 from the First National Bank yesterday and her daughter, Mrs. J. D. Jackson, 1548 Sixth Street, says that her mother often kept such sums of money at home under the mattress of her bed. Mrs. Jackson also says that she often warned her mother against such habits. The money was not under the mattress this morning.

Further inquiry showed that John Johnson did not appear for work as usual this morning and was later found by Policeman Patrick O'Hara in the railroad yards. He had with him $223.67 and a ticket to New York. He was known to be hard up but refused to account for the money and was given a berth in the county jail.

Samuel Benson, cashier of the First National, is sure that the two 100-dollar bills which were found on Johnson are the same bills that he gave to Mrs. Buckthorn yesterday afternoon. Johnson will be given a hearing to-morrow but it is already considered certain that he is the guilty party, the evidence being so strong.

(This story may be rewritten for local use and for a dispatch.)

## III

Sparks, resulting from the grounding of an electric wire, ignited a bucket of gasolene and fired the shop of the G. W. Smith Motor Co., at 228, 232 West street last night, five automobiles valued at $5,800 being destroyed and the building being damaged to the extent of 6,200 dollars by fire.

The insulation on the wires of an extension light that Edward Flasch, one of the repair men was using became cracked, the wire grounding as a result. The sparks fell into a bucket of gasolene standing nearby and in a few minutes the entire building was ablaze. G. W. Smith, proprietor of the garage, said that he was sitting in his office at the time of the explosion and tried to put the fire out with sand but could not get the blaze under any control. He then started to run out as many machines as possible.

Six cars, valued at $9,000 were saved.

## IV

Madison, September 25th, 1912; With a loud deafening roar that violently aroused hundreds from their beds of slumber the monster gas holder occuppying the southwest corner of South Blount and Main Streets at the gasplant of the Madison Gas and Electric Company collapsed very suddenly at 6:sO a. m. this morning, and now lies partly submerged in water, a total wreck. The damage will be fully 25,000 dollars, but there will be no interruption to the service the company's excellent reserve equippment being immediately brought into action for the emergency. The cause of the explosion was at first clothed in deep mystery before the officials of the company had time to make any investigation.

However it was definitely ascertained during the morning when Mr. John W. Jackson, the secretary and treasurer of the company, being interviewed by a Daily News correspondent this morning, stated that the immense quantities of snow on the roof of the holder was primarily responsible. The weight of the snow on one side of the holder causing it to drop down broke the wheel and pushed the holder off the foundation on which it was standing. There was a momentary blaze but when the tank settled down into the reservoir below the fire went out and the awful peril from this highly dangerous source was fortunately averted.

As it was dozens of windows at the planing mill on the opposite side of the street were all left intact. In fact no damage whatsoever outside of the holder resulted from the unfortunate accident.

Two workmen, Jacob Casey and Nelson Jones, were unfortunately caught beneath the wreckage and their bodies were removed later in the morning by the fire department. The tank was full when it collapsed and that it did not scatter destruction and take more innocent lives was one of the fortunate features of the accident and a great cause for congratulation among the officials of the company today.

(This story illustrates, among other things, excessive wordiness.)


**V**

After being chased by a young woman for several blocks, a man who gave his name as John Weber, was pursued through a saloon at 11-97th street by Policeman Arthur Brown and captured on the roof of a building adjoining the saloon, where the man had hidden behind a chimney. Weber

was arrested by the policeman and is held on a charge preferred by Charles Young, a grocer at 2145 Sixth avenue, of attempting to rob Young's grocery store. According to Young, just before he closed his store for the night last evening, a young man entered the store and asked for a pound of butter. "I thought," said Young, "that the man was just married and might be a possible new customer. I started for the back of the store to open a new tub but just as I turned to go, he hit me over the head with his cane. The blow dazed me but I still had sense enough to grab him by the collar. In the fight we both fell through the glass door at the front of the store and the d--n rascal got away." A young woman, who was passing the store, seeing the fracas, screamed and started to run after the young man. She followed him until he ran into a saloon. Then she ran up to Policeman Brown, who was standing at the corner of 97th st. and Sixth-av and told him that a robber had gone into the saloon. The policeman ran into the saloon, but found the man had left by the back stairs. The policeman followed up two flights of stairs leading to the roof, on the run, where he found Weber hiding behind a chimney. Weber refused to give his address.
After watching until she saw the robber taken away in the paddy-wagon, the

doughty young woman disappeared. Her name is unknown.

## VI

A burglar dressed in a Salvation Army uniform was arrested for attempting to burglarize Walter White's home, 16 West 62nd st. at about two o'clock last night. He gave his name as Julius Woll and his address as 129 23rd ave.
The caretaker at Walter White's said he was awakened at 1 o'clock by the noise of bureau drawers opening and he at once phoned to the station. An officer came and found the would-be burglar under the bed. After considerable scuffling the man was arrested and taken to the station.
The Salvation Army denied any connection with the prisoner but the landlady at his address said he had two uniforms and always wore one. He also carried a prayer book under his arm whenever he left his room. She also said that he had resided in her house for six weeks and owed four weeks board; also that he had not been there for two weeks. Inquiry proved that he was out regularly until three or four in the morning.

## VII

The wedding of Mr. James Henry,

1463 Seventh Street, and Miss Sarah Jones, last night at the home of the bride's parents, at 316 North Johnson Street, was a brilliant success.

Fifty guests were present and the presents which they brought all but filled the parlor. After the ceremony a seven-course banquet was served until 11:30 o'clock. Miss Sadie Jones rendered "The Rosary" to the accompaniment of Mr. John Field.

The bride wore a gown of pink taffeta and carried sweet peas. The bridesmaid, Lily Swenk, was dressed in white muslin. The groom and best man, Mr. Arthur Howles, wore conventional black. Rev. Stone of the First M. E. church officiated. The groom is a promising young lawyer of this city. His bride is one of the city's leading young society woman, being deeply interested in the Womans' Suffrage League. There marriage is the result of a love affair begun at the university and is the cause of heart-felt congratulations from their friends. After a trip to the Coast, the happy couple will reside in this city.

## VIII

"What we need in our universities are sportsmen and not sports," said President G. E. Gilbert of the Western University,

# GETTING THE SCOOP

in the convocation address yesterday afternoon at four o'clock. "The sportsman plays for the game, but the sport plays for the victory."

The President continued, "Before the battle, and during the battle, the sportsman can be told from the sport." It is the actions of the man, he said, when he is in the test that determine to which class he belongs. The President summarized the various college activities and showed how the two classes of men appear in each different activity. And in each, as the President said, "you can tell the sportsman from the sport."

"I think that this, the relation between the sportsman and the sport, is the truest analogy that can be applied to human life. Life as a sea, life as a battle, life as a river in which you must always paddle your own canoe upstream, life as a hill-climbing contest--all these analogies have their weaknesses. But life as a game is a true analogy."

The President concluded with a glowing tribute to our university.

## IX

### FAULTY LEADS

Evading the police by sliding down a rope fire escape from a hotel window, Joseph Matus, charged with robbing a lumberjack of $125, escaped the police temporily only to be arrested an hour later at the Chicago, Milwaukee and St. Paul depot.

----------

Ignited by the breaking of an electric lamp, a tank of whiskey containing 7,705 gallons exploded and threw Francis Tab, 120 W. 139th St., thirty feet against the opposite wall at the E. J. Jimkons Company, 40th street this morning.

----------

Fire of unknown origin started in the big lumber yards owned by Charles Johnson at 763 Clinton Avenue, yesterday afternoon. The yards and one million feet of lumber were totally destroyed. The entire district between Mitchell street and the South River was in danger of total destruction, according to fire Chief Casey.

----------

Fire starting in a shed on West street caused the total destruction of the First Baptist church and the death of two firemen killed by falling walls. Loss $120,000.

----------

Trade war is the only probable result of the abrogation of the Russian treaty, was the statement of the Hon. Frank J. Blank, secretary of State, before a large and enthusiastic audience at the opera house last evening. 1800 people packed the building to overflowing.

----------

John Jones, a workman, who was slightly injured when a thousand pounds of powder exploded and wrecked the Three-Ex Powder mill last night, was taken to the St. James hospital.

----------

The presence of mind and coolness of Mrs. J. B. Sweeny, 758 North Street, saved little Johnny Sweeny from death last night when she caught him by the coattail and dragged him from beneath the fender of a street car. Mrs. Sweeny was dragged 50 feet by the car and taken to the St. Luke's hospital in an ambulance that was hastily summoned.

----------

Falling through a street car window without receiving so much as a bruise was the unusual experience of Michael Casey last night on Main Street. Michael was not intoxicated--so he says.

----------

Recklessly driving his automobile over the curb on Smith street, Mr. James White, who resides at 764 Smith street, was fatally hurt by a careless chauffeur, who was unable to handle his machine and skidded at the corner near Mr. White's home.

----------

At a meeting of the Sane Fourth committee in the city library last evening at seven thirty, it was decided that Smithtown must pass a law forbidding the sale and use of cannon crackers.

# REPORTING FOR THE NEWSPAPERS

BY

CHARLES HEMSTREET

# PREFACE

Experience is the best teacher for the reporter, but he must know how to go about getting the experience: must have a foundation on which to build.

This work may serve as that foundation and as a guide for those reporters who have gained their experience in a desultory way, and who therefore fail to make intelligent use of it.

It will also give an idea of what the work of the reporter really is.

# CONTENTS

PREFACE
1. REPORTING
2. WHAT IS NEWS
3. THE NEWS COLLECTED
4. THE REPORTER AT WORK
5. A NEWS STORY ANALYZED
6. EVIDENCE : HOW WRITTEN
7. BEGINNING THE STORY
8. WRITING THE DETAILS
9. CONVENTIONAL EXPRESSIONS
10. PREPARATION OF COPY

# REPORTING

Writing for the newspapers is a business; nothing more. A would-be newspaper man must serve an apprenticeship much the same as though he were to be a bookkeeper or a shoemaker. He must learn just what to write, when to write it, and how to write it Above all he must learn of the things that should not be written. He must have a style, too; a newspaper style that is like nothing else in the world of writing.

The material of the newspaper writer is always awaiting him. There is usually more than he wants. His duty is to collect it. There need be no seeking for plot. Nature, in every phase, is there ready to be "written up" for the benefit of those who do not study it for themselves at close range. The task is interesting but not easy, for the writer must dig below the surface of things to extract the interest.

Any fairly well-educated person can become a reporter. It depends upon himself whether he is ordinary or exceptional; whether he is a mere machine, commonplace and conventional, or whether he is brilliant or unusual, writing of ordinary subjects with a dash and vigor that command and hold attention.

He must be able to gather news and write it. There are many reporters esteemed of the highest class who possess these qualities only to a limited degree. A man may have ability to collect news, and yet write of it so badly that his service is imperfect. Then, on the other hand, there are poor news-gatherers who write with perfect newspaper diction when the news is collected for them. Naturally, men of both types are useful to a paper, but it is when a man can both collect the news and write it properly that he becomes in the highest degree valuable.

Success depends upon the method which the reporter pursues. If he works with a definite object in view, he will make daily progress. But if he goes ahead aimlessly he will not make much headway.

Most young men enter the newspaper business with the hope and expectation of immediately becoming famous. When a bookkeeper enters a mercantile house it is with the one idea of making his living. But it seems that the newspaper business throws forth a certain glamour. There is a fascination in the idea that one's work will stand out for the world to examine and pass upon; that boys will rush through the streets loudly calling general attention to some article that one has written.

At the very start the hope of personal fame should be abandoned. To go into the business of writing for the newspapers as a means of earning a living is well and good, but a man's name is not going to be known throughout the land simply because he writes for the papers. As a rule, he is unknown beyond a very limited circle; the reading public knows nothing of him personally, but only the paper in which his work appears.

Newspaper work often leads into literary lines, as it gives an ease of expression that might not otherwise be obtained; but other things besides actual work on the newspaper must be done before the writer can hope to be recognized.

A reporter should have an eye quick to observe detail, and a knowledge of how to write plain facts in a simple manner. Accuracy and brevity should be cultivated, and the faculty of knowing how at a moment's notice to make a great deal out of very little and a little out of a great deal.

The reporter must keep in touch with men, women, and things, if he hopes to write sympathetically. If he has been a student of human nature before going into the business, it will be a great aid to him. If not, he must become one. This should not be difficult, for he will be thrown into contact with all sorts and conditions of men, and knowledge will come to him unconsciously.

An idea prevails that the reporter has but to record what has actually happened. He has to do more than this; for he must look below the surface for the vital causes that produce conventional effects. His power to do this depends upon the depth of his knowledge of human nature.

People witnessing occurrences and afterward reading of them in the newspapers find them not always accurate in detail as they have seen them. This is because the reporter has condensed and sifted out what is of interest and elaborated upon that. If he analyzes, it is with bold sweeps and dashes, retaining the main interest and casting out the trivial.

In all news items there are certain forms that may be followed. It is well, however, not to get into the habit of writing by form, as that leads to conventionality of expression. Most reporters are conventional and therefore commonplace and uninteresting. It is a fault that should be shunned.

Some reporters never get beyond certain conventional expressions, but resort to them over and over again. In a subsequent chapter many of these expressions will be given.

# 2
# WHAT IS NEWS?

The purpose of the newspapers is to print news.

What is news? Except those who write it, there are few who really know. Even those dealing with the reporter year after year seldom are able to judge of what an editor will print and what he will not even read.

News is something more than what has happened, or is about to happen. It is more than the account of an accident or peculiar incident; an interview with a prominent person or a report of an international event. These things go to make up news, but the news idea goes deeper still and has a broader scope.

News is that which will interest humanity at large. It affects masses rather than individuals. Thus it will be seen that an international event, for example, is always news, because it interests or affects a large number of people. Naturally the greater the number of people affected the greater the value of the news.

In collecting news, the reporter takes each fact presented and examines it to see that the human interest is there, whether the matter is local or general, whether it will interest many people and to what extent it will interest.

As the reporter works day after day, this process of reasoning becomes second nature to him, and he finally appears to disregard it and jump to a conclusion at once, recognizing by instinct rather than by judgment what is news and what is not. He has served his apprenticeship when his mind can render a decision instinctively, requiring only a flash of thought.

The human interest of a story may reveal itself in many ways. There is no way in which a person can be taught to recognize it save by experience. This experience may be obtained by constant reading of the papers, analyzing each item to see just what is in the story (everything that a reporter writes, whether a paragraph or a column, is a "story"), in what manner the news has been collected and how written up. It may also be obtained by accompanying the reporter on his work and then analyzing the story he writes. Still better is actual personal work, after the fundamental ideas have been mastered.

For those who desire to gain this experience by reading the papers, certain examples are given herewith. In each instance the illustration is of the most pronounced type so that there can be no mistaking the meaning. All the extracts given in this and subsequent chapters are from stories which have actually appeared in the daily papers.

The human interest may be embodied in the unusual or unexpected circumstances surrounding some ordinary happening; something unnatural and appalling; or in a commonplace accident or incident that occurs in a peculiar manner.

When the reporter understands what news is, he can appreciate its importance. In proportion as it is important, that is, in the proportion that it will affect the greatest number of people, must it be written up in detail.

The story of a man killed by falling from a window may be worth a "stick" or a column according to the attending circumstances. Here is a case where it was worth but a few lines:

"James Egelson, a carpenter, 37 years old, while intoxicated this morning fell from a third-story window at his home, 1621 Third Avenue. His skull was fractured, and he died before medical aid could be summoned."

The man was intoxicated and while in that condition he fell. If he had been walking in his sleep, after being at work for thirty-six hours, imagining in his dream that he was continuing his work; or if he had been forced to work while his wife lay dying at home, then the story would have been worth a great deal more as it would have had more of the element of human interest. There would have been compassion for the man and

# GETTING THE SCOOP

for the wife. Whether the man was killed or not in the least injured would not make the slightest difference in the length of the story. True, there is much human interest in death always, but the frequency with which it is recorded has made it commonplace as an item of news unless surrounded by unusual circumstances. The interest in the man and wife under the possible circumstances mentioned would be far greater than the knowledge of whether they are living or dead. Of course, if the wife were to die when told of her husband's fall, that would make a difference in the length of the story, not so much because of the woman's death, but in that the human interest would be heightened.

That death is by no means the acme of human interest in the eyes of the editors was aptly shown, a short time ago, by the accounts of two fires which occurred within a few days of each other.

In one, two people were burned to death, and three others so severely injured that they were removed to a hospital where they were confined for weeks. The damage amounted to ten thousand dollars.

In the second fire not a person was injured, and the damage was only five hundred dollars.

Still, the second fire was given twice as much space as the other.

The fatal fire occurred in a dyeing establishment. It was started by an explosion of benzine in the basement, and soon cut off the escape of twenty people who worked on the upper floors. Fireman extinguished the flames and found the dead and injured in the building. This was an ordinary story, the chief interest lying in the fact that several people were burned to death. The story was given half a column.

The other story, which was given a column, was of a fire in an Italian tenement at three o'clock in the morning. The flames broke out in a room where the tenants had erected a shrine of worship. Policemen had difficulty in arousing the sleeping people and they became panic stricken. Two children failed to get out of the building by way of the stairs, and when the smoke became too dense to permit of their leaving the room, they had to be taken to the roof by firemen by means of great

## REPORTING FOR THE NEWSPAPERS

hooks. When the fire was extinguished, it was found that jewelry that had been in the shrine room was missing.

Here was a story abounding in human interest. Not only were lives endangered, but rescues were made in a novel manner.

Here is the story, as printed in The World.

# FIRE! PANIC! THEFT!

## THRILLING RESCUE OF TWO GIRLS FROM A BURNING BUILDING.

"A fire broke out at 3.30 o'clock this morning in the three-story Italian tenement at 56 Mulberry Street, and there were a number of narrow escapes from death.

"When the fire had been extinguished, it was found that in a number of rooms where the firemen had worked, considerable money and jewelry were missing.

"The tenement was once painted white, and though the paint has long since worn from the bricks, the house still stands out prominently, far better than the others in the neighborhood. The building is well known to all the people in the street, as it is the residence of Sabina Romaic, the wealthiest man in Mulberry Bend. Romalo is estimated to be worth $90,000. He has a maccaroni factory in Mott Street. He leases the tenement house, and lives in it with his wife and six children.

"On the ground floor, Francisco Carro keeps a grocery store. On the top floor, Genero Romalo, a brother of the maccaroni manufacturer, lives with Barbara, his wife, and their five children.

"In a little hall bed-room on the top floor which faces the street, the Italians have erected a shrine to St. Joseph. It is a statue of marble, which was purchased by them a year ago. Around the neck of the statue was a heavy gold chain of elaborate workmanship and curious design, and pendant from it a massive gold locket. On the pedestal, there were four gold rings. It was in this shrine room that the fire broke out from some unknown cause.

"Policeman James Donlin, who has the Mulberry Street post, from Bayard to Worth streets, saw a glare of the flames through the shutters of the little room. He blew his whistle for aid, and rushed up into the building.

"The policeman stumbled through the dark halls and up the narrow stairs, but his cries of alarm had no effect. When he got to the top floor, the flames had already burst from the room of devotion, and were eating their way along the hall. Donlin broke in the door of Genero Romaic's room. Then his great trouble began. When the family were aroused to the fact that the house was on fire, they seemed paralyzed with fear, and not one of them would leave the rooms.

"Mrs. Barbara Romaic held her seven months old child, Nicholo, in one arm, while with the other she clung to the bedpost and refused to move. The policeman used force to take the child away from her. With it he ran down the stairs, and gave it to Policeman Moore, who was on the second floor landing trying to wake the other people. In the mean time, another policeman had turned in an alarm.

The rest of the people in the house were panic-stricken. The place was filled with the wild shrieks of the maccaroni manufacturer and his family as they tried to crowd down the stairs all at once.

"Policeman Donlin went again to the top floor to urge the people there to escape. Not one of them would move. Smoke filled the top of the building, and the policeman from inhaling this became faint. He started to go down the stairs for help, when he fainted and fell to the second floor. From there he was carried down to the street by Policeman Walsh. He was unconscious for ten minutes.

"Truck No.1 was the first to arrive. The firemen immediately ran a ladder up to the window of the shrine room, from which smoke poured. By this time the fire had got to the stairway on the top floor and cut off the means of escape for the members of the Romalo family there. The people had made their way to the front, but were at windows at the other end of the house from which the ladder had been placed.

"With pale and frightened faces they looked from the window screaming for help.

"Genero Romaic stood on the windowsill and yelled to the great crowd of people below that he would jump. They motioned to him to remain where he was.

"While the firemen were getting the ladder over to the proper window, other people had got to the roof. All were taken down the ladder with the exception of two of the children, Victoria Romalo, thirteen years old, and Theresa, her sister, eighteen years. They made their way to another window, and the firemen could not get near them.

"To the people in the street, it looked as though these girls would certainly perish in the flames, when suddenly two firemen appeared at the edge of the roof, directly over the window where the girls stood crying for help.

"The firemen, lying flat on the roof, lowered a swinging ladder which they hooked into the dress of Victoria, and raised her toward the roof. For a minute the girl dangled in the air forty feet above the ground. Not a sound was heard from the people below. Then the child was landed safely on the roof, and a great shout went up. Theresa was rescued in the same manner.

"The firemen had stretched lines of hose through the house and to the roof. While some of them worked on the flames, others were endeavoring to quiet the people in the large tenement house in the rear.

"These people were panic-stricken, and had fled by means of fire-escapes and the roof in their night clothes, although the fire could not by any chance have reached them. In half an hour the flames were extinguished, after having done $500 damage.

"When the Romalos returned to their rooms, they made a startling discovery. Every piece of jewelry that had been on the statue when the fire broke out had disappeared. Genero Romalo had also left 65 cents on his table, that was gone too.

Policeman Donlin said that he had not gone into the burning room, and that nobody had gone into it but the firemen.

"While a search was being made for the jewelry, Sabine Romalo rushed out of his rooms. He also had a loss to report. He had left a pocket-book containing fifty dollars on his table, and when he returned after the fire he found the pocketbook on the floor empty. He. had left his onehundred and-fifty dollar gold watch in his vest and that was gone.

"Romalo said the firemen had been through his rooms and must have seen the pocketbook. None of the firemen would admit that they had seen the missing things. Policemen Donlin reported the various losses at

# GETTING THE SCOOP

the Elizabeth Street Station, and the captain said there would be a thorough investigation."

Now see how the reporter has gathered his facts and what use he has made of them.

First, it is interesting to know something of the building where the fire occurred, so he has told that, and also something of the principal person living there.

Local color is a great factor in a story.

Next he writes of the statue in the shrine room. Then the stolen locket, chain, and rings are described. These facts the reporter gleaned from the people in the house and neighborhood.

Then follows a description of the first sight of the flames, the trouble which the policeman had in arousing the tenants and the panic which ensued. This matter was obtained from the policeman.

Then comes the account of the work of the firemen, and of the thrilling rescue of the girls; this information being obtained from interviews with several of the firemen.

Finally there is the complete record of the missing valuables and the explanation of how the losses were reported to the police.

Firemen were believed by many to have been responsible for the loss of the jewelry, but to have stated this as a fact would have been libel. So the story is told in so far as it is positively known, and the reader is left to draw his own conclusions.

---

Sensational features always give an added news importance to a story, even though the persons involved are unknown. Thus one suicide may be worth a column, whereas another can be disposed of in four lines. This, too, when both victims are in the same circumstances.

Here is a case where a suicide was worth little space from a newspaper man's point of view :

# REPORTING FOR THE NEWSPAPERS

"Henry Bosment, a French shoemaker, 60 years old, who had been ill with consumption for some time, committed suicide yesterday in his little shop in the basement of 192 Varick Street. He shot himself in the head and died instantly. Bosment was sitting lifeless on his bench when discovered by his wife. The couple had no children."

Two weeks before, in a crowded tenement within a few blocks of Bosment's shop, there had been another suicide. The man was an Italian fruit peddler. He was if possible of less importance than Bosment, but his death was given ten times the amount of space because of its sensational features. First he took paris green. The poison not acting quickly enough, he shot himself in the head. People in the house heard the report and ran to his room on the fifth floor. He heard them coming and when they reached his room he was standing on the fire escape, and before any one could prevent him had jumped to the pavement. When picked up he was dead. There was sensation in this triple attempt at self-destruction that made it a very good story.

The unusual is of great news importance. So that when a young woman of Brooklyn twisted her hair around her neck and strangled herself to death, the story was given nearly a column.

One would think that policemen above all others would know when they came across a bit of news. But they do not, not they. No day passes but the reporter realizes this fact. When there is an accident or a murder or anything requiring the presence of the police, they will tell you everything when questioned except the news there is in it. In the matter of small accidents the police never see anything. To them nothing is news unless somebody is killed. There may be in the occurrence a story that is worth a column, but the reporter will only get at it by the most persistent questioning, and sometimes not then.

In one case of this kind the policeman told a rambling story of a suicide, commonplace and conventional. The most inexperienced reporter would have at once seen that there was nothing more than a mere mention of it necessary. As the news-gatherer was about to leave the scene, the policeman remarked casually:

"Oh, yes, and this man was building a house to-day, and it fell down."

With this clew and by dint of questioning, the reporter found that the man had been a contractor; that he had secured the contract to build a little wooden carpenter shop, and that through some carelessness on the part of his workmen the house fell. The contractor grieved so over this that he straightway went home and committed suicide by taking carbolic acid.

As the story was first told by the policeman, the man was said to be a German living alone and no one knew of any reason why he should have wished to die. The policeman went on to tell of the particular kind of acid that the man had taken, and how it would eat through an iron plate if left for a long enough time. He seemed to think this of interest, but it was commonplace enough to the reporter, as hundreds of people kill themselves every year by drinking acid. The real point of the story a man taking his life for such a comparatively trivial matter as failure in his work escaped the policeman. Yet by his casual remark he unconsciously gave the clew, though the details had to be sought elsewhere.

Court clerks, judges, politicians, men who are constantly interviewed, are equally ignorant of what news is. These in particular are mentioned, as it would seem that after years of association with reporters they would learn something of the nature of their work. The ideas of the average citizen on the subject are still more vague. Speaking with a reporter they tell him all manner of things which they are sure he would like to write about, and he often makes enemies and has to give long explanations as to why the stories they suggest will not serve as news. Sometimes they offer a story that would advertise the man who tells it and which a paper would demand two dollars a line for giving publicity. Or perhaps they see something very interesting in a distinctly local matter that would not be of the slightest importance to the general public.

The reporter must learn first of all what news is, and use discrimination in writing it up.

# 3
# THE NEWS COLLECTED

Of the great number who read daily the results of the newspaper men's work, few give thought to the labor by which the news is collected.

This may be for the very simple reason that they have no desire to know anything about it.

Those who write for the newspapers have never made any secret of their method of work, and he who runs may read; yet to many people the workings of a newspaper office seems fairly mysterious. Naturally, news is carefully guarded until publication, that the people buying the papers may receive it fresh. Interested persons who try to suppress news are often puzzled when they see the matter appear in spite of their efforts. If the manner of collecting news were more generally known the difficulty in suppressing it would be better understood.

There is a prevailing notion that the editor of the newspaper each morning calls his reporters to him and starts them out over the city with instructions to look for news and gather it in wherever they happen to find it. In reality this work is done in a very different manner and under a perfect system. Yet the public can hardly know this of themselves, as only the results of the reporter's work appear in the paper and not the process by which they are obtained.

In New York, for example, there is not the smallest portion of the city that is not "covered" at all times - in other words, that is not directly under the eye of the reporter.

One class of reporters are known as Department Men. One of these is stationed at every point where routine news comes in every day. These men are everywhere in the courts, in all public department offices, at the headquarters of police, at

# GETTING THE SCOOP

the City Hall, the exchanges, and in Wall Street. Each man is responsible for the news in his particular department and for nothing else.

Then there are the men who do general work these look after such news as arises outside of the departments.

The first duty of the day of one of the office men is to read every paper published in the city. From these are clipped announcements of all events in which there will be news and which are to occur in the future; in fact, everything of interest. The announcements for the current day are taken out, and the others are pasted in an indexed book for future reference. The day's clippings are then sorted, and each subject is given to a different "general work" man to cover. He then collects the news relating to that one subject and writes a report of it.

There is always in the office an emergency man, sometimes half a dozen, ready to be called upon at a moment's notice should anything of unusual importance arise.

So it will be seen that every man has his especial work to do, and the editor knows at every moment exactly what each man is doing.

The number of men assigned to any special task depends upon the importance of the story and the various "ends" to be covered.

Perhaps this mere outline of the manner in which the men work is enough to indicate a system which is as perfect as can be, by which the news is collected and given to the public without loss of a moment.

The various newspapers have various sources of information, and the barest hint of the existence of a story serves to send, if necessary, a dozen men to different points to trace it.

News arising from casualties is the simplest to cover.

In the case of accidents whether important, as of the falling of a house, or trivial as of a man falling and being slightly hurt, all are at once telephoned to the Headquarters of Police by the policemen. From that point the record reaches the newspaper offices in a few minutes through the reporter stationed at Headquarters, and other men are sent out to get the story in detail.

It is a good thing for a new reporter to understand in the beginning that all the work is done by assignment, and that his duty is simply to do what he is told under the directions of a general in the person of the editor who directs the movements of the entire force.

A reporter cannot have too much general information. Sooner or later he is sure to have use for anything that he may know. If a man is assigned to an interview with a prominent foreign official, he will obtain it more easily and write of it more interestingly if he understands something of foreign affairs. Of course he should know as much as possible of United States politics, as of political matters he will often be called upon to write.

As an illustration of how little the news collecting system is understood by outsiders, take the case of a young man who was anxious to become a reporter.

For several weeks he called persistently at a newspaper office seeking employment. One Saturday afternoon he was told that he would be given a trial the following Monday.

Monday morning the young man failed to appear. At five o'clock in the afternoon, however, he hurried into the office, signs of agitation upon his face and in his hand a note-book. It was found that he had been working diligently for five hours. He had started out early in the morning to "hunt for news." In the neighborhood of an engine house just before noon he had heard an alarm bell. He knew from reading the papers that fires were news, and finding that this fire was some six or seven miles uptown he jumped on a car and in course of time arrived at the point whence the alarm had been sent out. There he found that there had been a slight blaze in a basement! With great industry he secured the names of the people in the house, the number of engines that had been on hand, a description of the house itself, and a vast amount of other information.

With this he had hurried to the newspaper office to report.

There he was told that the story of that particular fire had been telephoned to the office some four hours earlier, by

# GETTING THE SCOOP

the man in whose district it had occurred and whose special duty it was to cover it.

# 4
# THE REPORTER AT WORK

As has been said, few people know what really is news. Therefore the reporter must be most persevering in order to be a successful collector of it. Those whom he may interview, even though they be ever so ready and willing to assist him, will dwell on many irrelevant subjects, and it is only by persistent questioning that he will be able to extract the real news from the torrent of words poured into his ears.

Still more persistent must he be when he interviews a person who does not wish to talk and who tries by every means to hide that which he is asked to tell. In this case the reporter has before him a difficult task, and he must not be discouraged that he is compelled to ask many questions that seem at first thought useless. He must push his investigations until he is quite sure that no one coming after him can obtain any more information than has been given to him.

The questions to be asked will, naturally, be inspired by the nature of the information desired.

A general suggestion that might well be made just here is, never use shorthand in ordinary newspaper reporting. Many a man who would otherwise have made a good reporter has remained mediocre by attempting verbatim reporting, and many a good story has for this reason been spoiled. The mind, concentrated upon the shorthand notes, is diverted from the points of the story, and that which is of the most value is overlooked. In the writing out of the story there is a mass of notes to be gone over. Besides these objections there are often times when it is impossible to take notes of any kind, and when the mere suspicion that a reporter is at hand will serve to close the channels of information." Therefore to form the habit of taking copious notes is to hamper one's self in many ways.

Take as few notes as possible. Jot down names and addresses and train the memory to supply the rest. Then the whole attention can be given to every word that is said.

# GETTING THE SCOOP

If a speech or lengthy address is to be reported verbatim a special stenographer is always assigned to the task.

It is a popular belief that to be a real reporter one must carry a note-book. This is not the case. Note-books are used only by reporters in stories and plays. The few necessary notes can be taken on a bit of paper, and there is no need of letting every one you meet know that you are a reporter.

---

Here is an account of just how a reporter does his work, from the time he goes out on the story until it is published; how he conducts his interviews; what notes he takes and how he writes:

The first information came to the news gatherer when he was stationed at the Headquarters of Police, where, at seven o'clock in the morning, this bulletin was posted:

" Tenth Precinct.

"At 6:15 A. M. Officer Charles Muller brought here the dead body of unknown man, who died suddenly in front of 63 East Houston Street. About 35, dark hair, sack coat, light striped pants, brown soft hat, gray stockings. Supposed to be J. C. Carter of 61 Bond Street."

With this in mind the reporter started out to see what news there was in the occurrence more than that contained in the bulletin.

First he looked for policeman Muller and found him on post within a block of the spot where the body was first seen.

The following interview then took place between the reporter and the policeman:

**Question**. Officer, you found that man's body down the street, did you not?
**Answer**. The tramp? Yes.
**Q**. Was he dead when you found him?
**A**. Yes. There was a crowd around him. It was about half-past five.
**Q**. Do you know what he died of?
**A**. The doctor thought it was alcoholism.

# REPORTING FOR THE NEWSPAPERS

**Q.** Where was it you found him?
**A.** Down there in front of The Morgue, at No. 63.
**Q.** The Morgue?
**A.** That liquor store: that's what they call it, The Morgue.
**Q.** Why do they call it The Morgue?
**A.** I don't know, that's just a name it's got.
**Q.** Do you know anything about the man, who he is or his family, or anything?
**A.** No, I don't know. I believe he went into the saloon and asked for a drink and was thrown out. There was a letter in his pocket addressed to Carter, J. C. Carter. It said 61 Bond Street on it. I guess he's a lodging-house tramp. There were some other memoranda books, and fifteen cents in his pockets. That's all I know about him.
**Q.** You haven't been around to Bond Street, have you?
**A.** No, what do I want to go around there for? We'll just send the body to the morgue if nobody comes for it. Why don't you go down and see the people at the saloon.

This is all the policeman could or would tell, so the reporter went into the saloon to find out why the man had been thrown out. There the bartender was seen, and this is the interview which followed:

**Q.** What do you know about that dead man?
**A.** He's a bum. He came in here and asked for a drink. I wouldn't give it to him. I told him it was against the boss's orders to give drinks to bums. I won't sell drinks to bums. He monkeyed around for a few minutes, then he went out and fell dead right in front of the door.
**Q.** Did he have any money?
**A.** Yes, he had fifteen cents, but that don't make any difference. If I'd a sold it to him he'd a hung around all day.
**Q.** Did you put him out?
**A.** I told him he'd have to move on.
**Q.** Who owns this place?
**A.** Aaron Herzberg.
**Q.** Well, didn't he say anything when he asked for the drink?
**A.** No, nothing except "hurry up, I feel faint and dizzy," or something of that kind. I thought he just had the D. T.'s and was giving me a jolly. He was shaking, and looked as though he had been on about a three months' tear.
**Q.** What time was he here?

# GETTING THE SCOOP

**A.** It was just twenty-five minutes after five. I remember I looked at the clock just as he went out.

Number 61 Bond Street the reporter found to be a house in which there was a grocery store on the ground floor and a photograph gallery up-stairs. The gallery was kept by Bruno Schentner.

The grocery store was not open at that early hour in the morning, so the newsgatherer went up to the gallery. There he was met by a woman, who proved to be Mrs. Schentner.

She was interviewed.

**Q.** Have you a man named Carter working here?
**A.** Yes, he works sometimes. He is our agent.
**Q.** When did you see him last?
**A.** Last night. Did you want to see him?
**Q.** Are you related to him in anyway?
**A.** Oh, no. He just works here.
**Q.** Well, he died this morning.
**A.** Oh, my! I saw him last night.
**Q.** He died this morning. Do you know where he lived?
**A.** In some lodging house on the Bowery, I think. He got all his mail here.
**Q.** Has he any relatives that you know of?
**A.** No. Wait; there is a man that he has been going with a great deal. He will be here soon, if you could wait a few minutes. There he is now. Don't you see him over there sitting on the steps? He knows Carter better than any one else. I guess he will be able to tell you all about him. What did Carter die of?

"Dropped dead," the reporter answered briefly as he went through the door.

Across the street, sitting on a stone stoop, there was a man in a faded suit. The newspaper man approached and questioned him.

**Q.** Do you know J. C. Carter?
**A.** J. G. Carter I know.
**Q.** He works for Schentner?
**A.** Yes.
**Q.** Do you know where he lives?
**A.** No. What do you want of him?

**Q**. I want to find some of his relatives.
**A**. I don't know; if you want to leave any note for him, I will give it to him. I am waiting for him, he will be here before long.
**Q**. No, you will not give him any note, and there is no use waiting for him; he's dead.
**A**. Dead? Well, I'm not much surprised. I was a little afraid to go around with him; I thought he would drop dead. Did he drop dead?
**Q**. Yes.
**A**. Where?
**Q**. In Houston Street. How long have you known him?
**A**. About a year. He was an Englishman, as I am.
**Q**. How long had he been in this country?
**A**. He told me about four years. His relatives are wealthy.
**Q**. Is that so? Where do they live?
**A**. In England. I think his brother is a minister.
**Q**. Somewhere in England?
**A**. In a suburb of London; he has money.
**Q**. In what suburb, do you know?
**A**. No, I don't know, but he told me the name often. Let me see. Yes, it's in Hearne Hill. That's it. Carter was an educated man.
**Q**. He was?
**A**. Oh, yes. Nobody could talk to him for five minutes without finding out that he was a man of refinement. He was an elegant talker and a fine salesman, but booze killed him.
**Q**. He drank a good deal, then?
**A**. Always; he would make a few dollars, and then spend them on booze. Then he would hang the bartender up for a week. He had good positions; he worked for Jere Johnson.
**Q**. The real estate agent?
**A**. Yes, and he worked for William Bartman in Broadway, and a number of others, but he lost all of his positions by boozing.
**Q**. Is his father living?
**A**. No. His father died when he was about eighteen, he told me. He and his brother were just finishing their education. His mother died before that. His father lost all his money speculating.
**Q**. Did he ever hear from his brother?
**A**. Sure. His brother used to send him money. He was a great lace salesman. He worked for a London lace house and about nine years ago went to Australia for them. But

booze knocked him out, and his brother sent him to this country, to get rid of him, I guess.

**Q**. Was he a good-looking man?

**A**. Sure. He would have been if he did not drink so much. Where is the body ?

**Q**. At the Mulberry street police station.

This is all that could be gotten out of the friend, so the reporter left him. From the city directory he looked up the address of Jere Johnson and William Bartman.

Here are the notes the reporter took in getting the story:

> Aaron Herzberg.
> Bruno Schentner.
> Country, four years.
> Hearne Hill.
> Jere Johnson, 60 Liberty street.
> William Bartman, 174 B'way.

Besides these he had the police slip before him. Relying upon his memory for the rest, he wrote the story thus :

# HIS LIFE FOR A DRINK

## BARTENDER REFUSED TO SELL CARTER, WHO DROPPED DEAD

## BROTHER OF AN ENGLISH CLERGYMAN; HE WAS RUINED BY DRINK

J. G. Carter, an intelligent-looking Englishman, 34 years old, who is said to belong to a respectable family in London, fell dead on the sidewalk in front of Aaron Herzberg's saloon, 63 East Houston street, at 5:25 o'clock this morning, after the bartender had refused to sell him a drink.

Carter entered the saloon, according to the bartender's story, and ordered some whiskey, .laying the fifteen cents on the counter.

"Hurry up," he commanded, "I feel faint and dizzy."

"No, I cannot sell you anything. It is against the boss's orders to sell anything to bums. Get out and be quick," the bartender, according to his own story, replied.

Carter staggered to the door of the dingy rum shop, with an imprecation on his lips. He stumbled out upon the sidewalk, and fell in a heap at the curb, insensible.

When policeman Muller came up a few minutes later and elbowed his way through the crowd, he saw that the man was dead.

The body was removed to the Mulberry Street station house on a stretcher and the clothing searched for some means of identification. A letter addressed to J. G. Carter, 61 Bond Street, several memorandum books, and fifteen cents, were found.

Inquiries at 61 Bond Street elicited the information that Carter had been employed there by Bruno Schentner, a photographer, as a soliciting agent. He roomed in a Bowery lodging house, and received his mail at the Bond Street number.

He managed to make a living by canvassing for different business firms ; among others for Jere Johnson, a real estate agent at 61 Liberty Street, and William Bartman, jewelry dealer at 174 Broadway.

After the coroner views the body it will be sent to the morgue, and will undoubtedly be buried in Potter's Field.

From one of Carter's friends in this city it was ascertained that his family in London was at one time wealthy. Early in his life his mother died, and when he was eighteen years old and finishing his education at an English university with his brother, his father died. Before his death the elder Carter had met with some financial reverses, so the sons were left with nothing but their education.

Carter's brother had studied for the ministry, and he soon accepted a charge at Hearne Hill, a suburb of London. He is still there.

Carter entered a lace maker's establishment, and after five years became their head traveller. He sold lace in various European countries until 1885, when he went to Australia in the interest of his employers.

At first a moderate drinker, the habit grew upon him, so that in 1888 he was withdrawn from Australia and deprived of his position. From that time on his downfall was rapid. His brother at Hearne Hill helped him with money and advice, and finally four years ago he came to this country by means of money furnished by his brother. Here he prospered for a time, his command of language and his ability as a salesman

# GETTING THE SCOOP

procuring for him positions. But love of drink finally ruined him.

---

Another reporter did not see so much news in the story. This is what he wrote:

"James G. Carter, an Englishman 35 years old, dropped dead this morning in a saloon known as 'The Morgue' at 63 East Houston Street. He entered the place apparently suffering from an attack of delirium tremens, and asked the bartender to give him a drink. The bartender told him he had had too many already. 'All right,' said the man feebly, 'I'll have to try somewhere else' He turned toward the door, but had taken scarcely a dozen steps when he fell on the floor. A policeman who was summoned found that the man was dead.

"Carter was employed as a canvasser by a photographer named Schentner, of 61 Bond Street. It was said that he came of a wealthy family in England, and that his brother was a clergyman in one of the suburbs of London. The man was sent to this country because of his drinking habit. He died from a combination of alcoholism and consumption."

It needs only a comparison of the interviews with the written story to show how the news was separated from the useless information. The reporter has nothing to do with the head lines. They are written by the editor, or one of the desk men.

# 5
# A NEWS STORY ANALYZED

Newspaper stories are all similar in construction, however much their subjects may differ. An analysis of one is an analysis of all. All have component parts, divisions and subdivisions, which must be adhered to if the story is to be complete.

Thus a certain amount of sameness exists in them all, and the editors issue general instructions regarding their composition which must be followed.

Some papers permit more freedom of expression than others, and the reporter is able to disguise the set form, as the flesh covers up and hides the skeleton, but beneath the words the familiar framework stands out boldly enough to be easily recognized.

Different from a play, from a literary story, from any other style of writing, a news story begins with the news ; in other words, the culmination of the story is put first. The opening paragraph contains the climax. There is no leading up to a situation step by step until the point of interest is gradually reached, but, on the contrary, the first words reveal the entire situation and the rest of the story only leads in a circle to the opening lines.

There is a belief in the newspaper business that people as a rule do not care to read the papers very thoroughly, that they want to know exactly how much news there is in a story, but only if it interests them particularly will they read on for the details.

Those who do not desire the details can obtain the news quickly by scanning the opening paragraphs.

A general news story analyzed will show these divisions : THE INTRODUCTION: THE CAUSE: THE EFFECT: ATTENDING CIRCUMSTANCES and CONCLUSION.

These divisions may be defined as follows:

*Introduction* - The main facts of the story in brief. Giving an idea of what happened, where it happened, and the people concerned.
*Cause* - The incident or happening upon which the story is based.
*Effect* - The facts that make up the story, told in detail.
*Attending Circumstances* - Theories and incidents indirectly connected with the story.
*Conclusion* - The finishing touches necessary to bring the story to an end.

To understand clearly how a news story is analyzed, take the following account and study its divisions.

(News story from The World)

# FOUGHT SIX POLICEMEN!

## JOHN OTTO, A SUPPOSED LUNATIC, GIVES THEM A HARD TUSSLE

## FINALLY OVERPOWERED AND TAKEN TO BELLEVUE IN AN AMBULANCE

Six policemen had a pitched battle this morning with a man thought to be a maniac. It took place at Fifteenth Street and Second Avenue and lasted for over half an hour. The man is a veritable giant in strength and stature. Before he was subdued the clothing of two of the policemen was torn from their backs, one had a badly cut lip, and all bore marks of the combat, in the shape of bruised faces and bloody clothes.

The man gave the name of John Otto, says he is twenty-six years old and a porter.

It was just after three o'clock, when Policeman John Magner reached the southeast corner of Fifteenth Street and Second Avenue. A woman came up to him suddenly out of the darkness, and clutching him by the arm said :

"Sir, I have been assaulted; a man knocked me down."

"Where is he now?"

"I don't know; he went away."

Questioned further, the woman said she had left her house to go for a physician, when she met the man, whom she did not know, and he struck her.

The policeman noticed that she was a modest-looking, pretty woman, and that she was greatly excited.

Suddenly, as she talked, she turned around and uttered a shriek:

"There he is now!" she cried.

Magner turned at the cry, and there alongside of a railing before a brownstone house stood a tall man; his arms were folded, and he looked intently at the policeman and the woman. Magner went up to him.

"Who are you?" he asked gruffly.

In another instant the policeman was lying on his back on the pavement and the big man was on top of him. That was the beginning of the battle. Over and over the two rolled, but the policeman soon saw he was no match for the man. Time and time again the officer was struck in the face and choked. He called loudly for help, but the street was deserted, and there was no response to his cries. Speaking of it afterward the policeman said "His fingers were like living steel that every second tightened about my throat."

Magner would undoubtedly have been strangled had not Policemen Roach, Eaton, and Wren come running up the street. Then the fight was renewed, but the man proved a match for all four and they were forced to defend themselves against the continued attacks of the maniac, for it seemed impossible to subdue him. Three times he was hit on the head with one of the policemen's short clubs, but he fought on, the blood streaming down his face covering the policemen as they fought. The four kept up a continual outcry; the maniac did not utter a sound.

All the time the struggle was going on, the young woman stood nearby and looked on. Policemen Murphy and Boyle, who were in the adjoining precinct, further down Second Avenue, heard the cries, but for a time hesitated to leave their precinct. When the cries continued, however, they deserted their post and ran to the assistance of their comrades.

# GETTING THE SCOOP

Now there were six against one. It was terrific odds, and the man, weak from the loss of blood, was finally overpowered. Then five of the policemen held him down while Magner telephoned for an ambulance. It was feared that the man had been badly hurt; the policemen certainly were.

The man lay quietly enough until the ambulance came. Then he was manacled. He was considered safe, then, for a big leather belt was strapped around his waist, to which the manacles were attached by chains. The surgeon examined the man's head, and said he had only scalp wounds, but had lost a great deal of blood. When he was lifted into the ambulance his eyes were closed and he seemed unconscious.

"Can you take him alone?" asked one of the policemen.

"Oh, he's all right now," answered the surgeon. Just then the driver of the ambulance uttered a cry and disappeared from his seat. He was in the bottom of the vehicle with the maniac's terrible fingers about his throat. The man had broken the chains that held him!

Immediately the almost exhausted policemen were in the ambulance, holding the man. His wrists had the steel bands on them now, and he could not struggle as he did before, but he was not easy to conquer.

It was decided that three of the policemen should attend him to Bellevue Hospital. All the way the man fought. At the hospital he was put in a strait-jacket.

The policemen were treated for their injuries. Magner's lip was cut and his face swelled. The others were scratched and bruised. One of the sleeves had been torn from Eaton's coat; the uniforms of the other policemen were sad wrecks.

When the man had been taken to the hospital the woman disappeared. She had stood silently by until the end. One of the policemen thought he had seen the woman before, but he was not sure. Every effort was made to find her, but without success. It is believed that she knows who the man is. He would say nothing at the hospital after giving his name.

---

Analyzed, it will be found that the story was written in this manner :

In the Introduction is written the substance of the story; the fight, who fought, where they fought, who the man that fought the six policemen was, and the condition of the policemen when it was all over.

For the Cause there is the woman's appeal to the policeman.

For the Effect we have the story of the struggle in sequential detail.

Under the Attending Circumstances division there is the journey to the hospital in the ambulance and the disposition of the prisoner.

In conclusion, is the disappearance of the woman, the efforts made to find her, and the suggestion that she doubtless knew more of the maniac than she had told.

---

In some stories it will be found that the Effect is placed before the Cause.

The general rule to be followed is that if the effect can clearly be told without mentioning the cause then the Effect is to be placed before the Cause. In this way the latest news of the story is told first.

Sometimes it is necessary to write what is called a "running" story; for instance, when in a court or meeting of any kind the copy must be written as events take place.

The illustration herewith given of this form of writing is from the report of a billiard match between Schaefer and Slosson. Schaefer on the previous night, in stopping play, had left the balls on the table and was to go on with his unfinished run.

The reporter wrote this brief introduction before the game commenced :

"Jacob Schaefer, the little Wizard of billiards, who nipped victory out of seemingly impending defeat in the opening engagement on Monday night with Slosson the Student, his able rival, was the first to resume play in the big six-night balk-line match at Madison Square Garden Concert Hall last night. The Wizard had piled up an unfinished closing run of 120 on Monday night, and he had the privilege of prolonging it and having his opening inning added to the score of the seventeenth inning."

# GETTING THE SCOOP

Having written so much the reporter waited until the game opened. Then when Schaefer had finished his run he went on with the story:

"He opened with a spread draw at the bottom of the table, and managed to pick up 30 slowly before a miscue on a draw cut short the run at a total of 159, the highest thus far in the cue battle."

From this point the story was written and sent piecemeal to the newspaper office as the innings were played, thus:

"Slosson's opening effort of the night earned him a zero. He strove for the balk-line at his next chance and began some of that deft magic of delicate cue work that has brought him both fame and ducats."

And so on until the end. When the night's game came to a close a few lines in conclusion were added, and the copy was ready for the printer.

The "running" story is a difficult style of writing and not very satisfactory. But where there is little time and much to be written it is employed, as it is the quickest way of getting the news to the office.

# 6
# EVIDENCE: HOW WRITTEN

Court evidence is reported in various ways, and the fullness with which it is written up depends upon the importance of the case from a news standpoint; and this importance depends upon the human interest involved.

There are times when the evidence is taken verbatim, and others when the merest outline is necessary.

As an illustration take the following portion of the evidence which came up before a Senate investigating committee in New York City, and the manner in which various newspapers treated it in print.

Police Commissioner Sheehan was on the stand, examined by lawyer (now Recorder) John W. Goff. The evidence herewith given is verbatim and is a copy of the record of the court stenographer.

## EVIDENCE

**Question**. Did you ever say that the escape of Katie Schubert was made possible by collusion?
**Answer**. To be candid with you, Mr. Goff, I will tell that the day before she sailed I read in the papers that she was in Jersey City, and I said in the Board meeting that I thought she would never return to be a witness.
**Q**. Did it strike you as peculiar that she was allowed to depart without testifying against Inspector McLaughlin?
**A**. It certainly did. During the trials of Captains Cross and Devery I tried to bring out in her testimony the case against McLaughlin.
**Q**. You considered it a failure of justice?
**A**. In what respect?

**Q.** Why, a failure to prosecute a police officer on the testimony of a woman in your jurisdiction?
**A.** My associates acted honestly, on the advice of counsel for the Board, that the evidence against Inspector McLaughlin was not sufficient to convict.
**Q.** The evidence of Katie Schubert incriminated Captains Cross and Devery and Inspector McLaughlin. You say counsel advised the Board it was not prudent to put Inspector McLaughlin on trial: did you note the fact that charges were not made against him?
**A.** I did.
**Q.** Did you believe that some potent power was at work to induce Katie Schubert to sail for Europe in order to prevent the placing of Inspector McLaughlin on trial?
**A.** It was my opinion that McLaughlin ought to have been put on trial, and that Katie Schubert's testimony should have been taken. But I was bound to believe the counsel for the Board, Mr.
Wellman.
**Q.** What was your opinion of the Detective Bureau for allowing her to escape?
**A.** If she had been under the charge of the Detective Bureau, she would not have escaped. She was in the charge of counsel.
**Q.** Did it not impress you as ludicrous that the chief officer of the Detective Bureau should have made such a blunder as he did?
**A.** The newspaper accounts were very funny.
**Q.** Did you ever hear rumors or reports that other than pool sellers were paying the police?
**A.** I may have heard rumors or received anonymous letters. I received a great many. I received one yesterday while on the stand about you, Mr. Goff. I have it here. Do you want to see it?
**Q.** It is not necessary, Mr. Commissioner. It might not surprise you to learn that I have received bushels of letters about you.
**A.** I presume so.
**Q.** Well, let us see, let us see. Did you ever hear that the sailmakers in South Street were blackmailed by the police?
**A.** No.
**Q.** Did you ever hear that the West Side merchants were assessed by the police for the use of their sidewalks?
**A.** No.

**Q.** Don't you know that the merchants organized a Merchants' Protective Association, to protest against police blackmail?
**A.** I never heard of it, and I don't believe it. We never had any knowledge or information of the kind.
**Q.** Did you know the Italian fruit sellers were compelled to pay the police?
**A.** Only as it has been testified here.
**Q.** I am excluding testimony here. Did you know the police extorted tribute from the bootblacks?
**A.** I did not.
**Q.** Do you know that the Long Island clam diggers paid tribute to the police?
**A.** Where do they come in? I had not heard of that.
**Q.** I am only inquiring. Did you know that gambling houses paid protection money?
**A.** I may have read something like that.
**Q.** Did you investigate?
**A.** I could not investigate rumors.
**Q.** You investigated rumors about the pool-sellers, why not these rumors?
**A.** Because I had more definite information: because I was in the company of men who said pool-sellers were paying protection, but it could not be proved.
**Q.** Did you examine the Superintendent's last report, which stated that in New York City virtue reigned supreme; no green goods, no policy, no gambling?
**A.** The Superintendent's report speaks for itself.
**Q.** So you accepted the Superintendent's report that New York is an Eldorado of virtue, rather than the common reports as to the prevalence of protected crime?
**A.** I accepted the Superintendent's report.
**Q.** What do you do for your salary?
**A.** Oh, go ahead with your questions, Mr. Goff, and I'll answer you.
**Q.** But really, I want to know?
**A.** I work for my salary.
**Q.** What do you do?
**A.** I discharge all the duties of a Police Commissioner, as required by law.
**Q.** What are those duties?
**A.** I am at my office every day, and transact the business that comes before me.
**Q.** But what do you do?
**A.** A thousand and one things.

**Q.** But let us have details. You have testified here for three days as to absolute ignorance of everything concerning the prevalence of immorality and crime which as a Police Commissioner you should have known: you have testified that the Superintendent has refused to do his duty, and you have failed to compel him to; but even a knowledge by current report of police corruption has been satisfactorily offset in your mind by the assurance of the Superintendent to the contrary. Now what do you do for your salary?

**A.** I am in my office every day attending to my duties, seeing that the appropriation for the department is properly expended, and enforcing the criminal laws.

**Q.** This Committee has a right to know what you four gentlemen do to earn $20,000 a year; what do you do?

**A.** We see that the money appropriated for the department is spent properly.

**Q.** To see how $5,000,000 is spent; that is one thing; now tell us another.

**A.** We see that the police department does its full duty.

**Q.** The extracts from the rules and law show that the Police Board has absolute power to enforce the laws. What have the commissioners done to enforce the law?

**A.** We have enforced the law so far as it came within our judgment. The enforcement of law and order is in the hands of the Superintendent of Police.

**Q.** The evidence adduced before this Committee has established the fact that corruption runs riot in the Police Department. Do you still think that the Board has done its duty?

**A.** No knowledge of corruption has been brought to the knowledge of the Police Board since I have been a Commissioner.

**Q.** Do you believe the police force is free from corruption?

**A.** My belief is that this police force is the finest in the world, and that the citizens of this city are amply satisfied with the protection it gives them.

**Q.** It has been so testified here that ample "protection" is awarded.

**A.** Well, I think the people are satisfied.

**Q.** Satisfied? Do you think that the poor Greek, George Alexander, was satisfied, when he, after pawning his watch, to pay police protection, was driven out of honest business because he had no more watches to pawn for the police?

**A.** That is his story; perhaps it was a good thing to drive him out.

---

The fullest report of this evidence was printed by the Herald and shows how much of the testimony, questions and answers, can be caught by a good reporter without the aid of shorthand notes. Such notes as he did take were brief, embodying the main substance of the examination, and elaborated at the conclusion of the day's session.

**Q.** Did you ever say that Katie Schubert was allowed to depart for Europe unmolested?
**A.** I said that in my belief she would never appear to testify against any one.
**Q.** Did you believe that her departure was the result of collusion in order to avoid putting McLaughlin on trial?
**A.** I did not.
**Q.** Can you say why Katie Schubert was allowed to depart?
**A.** No, but during the trials you refer to, I repeatedly said that the same evidence applied to Inspector McLaughlin.
**Q.** Did you believe that some power was being used to keep Katie Schubert away in order to save McLaughlin?
**A.** I cannot tell you. I believe she should have been brought to testify.
**Q.** What is your opinion of the efficiency of the Detective Bureau in having permitted her to get away?
**A.** She was not in charge of the Detective Bureau, she was in charge of counsel for the department, Mr. Wellman.
**Q.** Did it not impress you as ridiculous that the chief officer of the Detective Bureau should have made the blunders he did?
**A.** The newspaper accounts were very funny.
**Q.** How about the payment of money to the police by the poolrooms?
**A.** Oh, I only heard rumors to that effect. I investigated the matter, but could get no evidence.
   Mr. Sheehan said that some of his information regarding the poolrooms was in the shape of anonymous letters. "For instance," he said, "I received an anonymous letter about you, Mr. Goff." As he said that he produced a letter from his pocket, and handed it to Mr. Goff for inspection.

"That is not necessary," said Mr. Goff, somewhat tartly;

"I may say that I have received bushels of such letters about you." "No doubt you have," was the response.

Mr. Goff then desired to know whether Mr. Sheehan had put the same degree of vigilance into his inquiries about alleged corruption in the police department that he would had a clerk in his own employ been similarly accused. Mr. Sheehan replied that he did all that he could have done under the circumstances.

"Well," observed Mr. Goff, "if you had a clerk in your employ, and you heard rumors regarding the way he was handling your money, would you wait for positive evidence before sifting the rumor thoroughly?"

"I told you, Mr. Goff," replied Mr. Sheehan, "that I did all I possibly could under the circumstances. I could go no further."

**Q.** Let us see, Mr. Commissioner. Did you ever hear that the sailmakers along South Street had to pay tribute to the police? A. I did not.

**Q.** Did you ever hear the same things about Broadway merchants?

**A.** No.

**Q.** Or the Italian fruit dealers?

**A.** No.

**Q.** Or the bootblacks?

**A.** No.

**Q.** Or the Long Island clam-diggers?

**A.** No.

**Q.** Or the gambling houses?

**A.** Well, I might have heard such a rumor.

**Q.** And you say you investigated it?

**A.** I couldn't investigate a rumor. I would not know where to start.

**Q.** Are we to understand that the reports of the captains, showing that virtue reigned supreme in this city, and that there was no gambling, lulled the Police Commissioners into a sense of security?

**A.** We relied upon the truth of the report made by the Superintendent of Police; we had to.

**Q.** You have stated that in order to procure protection, it would be necessary to go to a higher authority than a policeman; now in the face of such reports, were you not inclined to suspect the Superintendent?

**A.** I was not.

**Q.** By the way, what do you do anyhow for your salary?

**A.** I work for it.
**Q.** Yes, but what do you do?
**A.** All the duties devolved on me by virtue of my office.
**Q.** But it would seem from your testimony that you do nothing and know nothing.
**A.** I do my duty, I tell you.
**Q.** Give us a sample of what you do.
**A.** Anything that comes up.
**Q.** Tell us one thing?
**A.** Well, I see that the money of the department is properly spent.
**Q.** Oh, you do. Well give us something else?
**A.** I see that the Police Department does its duty.
**Q.** But what have the Commissioners done to enforce the law?
**A.** The enforcement of the law is in the hands of the uniformed members of the force.
**Q.** But the evidence before this Committee has established the fact that corruption has run riot there.
**A.** I believe that the police have given the citizens better protection within the last few years than they ever had before.

"Protection," said Mr. Goff. "Oh, yes, the citizens have got protection enough. The trouble has been that the police exacted too much for it. Take the case of George Alexander, for instance, who was driven out of his business."

"Perhaps there were good reasons for driving him out of the city," retorted the Police Commissioner. "You have only heard one side of the story."

---

The account printed in another paper was not so full. The editor did not desire so detailed a story, and while the reporter retained the form of the questions and answers, he gave only the most important news.

Here it is as it was printed:

As usual, the police investigators did not deign to do such a vulgar thing as to convene on time.

It was nearly an hour after the schedule time that the Committee began business in the Superior Court.

Commissioner Sheehan was on the stand, and lawyer Goff asked as a beginner:

"Do you not regard the escape of Kate Schubert as a miscarriage of justice?"

"In what respect?"

"Didn't it strike you as peculiar that she was allowed to depart without being asked about Inspector McLaughlin?"

"Yes, I said so at the time."

"Was not some potent influence at work to shield him?"

"I can't say."

"What is your opinion of the detective force in permitting her to escape?"

"I understand she was in the custody of detectives employed by the counsel to the Board and under surveillance of the Bureau."

"Did you ever hear rumors that other institutions besides the poolrooms were paying for protection?" continued Mr. Goff.

"I heard rumors. Why, I got anonymous letters. I got one yesterday afternoon about you. Do you want to see it?" and the Commissioner took it out of his pocket.

"It is not necessary. I have received bushels of anonymous letters about you."

"It would not be fair to charge the whole police force with taking that money from the poolsellers, when only a few did," said the Commissioner.

Counsel Goff asked why the Commissioner had not brought some to justice, when rumors were flying thick and fast.

"I couldn't fasten any crime on any official."

"Let us see, corruption was pretty general. Did you know the sailmakers had to pay?"

"No."

"Did you know merchants pay?"

"No."

"Did you know Long Island clamdiggers had to pay?"

"Where did they come in?" asked the witness.

"Never mind. Did you hear gambling houses had to pay?"

"I heard rumors, but I could not trace who paid it."

Then Mr. Goff, after several moments of profound meditation, said suddenly:

"What do you do to earn your salary?"

"Perform the duties devolved upon me as a Commissioner," answered the witness, who was on the alert, and Goff's little trick fell flat, as his others have.

The Commissioner said that he saw that the five million dollar appropriation for the police was properly expended.

---

The World reporter made no effort to get the evidence verbatim. He wrote a running story giving the outlines thus:

At the beginning of the proceedings, Mr. Goff again inquired the reasons of the failure to try Inspector McLaughlin with the captains. Commissioner Sheehan repeated that for his part he had been in favor of trying McLaughlin, and said that the day before Katie Schubert's disappearance he had heard that she had gone to Jersey, and that he had stated that he thought she would never come back. In spite of his belief that the Chief of the Detective Bureau had been fooled by the woman in the most amusing manner, the Commissioner preferred to believe that Assistant District Attorney Wellman was responsible for the fugitive witness.

Sheehan said that he had been brought to a dead stop in his investigation by something which he cordially agreed with Mr. Goff in describing as a Chinese wall, but which he would not describe more specifically.

Sheehan declared himself to be the most innocent little man in New York so far as knowledge of evil is concerned.

He swore that he had never heard of petty blackmailing of bootblacks, South Street sailmakers, peddlers, pushcart men, and Lord knows what. When asked if he had heard that there were gambling houses in every precinct in New York, Sheehan said he had heard that, but he did not know it except from rumor, and he could not investigate a rumor.

"Why," said Lawyer Goff, "didn't you institute some inquiries through the Superintendent?"

Commissioner Sheehan: "We got no report from the Superintendent, except some general reports."

Q. "And that lulled the Police Commissioners into quietude? The Superintendent's report made them disregard general rumors, and they relied on the Superintendent for the belief that New York was an Eldorado of virtue. What do you do anyway for your salary?" asked Mr. Goff.

"I work for it," said Sheehan.

After a deal of hammering Sheehan returned to the Superintendent again. Said he, "The enforcement of the laws is in the hands of the Superintendent."

# GETTING THE SCOOP

These three ways of taking the evidence should be closely studied.

For practice, it would be well to attend a court session, take notes in some one case and write them up after the three styles here shown. From the newspaper report of the same case it could be seen how the story written compared with the one printed.

These examples will also serve the purpose of showing how a sermon can be reported. If of great importance it is taken in full; then again it is sometimes condensed into a few lines embodying the main thought. Between these two extremes may be written stories of varying lengths. Lectures and speeches, in fact anything in the shape of an address, may be similarly treated.

# 7
# BEGINNING THE STORY

When every other detail of the business of reporting is thoroughly understood, there is still the introduction to the story to which many an hour of serious thought must be given. Too little attention is usually devoted to this detail, which is really the keynote of interest and which fixes the standard for all that is to follow.

One cannot be interesting and conventional at the same time, and the reader must be both attracted and interested at the start.

The brevity of the story should not be allowed to influence the style of the introduction. The same care should be expended upon the opening of a ten-line paragraph as upon a two-column story.

In writing an introduction, if the people concerned are of prominence, their names should be mentioned in the first line. Otherwise, precedence should be given to the circumstances on which the story is based. Do not use the names first, however, unless they are so well known that they will be at once recognized, as this is an ordinary and unoriginal beginning.

Here is an example of a purely conventional introduction:

"Charles Wittemann, 24 years old, of 300 East io6th Street, was arraigned before Magistrate Mott in the Harlem Police Court this morning, charged with having registered illegally on Saturday last."

This is the most commonplace opening that could be used. Hundreds and hundreds of times those same words have served to commence Police Court stories, with changes only of name, age, residence, justice, and charge. Few care what the man's name is, much less wish to know where he lives, or before what justice he was arraigned. On the other hand, there are many who would be interested in knowing of the charge on which the man was arrested. Therefore the news of the story as well as the point of interest is much better considered in this other introduction which was used by another paper for the same story, the same day:

"Acting under advice he had received from an officer of the German Reform Union, Charles Wittemann registered Saturday from his place of business instead of from his residence. Yesterday he was arrested for illegal registration."

This paragraph contains the story in a nutshell, so that any one at all concerned in matters political can read on and find out all about the age and residence of the offender, how he was arraigned in court, and what disposition was made of his case.

So many stories of fires must be written that unless especially on his guard the reporter after a time falls inadvertently into commonplace modes of expression. There is a partiality for telling how many stories high was the burned building, who saw the fire first, who turned in the alarm, and at exactly what time.

For instance the reporter who wrote the following introduction used all the commonplace expressions possible:

"Fire started this morning on the second floor of the five-story brownstone building 349 Broadway, and burned so rapidly that before the firemen could control it the building had been destroyed. The flames were discovered at 8:20 o'clock by Policeman Haggerty of the Leonard Street station, who sent in the alarm."

As a contrast to this, here is another introduction to the same story, which smacks of interest from the first word:

"Flames burned away the northwest corner of Leonard Street and Broadway at 8 o'clock this morning, and had penetrated well in toward the centre of the compact square of business houses before they were controlled. About $200,000 damage was done, but the property was well insured. The structures destroyed were old and out of keeping with those of the other three corners, so that the loss is expected to have a compensation in the erection of larger, more modern buildings."

It is commonplace to start a story with "A "or "An." Never under any circumstances commence with "Yesterday " or " Last week." If such a start is made the reader will imagine it is old news. These are days of up-to-date living and the news of to-day, not of last week, is wanted. If the occurrences happened last week, say so, but not in the first line.

One day, New York was astonished by the report of a bank defalcation, involving a large sum of money and sensational in character. Every paper in the city and throughout the country devoted columns to the story. The unusual importance of the news demanded a strong opening to the story.

This is the introduction The Sun used, quite an ordinary one giving a plain statement of facts. The news was told in the introduction, and the four columns which followed simply elaborated the opening:

"The National Shoe and Leather Bank, at Broadway and Chambers street, has been robbed of $354,000 by Samuel C. Seely, one of its bookkeepers, and Frederick Barker, a depositor.
"Seely fled a week ago Saturday, leaving a confession in his lawyer's hands. It is supposed he fled by steamship.
"Barker was drowned yesterday afternoon at his country home at Sand's Point. There is of course a strong suspicion of suicide. Barker, who was a supposedly wealthy and respectable lawyer in this city, past 60 years of age, had told his accomplice before the latter's flight that he was too old to run away himself, and would stay and face the music. It is alleged by Seely that Barker got all but $11,000 of the stolen $354,000."

Four and one-half columns were devoted to the story by the Daily News.

A clearer idea of the enormity of the theft was conveyed in this introduction. The unusual circumstances attending the crime were pointed out, a description of the two men concerned given, a hint as to what became of the money, and the bank's condition.

# GETTING THE SCOOP

"All New York was startled yesterday afternoon by the announcement of one of the largest bank defalcations of recent years. The National Shoe and Leather Bank had been a loser to the extent of $354,000, at the hands of Samuel C. Seely, one of its oldest and most trusted employees. Aside from the enormous amount involved in the defalcation the story of the crime is accompanied by some of the most sensational developments ever read. Seely was a bookkeeper, living modestly in an unpretentious house at 422 Halsey Street, Brooklyn, and from all that can be learned, was a man of exemplary habits. Nevertheless, there is no doubt that he has been stealing from his bank for a period of nine years. He is said to have had as an accomplice in the person of a Frederick Barker, a New York lawyer, who was a depositor in the bank.

"The story has a tragic side in the reported suicide of Barker, in the bay, near Sands Point, his summer residence, yesterday. Most of the money, it is said, was squandered in the promotion of a famous bicycle railroad.

"The shock of the announcement of the robbery was quickly tempered by the bank's statement that the institution was in a sound condition, and able to pay all depositors - a statement which was confirmed unanimously by all the members of the Clearing House Committee that had investigated the bank's accounts."

It will be seen that the writer of the News story was careful to avoid libel. As it was not a clearly established fact that Frederick Barker was an accomplice, the introduction states that he is "said to be." Nor was it more than a conjecture that Barker had committed suicide, so the account refers to the "reported" suicide. There was reason to believe that the money had gone into the railroad scheme, but this was not positively known, so could not be put down as a fact.

The Herald told in a crisp, pointed manner every detail of the story; who were those concerned in it, what became of the criminals, and described the condition of the bank. Although following the ordinary form, there was an individuality in the opening paragraphs that made them attractive.

They read :

"A defalcation of $354,000 in the Shoe and Leather National Bank, the flight of bookkeeper Seely who stole the money only to hand it over to a man who had him in his power; the search for the arch conspirator, who is said to be lawyer

Frederick Barker, and his death by drowning while the detectives were hunting for him, is the epitome of what is one of the most startling stories of crime unearthed in this city in many a day.

"The thefts began nine years ago and continued up to a few days before Seely took refuge in flight, having learned that a change in the system of ledger keeping would make further concealment of his crime an impossibility. And when it was discovered, the bank found itself with its whole surplus of $190,000 wiped out, and a deficit of $150,000, which the stockholders must make good.

The introduction to the story in the New York Press told the story in a brief, and interesting way:

"By a clever, carefully-planned and cold-blooded system, a bookkeeper of the National Shoe and Leather Bank has been robbing that institution for the past nine years. He was in collusion with a depositor, who has been doing business with the bank for thirty years, and the amount of money that they stole is declared to be $354,000 by the directors, and the National Bank examiner.

"The conspirators might have continued with their systematic robberies for many years more had the bank not decided about two weeks ago to change its system of bookkeeping in a small way. That would have put two other men upon the books that have been in charge of the guilty bookkeeper, Samuel .C. Seely.

"Quick to see the peril threatened, he disappeared, after making a partial confession to his lawyer, and his mammoth defalcation was discovered directly his books fell into an examiner's hands."

But it was left for the Morning Advertiser to give an introduction in no degree conventional, to disregard the ordinary rules, and to begin the story unlike any other paper.

In this introduction, Seely, the most important figure, was picked out and a good analysis given of the man around whom the greater part of the four columns that followed was written.

The Advertiser opening:

For the past ten years, when the bank examiners went to the National Shoe and Leather Bank to look over affairs, bookkeeper Samuel C. Seely stood at their elbows and helped, in an humble sort of way, fetching books, identifying ledgers, explaining the system of accounts. The eagle-eyed and sharp-witted examiners found him never obtrusive, never in the way, but always at hand and always obliging. So obliging!

Year after year the mild-mannered bookkeeper breathed a sigh of relief when the bank examiners left. He went back to his desk and plodded away. The bank officers considered him a model employee. They increased his salary. The United States Guarantee Company, surety on his bond for $7,500, considered him a model risk.

On Friday, Nov. 16, the bookkeeper went to the office of Lawyer Frank W. Angel, of No. 108 Fulton street, and said:

"Frank, I've taken some money that I can't replace. I'm in trouble."

"How much?" asked the lawyer.

"It's over $300,000 maybe $400,000 I can't hide it any longer."

Angel stared at the man incredulously, and then laughed at him. The bookkeeper twiddled his thumbs and looked reproachfully at his friend.

"Sam," said the lawyer, "your father was insane. Now you are insane."

"No; it's way over $300,000."

"You mean $300. You've worried over it until you are crazy on the subject. You imagine..."

"No; I've told you the truth."

# 8
# WRITING THE DETAILS

Brevity is best secured by adhering strictly to facts, telling them in a plain straightforward way without any attempt at literary picturesqueness. Those who read the newspapers do so not so much for the sake of passing time, as for the purpose of finding out what is going on in the world. The newspaper writer may have a grace of diction that is fairly dazzling, unsurpassed powers of description, and a remarkable gift of diving into the unfathomable; but the newspaper reading public will not appreciate these qualities half so much as a terse manner of recording the news. Facts, not words, are wanted. So the high-sounding phrases should all be left out and none but the simplest and most expressive forms used.

Do not use too many adjectives. Make the sentences short, crisp, to the point, using as few "ands" as possible.

But while all the facts must be written, they should not read like a catalogue of goods on sale. It is well enough to forswear superfluous elegance and eloquence, but the reader must be interested as well as instructed, and one's style must not be dry or dull.

A careful study of the best newspapers will show how facts can be plainly yet readably expressed.

A newspaper story should be a simple statement of fact and not an expression of opinion by the writer. Let the reader draw his own conclusions. The duty of the writer is to chronicle the occurrence, giving the views of interested people. If the papers desire to express more than this they will do so editorially.

The new reporter should compare every line of his that finds its way into print with the copy as he wrote it. He will then see exactly what changes have been made, where he has been ambiguous, where verbose. After a while he will know just what his editor does not want, and that is a great step in advance. Some reporters never learn what to leave out.

In reporting an interview it is usually undesirable to put down the questions of the reporter. These are best embodied in the answers, for he has at times to ask a great many that seem useless in order to lead the person he is interviewing into an admission that he would not otherwise make. Then, too, the public care only about the result of his labors, so that it is more than bad taste to introduce himself personally. Especially do not comment upon the manner in which the reporter has been treated. He may be well or ill received, but that is all a part of the newspaper business and depends upon the kind of people with whom he has to deal. The petty triumphs, victories, or failures of the reporter are not matters of news, and should be kept out of print.

---

The following examples are taken from the daily papers and will serve to show how general is the use of superfluous words, and how by omitting them a story can be made much stronger. In these cases the words in italics should have been omitted. All are mistakes frequently made.

"He is a bricklayer *by trade* and reputed a steady man, though he takes an occasional glass his friends say."

Besides the unnecessary words there is another common mistake in the construction of this paragraph. The man's occupation and his habits are commented upon in one sentence, whereas only one fact at a time should be taken up.

"But *in order that he might* prosecute the case, it was necessary that immediate action be taken."

The word "to" would have served for the italicized words. In the same way, "to" may often be used instead of "for the purpose of."

"Moore was arrested to-day *and locked up.*"

Of course he was locked up after being arrested.

"He says he does not fear the outcome of his trial *on* Tuesday." Never use "on" before the days of the week.

"*A man by the name of* Henry Tijon fell and sprained his ankle at the corner of Broadway and Bleecker Street, under peculiar circumstances, this morning."

Just six words too many in that one paragraph.

"Henry Hilbert, 27 years old, of 29 East Third street, *became involved in a quarrel* with his friend James Patterson," etc.

Why not say simply they quarrelled?

"The building was *completely* destroyed."

If it was destroyed, the destruction of necessity must have been complete. It is just as absurd to talk of a fire which has been "completely" extinguished.

"*Two men named* Harris Wilbur and De Witt Thomas were arrested," etc.

Everybody knows that Messrs. Wilbur and Thomas were not four men, and the three words are superfluous. Also sentences which start, "A man by the name of," are poor form.

"A *young* man 20 years old was killed this morning," etc.

Of course when this age is mentioned it is evident that he is a "young" man.

"It was a *very* fashionable wedding." The fact would have been better expressed had the "very" been omitted. This word should be used sparingly as it does not add force.

"The two-story stable of Henry Holt, at 361 East 89 Street, was *destroyed by fire* last night," etc.

By saying " burned " the sentence could have been made more terse.

"When the danger was over the young woman fainted *away*"

# GETTING THE SCOOP

"When he met *with* the man at the doctor's office, there was a disagreeable scene."

"Hastings went *along* with him, but it was under protest."

"It was fully two hours later when the boat pulled up alongside *of* the dock."

"Justice Simms asked him *over* again, if he had made the confession alleged."

"Opposite *to* that house is the residence of Mayor Van Wyck."

"First *of all* were the three men."

"Besides not being worthy *of* their esteem."

"John Hume, the most severely injured, fell *a distance of* fifty feet."

"Fire broke out *at an* early *hour* this morning in the two-story building," etc.

"The *dead* body of a man was taken from the East River this morning."

So much for useless words.

There are other errors so common that it should not be difficult to keep them in mind and guard against them.

For instance it is better to refrain from saying that a person lives "on" a street. "In" is better. People also travel "in" a train.

A woman is "married to" a man, so the announcement that "William Haines was married to Miss Louise Yeates last evening" is incorrect.

The other day the statement appeared that "President Martin differed with his colleagues."

This was a peculiar thing for Mr. Martin to do. In fact an impossibility. It must have been that he differed "from" his colleagues. It would have been better for him to have agreed "with" them.

"Mr. Wilber will locate in Chicago in the fall."

Properly speaking he could not locate. He might locate a certain house; or he might locate a man, but he could hardly locate himself.

"By his side there lay a 48 calibre Smith & Wesson revolver, of old pattern."

Now who cares what the calibre of the revolver was, who made it, or whether it was of old or new pattern? The fact that there was a revolver was all that was necessary.

Another misused word is "about." We read that "about four o'clock"; or, "In a room about ten feet square"; or, "A man about thirty years old."

Ordinarily the exact hour, or size, or age need not be told. Usually it does not make the slightest difference whether a certain incident occurred at 9:45 o'clock or earlier or later. Of course there are exceptions, as in the case of a murder where a few moments may make a great difference in the case of a man's proving an alibi, and the exact time would be of the utmost consequence. In this as in all else the reporter must use discrimination.

# 9
# CONVENTIONAL EXPRESSIONS

There are certain time-worn phrases which should be avoided as much as possible. Yet some reporters employ these ancient expressions in writing entire stories and their work is therefore commonplace and without individuality. It is, of course, less trouble to resort to the familiar sentences, but yielding too often to the temptation one is presently unable to throw off the tyranny of habit.

The following examples are taken from newspapers published within a few days of each other. They are in constant use and can be picked at random from any issue of almost any newspaper.

"James Henner, the well-known clubman, was arrested last night for assaulting Timothy Brown, the prominent banker."

For the unoriginal reporter ordinary people do not exist. Everybody is "well known," "prominent," "influential," or "well-to-do." In the same way they will write of "The beautiful and accomplished" daughter of John Brown, from mere force of habit and not that it is in any way certain that the lady possesses these qualities.

"A large and appreciative audience witnessed the performance."

This is not only conventionally expressed, but the word "appreciative" often conveys an untruth. People do not always appreciate a performance even though they applaud it generously. They may simply enjoy it.

"Springing to his feet, with madness in his eyes, Caperruto whipped out a revolver and fired at the departing woman."

Many reporters seem to think that the only way for a man to draw a knife or revolver from his pocket is to "whip it out."

"It bids fair to be a great success."

This is not only time-worn but has no meaning save that accorded by conventional usage.

"The worst storm in many years passed over the city this morning."

This is much used and is rather sweeping. The conditions under which the reporter viewed the storm may have made it seem to him one fierce beyond precedent, but this is an extreme statement. In this particular case it was incorrect, for the weather reports showed that the storm was not an unusual one. The reporter had doubtless many times employed this stereotyped expression in reference to fires, murders, and accidents, changing only a few words to suit each occasion.

"All in all it was a scene that beggars description."

This statement has outlived its usefulness, and is as bad as its companion "in an instant pandemonium reigned."

"She fell backward from the window, turned once in the air, and in an instant she had struck the ground with a dull thud."

"Dull thuds" only appear in the copy when the writer lacks the power of otherwise describing sound.

The subterfuge "et cetera" is invariably employed when the writer cannot think of anything more to say.

People who have "disappeared as completely as though the earth had opened and swallowed them" have been too often alluded to; as have those others "drowned like rats in a hole."

So limited is the vocabulary of many reporters that they have but little choice in the selection of adjectives and other qualifying words. To these everything in the nature of an accident is "sickening," "awful," "ghastly," "terrible" or "appalling."

Over and over these words are used in comparatively trivial instances, until when some real catastrophe occurs deserving the strongest possible treatment, all the emphatic expressions have been so often used that there is no power in them, and they become trivial in the writing.

Abuse also destroys the value of the words "pretty," "grand," "splendid "and "lovely."

In many cases the story is stronger if adjectives and adverbs are omitted, or at the most used sparingly. In all cases the use of the right word in the right place is to be striven for.

# PREPARING "COPY"

When writing manuscript, or "copy," the reporter too often forgets that somebody else has to read it.

Write legibly.

It is safer to print proper names, as mistakes in these are easily made and may cause much awkwardness.

Do not forget to cross the t's and dot the i's.

To save time there are signs that may be used to indicate certain desired corrections. Three lines beneath a small letter will show the printer that he is to set it as a capital.

A line drawn obliquely through a capital letter from right to left makes it a small letter.

Put a ring around all periods.

Put paragraph marks at the beginning of all paragraphs.

Three lines beneath words or sentences show that they are to be printed in large capitals. Two lines indicate small capitals. One line, italics.

Figures to be spelled out in the printing should have a ring about them, and this applies to abbreviated words that are to be printed in full.

A double cross at the end of each story indicates its conclusion.

Make your meaning absolutely clear, and bear in mind that the slightest mark has a meaning for the printer, and that

# GETTING THE SCOOP

he has neither time nor inclination to ponder over your work in an effort to find out what you are trying to express.

www.ingramcontent.com/pod-product-compliance
Ingram Content Group UK Ltd.
Pitfield, Milton Keynes, MK11 3LW, UK
UKHW021318180426
11947UKWH00015B/1298